Early Modern Military History, 1450–

Also by Geoff Mortimer

EYEWITNESS ACCOUNTS OF THE THIRTY YEARS WAR 1618–48

Early Modern Military History, 1450–1815

Edited by

Geoff Mortimer
St Edmund Hall, Oxford

First published 2004 by
PALGRAVE MACMILLAN
Houndmills, Basingstoke, Hampshire RG21 6XS and
175 Fifth Avenue, New York, N.Y. 10010
Companies and representatives throughout the world

PALGRAVE MACMILLAN is the global academic imprint of the Palgrave
Macmillan division of St. Martin's Press, LLC and of Palgrave Macmillan Ltd.
Macmillan® is a registered trademark in the United States, United Kingdom
and other countries. Palgrave is a registered trademark in the European
Union and other countries.

ISBN 1–4039–0696–3 hardback
ISBN 1–4039–0697–1 paperback

This book is printed on paper suitable for recycling and made from fully
managed and sustained forest sources.

A catalogue record for this book is available from the British Library.

Library of Congress Cataloging-in-Publication Data
Early modern military history, 1450–1815 / edited by Geoff Mortimer
       p. cm.
    Includes bibliographical references and index.
    ISBN 1–4039–0696–3 – ISBN 1–4039–0697–1 (pbk.)
      1. Europe – History, Military. 2. Military history. I. Mortimer, Geoff, 1944–
D25.P35 2004
355′.009′03—dc22   2004047837

10 9 8 7 6 5 4 3 2 1
13 12 11 10 09 08 07 06 05 04

Printed and bound in Great Britain by
Antony Rowe Ltd, Chippenham and Eastbourne

Contents

References

All references in this book are given in smaller print within the text rather than as notes. The date/author system is used, quoting the author's name, the year of publication, and where relevant the particular page or pages referred to, for example (Smith, 1999, pp. 127–35). Details of the corresponding works are given at the end of each chapter.

Notes on the Contributors

Black, Jeremy, Professor of History at the University of Exeter. Author/editor of *War: An Illustrated World History* (2003), *European Warfare 1494–1660* (2002), *Western Warfare 1775–1882* (2001), *War: Past, Present and Future* (2000), *European Warfare 1453–1815* (1999), *War in the Early Modern World* (1999), and a large number of other books on early modern military history and other historical topics.

Cogliano, Francis D., Reader in American History at the University of Edinburgh (PhD Boston, Massachusetts). Author of *American Maritime Prisoners in the Revolutionary War: The Captivity of William Russell* (2001), *Revolutionary America 1763–1815* (2000) and *No King, No Popery: Anti-Catholicism in Revolutionary New England* (1995).

Forrest, Alan, Professor of Modern History at the University of York. Author of *Napoleon's Men: The Soldiers of the Revolution and Empire* (2002), *The French Revolution* (1995), *Soldiers of the French Revolution* (1990), *Conscripts and Deserters: The Army and French Society during the Revolution and Empire* (1989), and a number of other books on this period.

Glete, Jan, Professor of History at Stockholm University. Author of *War and the State in Early Modern Europe: Spain, the Dutch Republic and Sweden as Fiscal–Military States 1500–1660* (2002), *Warfare at Sea 1500–1650: Maritime Conflicts and the Transformation of Europe* (2000) and *Navies and Nations: Warships, Navies and State Building in Europe and America 1500–1860* (1993).

González de León, Fernando, Associate Professor of History at Springfield College, Massachusetts. Author of articles in a number of journals, including *The Journal of Modern History* and *The Sixteenth Century Journal*, and of chapters in recent monographs on early modern military history. His book on the Spanish Army of Flanders is forthcoming.

Harding, Richard, Professor of Organisational History at the University of Westminster. Author of *Seapower and Naval Warfare 1650–1830* (1999), *The Evolution of the Sailing Navy 1509–1815* (1995), and *Amphibious Warfare in the Eighteenth Century: The British Expedition to the West Indies 1740–42* (1991). Co-editor of *Precursors of Nelson: British Admirals of the Eighteenth Century* (2000).

Mortimer, Geoff, Lecturer in German at St Edmund Hall, University of Oxford. Author of *Eyewitness Accounts of the Thirty Years War 1618–48* (2002), and articles on this period in a number of journals, including *The English Historical Review* and *German History*.

Murphey, Rhoads, Reader in Ottoman Studies at the Centre for Byzantine, Ottoman and Modern Greek Studies, University of Birmingham (PhD Chicago). Author of *Ottoman Warfare 1500–1700* (1999) and many other books, chapters and articles on Ottoman history.

Rogers, Clifford J., Associate Professor of History at the United States Military Academy, West Point. Author of *War Cruel and Sharp: English Strategy under Edward III 1327–60* (2000), *The Wars of Edward III: Sources and Interpretations* (1999), and other publications on fourteenth-century England and the age of the Hundred Years War. Editor of *The Military Revolution Debate* (1995), and co-editor of *Civilians in the Path of War* (2002) and *The Journal of Medieval Military History*.

Showalter, Dennis E., Professor of History at Colorado College, Colorado Springs. Author of *The Wars of Frederick the Great* (1996) and several other books on German history, including *German Military History 1648–1982: A Critical Bibliography* (1984).

Wilson, Peter H., Professor of Early Modern History at the University of Sunderland. Author of *Absolutism in Central Europe* (2000), *The Holy Roman Empire 1495–1806* (1999), *German Armies: War and German Politics 1648–1806* (1998) and *War, State and Society in Württemberg 1677–1793* (1995).

Introduction: Was There a 'Military Revolution' in the Early Modern Period?

Geoff Mortimer

Fashions in historical studies come and go, leading Jeremy Black to observe a few years ago that 'military history has not played a major role in the academic community for decades, and scholarly work on modern forces and warfare is also limited' (Black, 2000, p. 1). He identifies two reasons: firstly an overt interest in war may be seen as lacking in political correctness and akin to militarism itself, and secondly some scholars view war as little more than a symptom, preferring to concentrate on the fundamental forces driving history which give rise to it. Nevertheless an impressive range and quality of specialist work has been published in recent years by historians active in this field, while a considerable number of studies addressed to a more general readership are to be found on the booksellers' shelves. This is not surprising, as if war is indeed only a symptom it is nevertheless a very prevalent one, almost as old as mankind but showing few signs of decline in the nuclear age. Politically correct or not, it is difficult to avoid for long in most mainstream historical studies, and it is moreover a subject which attracts continuing interest among both students and the wider public.

Misunderstandings about military history may well originate in a rather limited view of the concept, reminiscent of old schoolroom approaches to battles and dates: 1066 and all that! The history of war, or of individual wars and campaigns, certainly belongs to – but does not comprise – military history, which is much more deeply inter-related with other core parts of historical analysis. Two well-known maxims make the point. Clausewitz famously observed that 'war is nothing but the continuation of the political process with the inclusion of other means'. In other words it cannot be separated from the events and conditions giving rise to it, or from the consequences stemming from it. Almost two thousand years earlier Cicero complained that 'the sinews of war are unlimited money' – a conclusion which has lost none of its force with the passage of time. Hence war cannot be separated from economics, and military history, economic history and political history have strong links. It is also useful to remember that actual war is only part of the story. The concept of deterrence is by no means a modern invention, and the balance of power was central to politics in much of the early modern world. Military power was (and is) closely linked to political status. Prussia, for example, built itself up from insignificance in 1648 to be a great power a hundred years later, largely by developing a substantial army, although for most of this period it made little use of it.

The foregoing thoughts suggest the approach adopted in this book. Clearly this cannot incorporate all the political and economic factors bearing upon the military history of the period, but nor can such matters be entirely passed over in order to focus exclusively on wars, weapons, military organization, grand strategy and battlefield tactics. A balance is sought in which attention is drawn to each aspect at appropriate points, although considerations of space preclude going into too much detail or aiming at comprehensiveness, while in dealing with a period of some 350 years a selective approach is inevitable (as no doubt is the consequent criticism that the wrong things have been selected or left out). The aim is to show how the nature of military power and its deployment developed, and hence the emphasis is on change, with examples – essentially those in the forefront at the relevant time – chosen to demonstrate how this took place. These are presented in broadly chronological order, and are discussed at chapter length by academics expert on each topic, while the references provide wider reading lists to facilitate further study.

Periods are always problematic in history, and the use of the date 1450 in the title must be viewed as arbitrary. Nevertheless the transition from the medieval to the early modern period (however these are defined) marks a logical starting point for this book. Maurice Keen has noted 'the very slow rate of technological advance in the art of warfare during the Middle Ages', adding that 'around 1500 shifts in conditions ... were beginning to accelerate', notably with the development of professional standing armies and the effective deployment of gunpowder weapons (Keen, 1999, pp. 5, 8). Change continued to characterize the next three hundred years, but underwent an order-of-magnitude shift after the mid-nineteenth century, with the advent of the machine gun and the explosive shell in place of the musket and the cannon-ball, the dreadnought in place of the sailing ship of the line, and vast new armed forces of unparalleled size to use these weapons. There are thus technical grounds for ending this book with the Napoleonic wars, before these further changes started to become significant and to require discussion, which must be left for another volume.

The geographical area to be covered is another contentious issue in a book of this kind. Black has argued against a 'Eurocentric' approach, reminding us that 'conflicts which did not involve Europeans were important and have much to teach us', whereas Geoffrey Parker added the rather provocative subtitle *The Triumph of the West* to his *Cambridge Illustrated History of Warfare* (Black, 1999, p. 5; Parker, 1995a). Considerations of space rather than principle have dictated the balance between these positions. Hence, while most of this book is indeed Eurocentric, two chapters deal with the wars of the Ottoman Turks and another with those in North America, although both of course had a substantial European involvement, leaving it to Black himself to give a wider view in the final contribution.

Was there a 'military revolution' in the early modern period?

No book on the military history of this period can entirely avoid the 'military revolution' debate, which has flourished since Michael Roberts first argued the case in 1955 (Roberts, 1995, is the most convenient source for a number of the seminal papers). Indeed it was initially intended to devote a chapter to the subject, but circumstances and space limitations combined to prevent this. A brief comment here must therefore suffice, if only to indicate a view that this debate has outlived its usefulness, so that a chapter on it may not have been necessary after all!

Roberts viewed changes in warfare during the late sixteenth and early seventeenth centuries as so large as to amount to a revolution, focusing on the growth of firepower from disciplined and drilled infantry, the much increased size of armies, bolder strategies designed to seek and win decisive battles, and the growth in size and importance of supply and support functions. Although nominating the period as 1560 to 1660, Roberts saw the full development of these features mainly in the campaigns and methods of Gustavus Adolphus during his 1630–32 invasion of Germany. In more recent years Parker has been the leading protagonist of an early modern military revolution, but he places it earlier, firmly in the sixteenth century, with elements stemming from a still earlier period (Parker, 1995b, 1995c, 1996). To Roberts's characteristics of revolution, which he broadly retains and develops, Parker adds emphasis on the growth of siege warfare – a feature he sees as driving the increase in army size – and of sea power, the latter having added significance in the light of his conclusion that a major effect of this revolution was the rise of the west, based on the military superiority of Europeans over non-Europeans. In a broadening debate others have argued for a military revolution in the fifteenth century or even earlier, or have seen revolutionary elements both then and significantly later, in the latter part of the seventeenth century, marked technologically by the introduction of the bayonet and politically by the rise of great power states capable of financing large standing armies.

Most of these developments are discussed in one or more chapters in this book, and there is no doubt that cumulatively they produced a great change in the nature and scale of warfare. However the word 'revolution' as normally understood implies not only decisive change, usually of lasting significance, but also that change takes place suddenly or over a relatively short period of time. In historical terms revolutions mark discontinuities, and as such are essentially the opposite of evolutionary processes in which change occurs more gradually, whether semi-continuously or as a series of smaller steps. In the context of the military revolution theory, the fact that historians point to a variety of significant factors and suggest a number of different periods, all with long timescales, is more suggestive of evolution than revolution. Parker has countered this argument by pointing out that 'both the scientific and the industrial revolutions lasted well over a century', even if, as he concedes, 'one might disqualify the "agricultural revolution" … on the grounds that it occurred in prehistoric times' (Parker, 1995c, p. 339). Here he overlooks the fact that in all these instances the word 'revolution' is employed in an essentially metaphorical sense, and by analogy the same applies to the so-called military revolution. The changes, taken over a long enough period, were indeed dramatic, almost as though the results of a revolution, but the other factors associated with revolution in a literal sense simply did not apply.

One could dismiss the foregoing as a semantic quibble if it were not for one further point. The term 'revolution' also clearly implies that the change in question was exceptional. However in military history, as in various other branches, particularly scientific history, it can be argued that change is the norm, and moreover that change tends to accelerate. The very fact that supporters of the military revolution theory disagree about when it occurred makes the point. Change was occurring at all these times; the only question is which precise aspect might be deemed to be decisive and hence revolutionary.

The growth in size of armies can be taken as an example (a topic which I discuss further in Chapter 6). Roberts made this one of the central features of his military revolution, and Parker amplified the point by noting a tenfold increase in numbers of soldiers between 1530 and 1710, both in total in European state armies and at individual battles, giving as examples Pavia in 1525 and Nieuwpoort in 1600, each involving 20,000 men, as compared to 200,000 at Malplaquet in 1709 (Parker, 1995b, p. 43). However such changes neither started in 1530 nor ended in 1710. Keen quotes Jean du Bueil saying to Louis XI in 1471: 'War has become very different. In your father's days, when you had eight or ten thousand men, you reckoned that to be a very large army: today it is quite another matter. One has never seen a more numerous army than that of my lord of Burgundy' (Keen, 1999, p. 273). Turning to later periods, the French *levée en masse* raised an army of some 700,000 in 1794, 85 years after Malplaquet, while Napoleon conscripted more than two million men between 1800 and 1814 (Forrest, 2000, p. 65). Another hundred years on even this looked modest compared to the armies of the First World War, with over two million soldiers involved in the battle of the Marne in

September 1914, and some 65 million men mobilized during the conflict (Murray, 1995, p. 269; Bourne, 2000, p. 137). These numbers, huge as they are, were in turn surpassed by those of the Second World War, when, to give just one figure, the Red Army was operating with four million troops in the winter of 1942–43 (Murray, 1995, p. 328). The comparisons would be even more dramatic if account were to be taken of the growth in firepower available to the individual soldier, sailor or airman, which has of course led to equally striking reductions in combat army size in recent years. On this basis a military revolution, in terms of troop numbers, could be postulated for each hundred years or so, and similar arguments could doubtless be deployed in respect of tactics and technology. The more reasonable view is that given above, that change tends to be continuous, and to accelerate over time. As to whether there was any more definable military revolution in the early modern period, then – to use the catchphrase of Professor C.E.M. Joad on the BBC's *Brains Trust* in the 1940s – it all depends on what you mean by a revolution.

References

Black, J.M. 2000. *War: Past, Present and Future*, Stroud.

—— 1999. *Warfare in the Eighteenth Century*, London.

Bourne, J. 2000. 'Total War I: The Great War', in Townshend, 2000, 117–37.

Forrest, A. 2000. 'The Nation in Arms I: The French Wars', in Townshend, 2000, 55–73.

Keen, M.H., ed. 1999. *Medieval Warfare: A History*, Oxford.

Murray, W.A. 1995. 'The West at War 1914–18', and 'The World at War 1941–45', in Parker, 1995a, 266–97 and 320–39.

Parker, G. 1996. *The Military Revolution: Military Innovation and the Rise of the West, 1500–1800*, Cambridge.

—— 1995a. *The Cambridge Illustrated History of Warfare: The Triumph of the West*, Cambridge.

—— 1995b. 'The "Military Revolution, 1560–1660" – A Myth?', in Rogers, 1995, 37–54.

—— 1995c. 'In Defense of The Military Revolution', in Rogers, 1995, 337–65.

Roberts, M. 1995. 'The Military Revolution, 1560–1660', in Rogers, 1995, 13–35.

Rogers, C.J., ed. 1995. *The Military Revolution Debate: Readings on the Military Transformation of Early Modern Europe*, Boulder.

Townshend, C., ed. 2000. *The Oxford History of Modern War*, Oxford.

1

The Medieval Legacy

Clifford J. Rogers

The armies and navies inherited by the sixteenth century were conquering armies, though in the new era they soon became very different in role – less so in form. Conquering Naples in 1494, Charles VIII of France wielded forces forged in a dark time by his grandfather, and tempered and tried by the internal conquests of Normandy, Gascony, Brittany and Burgundy. When Gonzalo de Cordoba, 'El Gran Capitán', reached the peninsula to make the Spanish riposte, he and his army had also been shaped by the developments of the latter part of the Hundred Years War, and hardened in the decade of invasions launched to subdue the 250-year-old Emirate of Granada. On the other rim of the Mediterranean, Ottoman armies were grinding forward in the Balkans, seizing Serbia, the Morea, Bosnia, Herzegovina and Negroponte (Euboea) between 1459 and 1470, and even smashing their way into Otranto in southern Italy in 1480, only to ebb back on the death of the sultan a year later.

The Middle Ages are traditionally defined, in America at least, as ending in 1453. Of course everyone realizes that there was no hard division which suddenly occurred in that year, but for military historians in particular the events of 1453 were indeed of great importance, even epochal. At one end of Europe Bordeaux surrendered to a French army, bringing an end to the Hundred Years War, the crucible of the most important military developments of the late Middle Ages. Far to the east Mehmed the Conqueror fully earned his sobriquet when he captured Constantinople, thus dealing the death blow to the Eastern Roman Empire. Elsewhere the smallest and shortest-lived of the European 'Gunpowder Empires', the Burgundian state, hammered down three castles with artillery and won a major battle, thereby restoring its authority over the rich and populous city of Ghent, which had rebelled rather than submit to a tax increase and interference with its municipal levies. The French and Ottoman armies shared important characteristics with one another, and with Burgundian and Spanish forces that would soon make their own bids for conquests of great importance – though only the latter would succeed, when Ferdinand and Isabella destroyed the last Islamic state in Iberia between 1482 and 1492. There were of course significant evolutionary developments in military structures and methods between 1453 and, say, 1529, but most of them were essentially refinements and extensions of the patterns already established in 1453. In other words the armies of Charles VIII and Gonzalo de Cordoba were essentially legacies of the Middle Ages in their structures and their methods. To understand the wars of Italy and the early modern military revolution, then, we have to understand the conquering forces of 1453, and how they came to be the way they were.

Throughout the late Middle Ages France had three or four times the population and economic strength of England, yet for the first hundred years of the Hundred Years War the French suffered many more defeats than they gained victories. Indeed when it came to full-scale land battles it could be argued that the French did not win a single one during that period, whereas the English gained decisive results at Crécy, Poitiers, Agincourt and Verneuil. (The French did win at Baugé in 1421 and Patay in 1429, but these involved substantially smaller forces than the others mentioned, and had no king or regent fighting on either side.) During some phases of the war, notably under Charles V, the French had nonetheless managed to make some gains by avoiding battle and using their superior resources to occupy territories castle by castle and town by town. This method worked well enough during periods when the French leadership was strong and the English leadership was weak, provided that it was directed at the reconquest of areas recently captured by the English, where the lords of the castles and the bourgeoisie in the towns were not averse to returning to Valois rule. Despite their huge advantage in resources, however, the French armies of this period were never up to the task of seizing English Gascony, as demonstrated by their ultimately unsuccessful efforts in 1337–40, 1377, 1403–07 and 1442 (see Labarge, 1980, for summaries of these campaigns). In 1450–53 things were very different. The last two major battles of the war, Formigny in Normandy and Castillon in Périgord, were the first two to be won decisively by the French. Even before the first of those battlefield successes, however, Charles VII's captains had demonstrated a new ability to make rapid conquests in Normandy. Then in 1451, without needing to fight a real battle in the south, the French overwhelmed the defences of Gascony and occupied Bordeaux, a feat they had attempted unsuccessfully many times before. Castillon, two years later, sealed and solidified the conquest, but did not drive it.

The forces which accomplished this remarkable turn-around were created between 1439 and 1448, and were carefully designed to solve a variety of political and military problems, and to put into effect lessons learned from experience and reinforced by the study of old Roman institutions and practices.

The problems were those of conquest. The solution was a combined-arms force of well-equipped, well-trained and well-disciplined soldiers, principally the famed *compagnies d'ordonnance* and the skilled gunners of the royal artillery.

An age of strong defence

In western Europe, especially from the twelfth to the fourteenth century, the conquest of a province, much less of a country, was a daunting prospect. The eleventh century had been a great period of conquests, with the Norman occupations of England, southern Italy and Sicily, the Reconquista in Iberia, German expansion to the east, and the establishment of the crusader states in the Levant. In all of these cases, however, the defeated enemies had been at a disadvantage in battle, and the territories seized had been only lightly fortified. Thereafter, as stone castles sprang up at every major road junction or river crossing, the strategic defender's position improved greatly.

In such an environment conquest required either many sieges or mass defections by the people who controlled the fortifications. Realistically, in fact, it took both. Each major siege was an expensive, time-consuming and difficult task, and attempts to capture a major castle or a fortified town often failed. Assaults typically required the attackers to cross a palisade and a moat while under heavy fire from above, then to climb siege ladders and somehow, from those unsteady platforms, to outfight the defenders on the stone walkways at the top of the walls, all the while suffering from enfilading fire from the projecting towers on either side. If resisted by a suitable garrison such assaults rarely succeeded. That forced the besiegers to turn to slower methods. Siege engines, mainly counterweight trebuchets, were not usually able to batter down walls efficiently enough to cut holes for direct attacks. The besiegers' projectiles could, however, demolish machiolations, merlons and tower-tops to help clear the way for renewed attempts at escalade. Moreover, broad sections of walls could be brought down, with the suddenness necessary to prevent the defenders from constructing a second line of defence behind the gap, by mining. This involved tunnelling up to the wall, then along below it, while holding up the stone with wooden supports. When this work was far enough extended the tunnel would be filled with combustible material (or eventually gunpowder) and set afire; once the timber props burnt away, the fortifications would tumble down. But this process, like the other major option – to starve the defenders into submission – was very slow.

Every day that went by during these long processes posed challenges and risks for the besiegers. The first problems that had to be overcome were ensuring the flow of money and troops. If the large sums necessary for an army's wages could not be found, the siege was likely to fail; it was lack of funds that ended Edward III's siege of Tournai in 1340. Even if sufficient money was available, a siege might fail because there was simply not enough food and forage coming in to sustain the soldiers and their horses, as in the same king's siege of Reims in 1359–60. Disease might ruin a siege army, as at Gibraltar in 1350, while internal conflicts between reluctant allies could shatter it, another factor contributing to Edward's failure to capture Tournai.

Sieges that did not simply fail might be broken. Depending on the situation, if a relief army arrived it might be able to cut the besiegers off from supplies. In that case they would have to come out from their field fortifications and fight in the open, and if they lost, the siege would be over. Of course the defenders of a threatened place could also choose to fight even before the siege began. The 'home-field advantage' meant that the invaders had to be very strong to have any chance. This was especially true from the fourteenth century onwards, as infantry forces, including urban militias, improved in quality to the point where they could be a major factor in battle. Think of the situation in economic terms. A powerful prince planning offensive operations could raise an army of two or three thousand men-at-arms (armoured soldiers, each provided with several horses, and well trained to fight either as heavy cavalry or on foot) and a force of infantry several times as large. It could take a substantial effort even from a whole kingdom to find that many troops willing to undertake a long-term offensive operation, and to raise the funds necessary to pay them for the time required to assemble, to travel to the target city, and to hold the field for the months a siege might take. (Even if the campaign proved to be a short one, the budget and therefore the size of the army would usually be determined by the expectation of a long one. As late as 1409 one authority recommended planning for sieges lasting six months each.) The defenders, on the other hand, faced with a threat to their homes, could be expected to contribute a much greater proportion of their financial resources and manpower. Furthermore if they were willing to risk battle they would only have to pay wages (including those of mercenaries or allies, if they were available) for a short period, just long enough to forestall or break a siege. Thus they could hire far more troops with a given amount of money.

The dramatic difference these considerations made can be illustrated by contrasting two simultaneous campaigns undertaken by Edward III, the siege of Calais and the response to the Scottish invasion of 1346. The siege of Calais, which lasted from October 1346 to August 1347, had to be maintained by an army large enough to stand up to a French relief army. Because the English had just won the battle of Crécy that was not as demanding a requirement as it otherwise would have been, but still the besieging force averaged somewhat over 10,000 men (Rogers, 2000, p. 273). Sustaining this force required the full attention of the English government, which had to organize a massive logistical effort and exert pressure by a host of means to keep the manpower up to sufficient levels. All in all it was the greatest single task the English crown had ever undertaken. In wages alone the cost of the operation (including the preceding campaign across northern France) amounted to over £127,000, the majority of which represented the expenses of the siege proper (Grose, 1812, p. 261). This sum exceeded the total revenues of the English crown for the first four years of Edward's reign combined. Although the siege did succeed (unlike the even more expensive though shorter siege of Tournai in 1340), and the capture of Calais was far from trivial, the ratio between the scale of the effort and the extent of the gain offers a powerful example of the difficulty of conquest in the fourteenth century.

While the siege was in progress the Scots invaded England to aid their French allies, thinking that with the royal army overseas and other substantial forces committed to Brittany and Aquitaine they would find only priests and shepherds to oppose them. Instead they were promptly met by an army which had been rapidly assembled almost entirely from the resources of the northern counties of England. The retinues of the northern magnates, including the small standing forces maintained at government expense by the Wardens of the Marches, amounted to something like 500 men-at-arms and an equal number of mounted archers. The rest of the army of around 9000 men was composed of arrayed troops, the majority of them mounted archers. The service of the 4328 soldiers in the Lancashire and Yorkshire contingents cost the Crown a mere £308 for four or five days' pay. The remainder of the army seems to have cost Edward III nothing at all, since its duration of service did not exceed the eight days provided at the expense of the county communities. Within that period they defeated the Scots at the battle of Neville's Cross, captured King David, and effectively ended the Scottish threat to northern England for a generation (Morris, 1914; Rogers, 1998).

The same logic of disparity helps explain how the city of Staveren could defeat the expeditionary army of the wealthy Count of Hainault, Holland and Zeeland in 1345, and how the people of Liège could defeat their bishop and his allies at Vottem the following year. Another good example is the failure of the anti-Hussite crusades of 1420–31. A whole series of armies, built up from the resources of nearly all of Europe, were routed time and again by inexpensive local forces, whose high level of commitment helped compensate for their relatively low level of training and equipment. In 1499 the Swiss put over 34,000 men into the field out of a total population of around 800,000; this was more than double the size of the largest army any English king took to France during the Hundred Years War, at a time when England's population was around five million. The Flemings, Scots and Frisians employed similar *levées en masse*, with comparable results (Winkler, 1982, pp. 101–7; Verbruggen, 1997; Rogers, 2000, pp. 40–1).

Even if circumstances allowed the besiegers to continue operations without leaving their camp (for example if their perimeter included a harbour and they were being supplied by sea, as in Edward III's siege of Calais in 1346–47), or if their opponents could not muster a force strong enough to face them in regular battle, they were still vulnerable. A siege line typically had to extend several miles to encircle even a fairly small town. This left the besiegers vulnerable to defeat in detail; even a weak relief army could sometimes hit a portion of the lines in a surprise night or dawn attack, then roll up and defeat the besieging army. The relief force under such circumstances typically enjoyed major home-field advantages from knowing the terrain and having the assistance of local partisans. Just such operations led to the failure of the French sieges of Auberoche in 1345 and La Roche Derrien in 1347, and indeed to the failure of the whole efforts to subdue Guienne and Brittany of which those sieges were a part.

Finally, attempts at conquest were often frustrated by the recall of the invasion force to deal with counter-strikes or other crises in different theatres of operations. The future John II's attempt to capture Aiguillon in 1346, for example, was aborted by his father's defeat at Crécy, despite the solemn oath the prince had sworn at the start of the siege to see it through to the end. And even when the besiegers managed to keep their army together for the necessary length of time, avoided destruction by disease or a relief army, and captured a substantial town or a key castle, they were likely to nearly bankrupt themselves in the process.

An invading army that kept concentrated could only expect to complete two or three major sieges in a year, even if all went well. The enemy, meanwhile, could gain ground elsewhere in the theatre of war, or stage a recovery during the period of financial exhaustion that was likely to follow a major offensive operation. If the invading army tried to accelerate the process of conquest by conducting several siege operations simultaneously, it faced a very serious risk of defeat in detail, of the sort Henry of Grosmont inflicted on the French around Bergerac in 1345. There was also something of a self-fulfilling prophecy at work. If the inhabitants of a walled town expected an invasion to be successful, and were summoned to surrender, they were likely to make a deal to do so on favourable terms. But if they thought that they could resist effectively they might well choose to fight, and if they did they were fairly likely to succeed, and almost certain to prevent any extensive conquests by the enemy. This was especially important because during a major siege the invaders would normally send out detachments to try to persuade neighbouring strongholds to surrender if the main operation was successful. These negotiations rested on the threat that any town that refused such an arrangement would be next in line for attack, and would be treated harshly if captured. Such a threat held little terror if it were presumed that a single major siege was the most that could realistically be carried through in one campaigning season.

Offensive strategy

Considering all these difficulties and perils, it is easy to see why the major French efforts against Gascony in 1337, 1339, 1345–46, 1377, 1403–06 and 1442 all failed to complete their mission and capture Bordeaux, while any number of other offensive operations elsewhere in Europe likewise failed in this period. The defender's advantage in warfare was so huge that it was almost impossible to surmount it, even when the attacker was three or four times as strong in absolute terms. When large areas did change hands it was usually in the wake of a major battle, but for that very reason belligerents attempting conquest were often met by foes who refused to oblige them by fighting in the open field.

Faced with these problems, aggressive powers often turned to the main strategic alternative to siege-based conquest: the *chevauchée* or 'war-ride'. The two different styles of warfare coexisted; the same armies and the same commanders would employ each at different times and under different circumstances. There was the war of fortresses, and there was the war of *chevauchées*. The former focused on major sieges with the full apparatus of encirclement, bombardment, sally and assault. It also included the tangled struggles of small garrisons spread throughout networks of fortifications, as they raided cattle, sprang ambushes, intercepted supply columns, attempted night escalades and so on. These elements of 'little war' were sometimes the endemic wrestling of frontier zones, and sometimes directed towards the support or frustration of a major siege. The *chevauchée* was a slashing mounted invasion of enemy territory, characterized by widespread devastation and burning. An army of six, ten or twelve thousand on *chevauchée* typically created a zone of ashes and tears around fifteen miles wide, and dozens or hundreds of miles long. Within this area the strongly fortified towns and the castles of the countryside would be packed with refugees. Unwalled or ill-defended settlements and individual manors would often be emptied out three times: first by their fleeing inhabitants, next by the army charged with defending the area and its hangers-on, and finally by the foragers and outriders of the invading force. Peasants too slow to evacuate would sometimes be rounded up and herded along with the stolen livestock, to be ransomed later for whatever small sums their more fortunate relations and neighbours could raise. All the devastation inflicted by such operations served to weaken the enemy regime economically and politically, and to pressure the defenders either to give battle or to seek peace. The defenders, meanwhile, would have as strong a force as they could spare from the defence of their strongholds assigned to shadow the invaders, warily watching their movements, laying ambushes for scouts, stragglers and foragers, and otherwise doing their best to minimize the damage inflicted on the countryside. This pattern of events was also often re-created on a smaller scale by the garrison raids that were a major feature of the war of fortresses.

Grand battles were less common than sieges and *chevauchées*. The possibility of a general engagement remained important in nearly every campaign, however, even when that possibility did not become a reality. Belligerents on the strategic offensive typically hoped for an opportunity to win a decisive tactical victory, which would clear the way for siege and ravaging operations to be conducted with much greater dispersal, and therefore speed and effectiveness. The defenders, on the other hand, often preferred to avoid battle, and to employ a Vegetian defence-in-depth strategy. By strongly holding the well-fortified towns and castles, emptying out the countryside as much as possible, and hemming in the invaders with small detachments harassing their supply lines and cutting up their outriders, the defenders could prevent their enemies from making any easy conquests. Though very effective, this strategy was also difficult to sustain. It enabled the defender to limit, but not to eliminate, the devastation of his lands. To put a stop to the ravaging the only real option (other than surrender) was to destroy the invading army in battle. Defeat deep in enemy territory was usually catastrophic. Thus an army conducting a large-scale *chevauchée* had to be ready to face a battle, and that requirement was as important in shaping the army and its commander's strategy as were the demands of efficient pillaging. Similar logic applied to siege-based schemes of conquest. Very often major sieges would run their course without a battle, but the besieging army had always to be ready to fight off a relieving army.

The structures of armies

Thus the structures of fourteenth-century armies were moulded by the demands of siege operations, open battles and ravaging or counter-ravaging operations all at once. Yet the different modes of strategy called for different emphases and balances of troop types. The elements were quite consistent across Europe, though there were regional specialities such as the longbowmen of England and the *jinetes* (light cavalrymen) of Iberia. Almost everywhere there were three main categories of soldiers: men-at-arms, mounted infantry and simple infantry.

The men-at-arms were mostly knights and esquires drawn from the lower nobility; they were by definition well-armoured and well-equipped, and mounted and trained sufficiently to fight effectively as heavy cavalry. Men-at-arms were always accompanied by non-combatant pages (a minimum of one for every two men-at-arms, but usually one to one) and had to provide themselves with three or more horses, typically at least one expensive battle charger, one riding horse and one pack horse. Very often, being nobles, even simple men-at-arms brought much more substantial stables and households of servants on campaign, as well as retinues of lesser soldiers.

Men-at-arms were able to fight very effectively on foot as heavy infantry, and over the course of the century this became more and more their normal battlefield role. This was the result of a chain reaction to cavalry charges which suffered crushing defeats. By the time of Poitiers in 1356 the large majority of the French men-at-arms fought on foot. In doing so they were imitating the English, who had defeated them at Crécy ten years earlier. The English in turn were imitating the Scots, who had beaten them at Bannockburn in 1314, while the Scots had been inspired by the victory of the Flemish communal infantry at Courtrai in 1302. Still, at Poitiers (just as at Agincourt in 1415) the French began the battle with substantial flanking and reserve contingents who remained mounted. Furthermore even the men-at-arms who fought on foot, if victorious, mounted for the pursuit. This was an extremely important tactical function, since the defeated often suffered more losses in the chase than in the battle itself.

During ravaging operations, too, the men-at-arms' service as heavy cavalry was extremely important. Much of the actual work of pillaging and burning was conducted by other sorts of troops, but it was vital for their success that they be supported by men-at-arms. Mounted infantry might be very effective in large numbers and tight formations in battle, but small bands of such troops could still be ridden down and hacked up fairly easily by lancers, if caught without such support. Similarly, true cavalry played a crucial role in siege operations. Many historians have made derisive quips about the inability of mounted men to attack fortifications, but it must be remembered that sieges very often became races to starvation. Besieging armies required vast quantities of supplies every day, and unless water transport was practical this meant long trains of slow-moving wagons and pack animals. It made no difference if the wagons had been loaded by foragers, government officials or merchants seeking profits; the supply lines had still to be protected by cavalry. Furthermore it remained the men-at-arms who normally carried out spearhead assaults over walls or through breaches, albeit without their steeds.

For all these reasons men-at-arms were valued more highly than any other soldiers by medieval commanders. Even though in the fourteenth century an esquire cost twice as much in wages as a mounted infantryman or light cavalryman (and four times as much as a true footman) governments were constantly making efforts to increase the proportion of men-at-arms in their armies. The cavaliers' proportional contribution to overall army numbers varied greatly from country to country, while tending to rise from the beginning to the middle of the fourteenth century, and then (in some areas) to fall again. The balance between these elite fighters and other types of soldier also depended on the purpose for which a given army was raised. Forces intended for offensive operations, especially *chevauchées*, might typically include 25 or even 50 per cent men-at-arms. Shadowing forces might have an even greater proportion of men-at-arms, while garrisons emplaced mainly to defend a fortification (as opposed to garrisons intended to defend or cut supply lines, to dominate a region or to conduct or guard against raids) might have very few. Urban contingents and armies drawn from poor, mountainous or heavily forested areas (like Switzerland and Scotland) usually contained only a small proportion of men-at-arms.

In Iberia light cavalrymen known as *jinetes* were employed in large numbers. The French *varlets* or *gros valets* also served as true light cavalry in at least some cases; they were normally equipped with brigandines or mail haubergeons, supplemented by plate protection for head, neck and hands, and mounted on horses whose descriptions and values indicate that they were meant for use in combat. The English seem not to have employed any such troops, though it is possible that the 'hobelars' who were fairly numerous in the 1330s could fight on horseback. Mounted infantry, on the other hand – that is, soldiers who rode to the battlefield but had neither the training nor suitable mounts for fighting on horseback – went from being rare to extremely important over the course of the century. The Irish and Scottish led the way in this, but it was the example of the English mounted archers, superb fighters, which eventually inspired widespread emulation. In the 1330s it was normal for English military retinues to include around one mounted archer for each man-at-arms; later, as it became more difficult to recruit the latter, the ratio often rose to three or four to one. These troops were much cheaper and usually easier to raise than men-at-arms; like light cavalrymen, they normally received only half the pay of a regular man-at-arms, and could be drawn from any social class. In battle, under the right circumstances and as part of a balanced combined-arms force, English longbowmen were at least as effective, man for man, as knights and esquires. They were also invaluable in assaults on second-rate fortifications, where their covering fire could sweep the ramparts of defenders, allowing other troops to stage successful escalades or demolish walls with picks and rams.

Even when longbowmen were not available, other forms of mounted infantry – typically crossbowmen or spearmen – were widely employed. On *chevauchée* their inexpensive hackneys gave these troops the mobility to keep up with the men-at-arms. Measured by linear distances, fourteenth-century armies, even all-mounted ones, tended to advance in reasonably short stages, typically averaging around twelve to fifteen miles a day, but many of the individual soldiers actually went much farther, often swinging out five miles or so from their divisions' main lines of march in order to plunder and burn. Thus if the army pushed forward 15 miles some of its members might well have covered 25 miles that day, a rate which only horsed troops could sustain. Without a large proportion of mounted troops an invasion force would have to move much more slowly and lay waste a much narrower band of territory.

That in turn would make it more difficult for the army to supply itself, and reduce the damage and provocation inflicted on the enemy.

True footmen were not as useful as mounted infantrymen, especially for offensive operations, but they had two key advantages: they were even cheaper, and under the right circumstances they could be available in very large numbers. An army raised for a major siege would normally include a large proportion of simple infantry. The siege lines had to remain heavily manned at all times, while other soldiers were needed to dig, and to fill out the ranks in case a relief army arrived to attempt to break the siege by battle. No horses were needed for these duties, and since each horse had to be provided with forage, and each rider's wage had to reflect the capital and maintenance costs of his mount, it was obviously preferable to hire footmen for jobs footmen could effectively perform. In areas like Flanders and Italy, where wars often centred around the large towns as protagonists and targets, and when operations were typically conducted mainly within relatively short distances, infantry drawn from town militias often formed the great bulk of armies.

Except among the English (and later the Scots and Welsh), who favoured the longbow, the predominant type of infantryman was a soldier armed with a spear or pike. Spearmen often used large shields, which might 'cover them up to their noses' whereas those employing the longer pike or other pole-arms typically needed both hands free to employ their weapons. Although 'lances afoot' or *armati* with armour comparable to that of a man-at-arms were not unknown, it was more common for an infantryman to be equipped more lightly, with a mail haubergeon or hauberk and an iron cap, together with a quilted gambeson composed of many layers of canvas, or a jack, brigandine, or more rarely a coat-of-plates, the latter three all being various forms of protection composed of thin iron plates riveted into cloth or leather coverings. (The defensive equipment of mounted infantry was similar, though tending to the higher end of the scale.) The spearmen were typically supplemented by smaller numbers of three other types of soldiers: crossbowmen, *paviseurs* and various forms of what might be dubbed 'strikers', that is men armed with halberds, *goedendags*, battle axes, bills and the like. In a formation of pikemen or spearmen, the strikers would be interspersed among the front rank or ranks. From there they could hit out at enemy troops, especially cavalrymen, who were halted by the serried points of the longer pole-arms or who tried to push in among them. The role of the crossbowmen was essentially the same as that of the longbowmen. In battle they attempted to clear away the enemy missile troops. If successful at that, they could employ their fire to wear down the strength of a stationary enemy force, or to weaken and disrupt an advancing one before retreating out of its way. Even if defeated, an advanced force of crossbowmen would still serve a useful purpose, screening the other soldiers from harassment for as long as it was able to hold the field. *Paviseurs,* equipped with very large shields to protect their partners as well as themselves, were very often paired with crossbowmen to make the latter less vulnerable during the relatively slow reloading process. Unlike longbowmen, however, crossbowmen were not expected to be able to stand up to a serious attack of infantry or cavalry, even with the aid of the *paviseurs*.

Across the lines of such functional divisions, troops could also be categorized by the ways they were raised for service. By the 1340s traditional feudal service had essentially disappeared in France, England and most other areas. All soldiers were paid, from foot archers to princes. Native troops serving their own sovereigns were mostly recruited in one of two ways; to use the English terminology, they were either volunteers serving in retinues, or arrayed troops who had been called into service by royal authority. The retinues were normally composed of men-at-arms and mounted infantry (or *gros valets* in France) who had contracted to serve for one or more quarters. The companies of great lords and of important professional captains might contain hundreds or even – in a few cases – thousands of men, including many men raised by subcontracts. Individual knights and esquires often enlisted to serve under friends, relatives or lords, but they could also enter the army on their own account, serving as the head of a retinue of just a few men. Their terms of service were fairly standard; sometimes they were spelled out in writing in a letter of indenture (roughly the same as the French *lettre de retenue* or the Italian *condotta*), but these written agreements were usually dispensed with if the king was leading the army in person. Heads of retinue were usually given their men's pay in advance. In addition to their daily wage, men-at-arms normally received a lump-sum bonus known as a *regard*, typically equal to 50 or 100 per cent of an esquire's pay. In the former case (the norm from the 1340s to the 1370s) troops were theoretically expected to surrender half of their war gains from plunder and ransoms to their captains, who in turn provided the same proportion to the king, but on the other hand the men were entitled to replacement costs if their principal warhorse were lost on campaign. With the higher *regard* the captain's share of profits fell to a third, but the troopers lost their right to *restor* for dead horses (Ayton, 1994). Soldiers were generally required to stand muster at the start of their service, and twice a month or so if stationed in garrison. At musters the men would 'show' (*monstre* in French, hence the English word) their mounts, armour and weapons; if these were not up to par they would be fined or have their wages reduced. Contract forces of this sort were the norm for garrison service, and also provided most of the men-at-arms and mounted infantry for major offensive expeditions.

When an enemy invasion was expected, the defending ruler, if he had sufficient warning, would usually build the core of a field force by the same means. Once the attacker had begun operations, the defender might supplement his army by drawing forces out of garrisons not directly threatened, though this would be counterbalanced by sending detachments from the main force to stiffen the defences of fortified places which were in the invader's zone of operations. Meanwhile the defender would typically issue a general summons requiring all those in the affected area who were able to bear arms to join his army. In practice most people would pay a monetary fine in lieu of personal service. Especially if the invasion took the form of a *chevauchée*, only mounted men would be of much use anyway, since only they would be able to keep up with the pace of manoeuvre. Noble men-at-arms, however, could be expected to turn out in significant numbers. In areas with strong traditions of broad military service, such as Scotland, northern England, Gascony, Switzerland, Flanders, Frisia and many parts of Iberia, quite large forces of reasonably effective infantry could also be raised. If the invaders settled down into a siege or if they were expected to march straight to battle, so that mobility was not as much of an issue, such troops could form large portions of defensive field armies. Especially in the former case, when a relief army was to be prepared, contingents of urban militiamen might be requested or demanded from a wide area – though more often requested than demanded, since most significant towns had charters limiting their military obligations to local operations. In England such armies were raised by com-missioners of array, who were empowered to select the fittest, strongest archers from each community, up to a specified number, and to compel them to serve. Such arrayed forces could also be used in some cases for offensive operations, particularly within the British Isles. The use of substantial contin-gents of arrayed troops for the Crécy–Calais campaign of 1346–47 was, however, the exception rather than the rule for overseas operations.

In addition to these two basic categories of native troops – those raised by contract and those gathered by array or general summons – armies often con-tained substantial bodies of paid mercenaries from other lands. Usually these were volunteers, organized under their own captains in areas with at least some loose alliance with the power they agreed to serve. The French, for example, often employed large numbers of Genoese crossbowmen. In Italy such *condottieri*, drawn from all over Europe, formed especially large propor-tions of most armies. Foreign troops were typically retained in much the same way and with basically the same conditions as the indentured native forces.

Tactics and strategy in transition

In the twelfth and thirteenth centuries battles had normally, though by no means always, been won by cavalry charges. By the middle of the fourteenth century a whole series of battles from Courtrai to Crécy had witnessed mounted men-at-arms suffering crushing defeats at the hands of men fighting on foot. Infantry in close order (unlike cavalry) are most effective fighting on the defence. The inherent strength of a tightly arrayed force of footmen was normally increased still further by the use of various forms of obstacles, including hedges, agricultural ditches, streams, lines of baggage wagons, belts of horse-tripping potholes, hastily dug trenches and the like. These were almost invariably used to protect the flanks, and sometimes also to cover the front of a formation. Frontal attacks into these defences were often made, but almost never succeeded.

It was relatively easy for the side on the strategic defensive to employ such defensive tactics, simply by taking up a blocking position between the aggressor and his target. However invaders could sometimes use the pressures of siege or *chevauchée* to impel an enemy into taking the tactical offensive (as the English did at Halidon Hill, Crécy and Poitiers), but this was a tricky proposition and required skilled generalship. Since siege operations were so difficult and costly, *chevauchées* were generally the preferred means of offensive warfare. Thus mounted infantry, which had the mobility to outdistance or bypass defensive blocking forces of simple footmen, but also the combat effectiveness to win battles if attacked, became increasingly popular for armies of invasion. Faced with fast-moving enemies, defenders too had to rely on cavalry and mounted infantry who were capable of rapid manoeuvre. This meant a general trend towards armies more and more composed of contract retinues, with less and less reliance on troops raised by general levy. The interminable wars kept significant numbers of troops in constant, or at least frequent, service in frontier garrisons, and also spawned large mercenary companies. Both these developments offered more opportunities for men of all social ranks to make careers in arms. The Black Death, which hit in the middle of the fourteenth century, contributed to these phenomena. Minor lords found that the real revenues produced by their lands declined with the impact of inflation and falling rents; military service offered an excellent way for them to tap into the rising wealth of the urban and village middle classes to subsidize their noble lifestyle, whether through the medium of royal taxation or through pillage and the exaction of *appatis* (protection money).

By the turn of the fifteenth century, however, the grand *chevauchée* had lost much of its lustre as a method of offensive warfare. Taking their example from the Scots, the French had re-learned the effectiveness of the Vegetian, battle-avoiding strategy, and all across Europe heavy expenditure on fortifications, both urban and seigneural, reduced the impact of ravaging.

Tactics continued to favour the defence, and formal sieges continued to be long and expensive. One change did favour the offensive in siege warfare; the steadily growing strength, revenues and administrative capacities of central governments increased armies' staying power, which reduced the chances of sieges simply failing due to lack of money or supplies. Still, conquest remained extremely costly and difficult. It was only the combination of French errors in the Agincourt campaign and the political divisions in France deriving from Charles VI's madness that made Henry V's occupation of Normandy possible. Venice was able to make significant territorial gains in the wars of 1404–05, 1411–12 and 1418–20, but the scale was much smaller. Offensive wars aimed at territorial aggrandizement were more likely to end in failure, as with the Angevin and Imperial invasions of Italy in 1391 and 1401, the Castilian invasion of Portugal in 1385, the Austrian attempt to subdue Switzerland in 1386–88, the Ottoman sieges of Constantinople in 1396 and 1422, or the five Hussite Crusades. When conquests were made, they rarely extended much beyond a single town and its environs; the major Castilian offensive against Granada in 1407 led to the capture of Zahara, but then ended in failure with an attempt to capture Setenil. In 1410, in a follow-up operation, the border fortress of Antequera fell after a siege of nearly five months. There the effort at conquest halted for a generation, with relatively small return for such great effort. By 1482 Zahara was back in Moslem hands, and Granada was not significantly smaller than a century before. The picture was little different from what it had been in the 1340s, when a major battlefield victory at Rio Salado and an international crusading effort enabled Alfonso XI to capture Algeciras after an exceptionally difficult two-year siege, but not to capture neighbouring Gibraltar. That took until 1462. Similarly even the great Polish victory over the Teutonic Knights at Tannenberg in 1410 led to no sweeping territorial losses by the order, which successfully defended its great stronghold of Marienburg. The French siege of Arras in 1414 simply failed, as did Philip the Good's siege of Compiègne in 1430.

All this really started to change with the French reconquest of Normandy in 1449–50 and the conquest of Guienne the following year. The French and Burgundian suppressions of the revolts of Gascony and Ghent in 1453 only confirmed the change. The Burgundian conquests of Guelders and Lorraine in 1473–75, the Spanish conquest of Granada, the Ottoman seizures of Constantinople in 1453, Serbia in 1459, Bosnia in 1464 and Herzegovina in 1467, and even Charles VIII's drive to Naples in 1494 were cut from the same cloth. Two key developments served to tip the balance between offence and defence: the creation of permanent standing forces and improvements in artillery design.

Both of these were natural evolutionary progressions of trends dating back at least to the mid-fourteenth century, if not the late thirteenth. But at a certain point evolutionary change had revolutionary implications. Let us first consider gunpowder artillery. Cannon were first employed in Europe as early as 1326, but it was not until the 1370s that they became truly formidable weapons, throwing stones of 300 to 400 pounds or more. These great guns, however, were essentially what we would today call mortars. Their short barrels spat out stone balls at a high trajectory and low velocity, making them more suitable for demolishing buildings inside towns than for breaching fortifications. By the 1420s and 1430s we see true cannon with much longer barrels, which fired large projectiles much more rapidly and accurately; these guns were capable of knocking down the walls of many towns or castles within a few short weeks (Rogers, 1995, pp. 64–76). Even a badly breached wall was not easy to attack, and determined defenders could still beat off assaults, as the garrisons of Beauvais, Neuss and Rhodes did in 1472, 1474 and 1480. Still, what had been the general rule became the exception, and what had been the exception became the rule. Rouen, which took Henry V six months to capture in 1418, fell in days in 1450. In 1415 it was considered almost miraculous that the English were able to take Harfleur in just six weeks; in 1450 the French managed the job in 17 days. To reach Ghent in 1453, Philip the Good had first to deal with the castles of Schendelbake, Poeke and Gravere; all three were reduced so rapidly that the advance on the main target was not seriously impeded, even though the duke's brutal policy of executing the defenders ensured that they were not surrendered lightly. Dinant, which had been besieged without success 17 times before, was pummelled into submission by Burgundian guns in just one week in 1466 (Vaughan, 1975, pp. 129–56; Hall, 1997, p. 121). It only took three days of bombardment in 1484 before the walls of Setenil, which had halted the Spanish offensive of 1407, were 'reduced to great chunks of rubble' (Cook, 1993, p. 51).

Although the new artillery created unprecedented potential for conquest, it could not, of course, do its work against enemy walls unless it could be brought up to them. Thus the role of battle in defensive strategy became vastly more important, with the Vegetian style of defence declining proportionately. As Guicciardini put it, 'whenever the open country was lost, the state was lost with it' (Rogers, 1995, p. 74). In other words, almost the only way for a strategic defender to prevent total defeat was to fight and win an open battle. Such battles normally took one of two forms; either the defender had to block the enemy army and its artillery as it approached its target, or if he could not manage that he had to attack the aggressor's siege lines and drive him away. Artillery, in addition to its role in battering down fortifications, was coming to play a greater role in the field, and this too tended to facilitate successful invasions. The two possibilities are illustrated in the two main battles of the French conquests of 1450–53. Formigny was of the first type; the English, as in so many other battles, formed up in a defensive array, playing to the strength of their longbowmen. The French proceeded to take advantage of their superior artillery to bombard their enemies until they had to break formation, leading (after some hard fighting) to the biggest English battlefield defeat of the war thus far. At Castillon in 1453 an English relief army arrived after the siege of the town had begun. The English were thus compelled to take the tactical offensive, and their attacking columns were shredded by French guns. This defeat essentially brought the Hundred Years War to a close.

These two battles were not, of course, won by artillery alone. Another crucial ingredient of French success was the creation, between 1439 and 1448, of a whole new military structure for France. The centrepiece of these army reforms was the formation of the *compagnies d'ordonnance* in 1445 (Solon, 1970; Contamine, 1972). In 1450 there were 20 of these companies, each composed of 100 *lances fournies*: one man-at-arms, one swordsman (*coutillier*) on a 'fighting horse', who seems to have filled the role once carried out by a squire, two well-equipped archers, a valet, and a page to manage the horses. The soldiers of these ordinance companies were an elite group, selected from the much larger body in royal service in 1444 on the basis of their physique, skill, valour, equipment and military experience. Even in peacetime these companies were kept at full strength and earned full pay, making them the first real national standing army in Europe. Most French walled towns of any size had 10, 20, 30 or more lances stationed in them and supported by their taxes, and in addition to maintaining their readiness to fight in war, these men enforced royal authority and performed some police duties. Louis XI later observed that armies composed of new troops can collapse of their own weight without even seeing the enemy (Solon, 1970, pp. 208–9). With these hardened warriors there was little risk of that.

These ordinance companies formed the solid core of the French army on campaign, but by no means were they the full strength of the military establishment, not even of the standing forces. There were also large numbers of men in the 'little lances', less well mounted and equipped, and intended mainly for defensive garrison service. For the conquests of 1449–53 the cavalry and mounted infantry of the lances were supplemented by a sort of ready militia, the 'free archers', who kept themselves prepared for service in exchange for tax exemptions. Each parish was to support one free archer. Later in the century Louis XI employed strong contingents of Swiss and other mercenaries to round out his forces when needed. Finally there was the impressive independent structure of the royal artillery, organized by Jean and Gaspard Bureau. In the second half of the fifteenth century the great wrought-iron bombards were largely replaced by cast-bronze cannon of smaller bore but – thanks to stronger powder charges and cast-iron balls with three times the density of stone – of comparable hitting power. This greatly increased the operational mobility of the artillery, speeding up campaigning still further.

The success of this military system in 1449–53 left France, according to one contemporary, 'the envy of the world'. Envy inspired emulation, sometimes coupled with improvement. The dukes of Burgundy and Brittany created their own ordinance companies, in the former case justified by the assertion that without them Burgundy would lack 'a proper military defence' (Solon, 1970, pp. 227–8, 222, 254). The Burgundian companies were structured by an elaborate chain of command and required to engage in regular field training, and their officers received formal commissions and printed copies of their ordinances. By the 1470s Venice and Milan had ready militia forces, *provisionati*, somewhat similar to the free archers, and as early as 1456 the latter state reportedly had 12,000 cavalry in standing squadrons (Mallett, 1974, pp. 108–18). The Spanish national army developed somewhat later and with greater differences from the French model, but still along the same general lines (Stewart, 1961). By 1472 the Ottoman sultan had 10,000 full-time infantrymen in his corps of Janissaries, and Matthias Corvinus of Hungary matched them with his own standing army.

Permanent forces, mostly of mounted men, who could be set into motion at short notice, ready forces of well-equipped infantry who could be mobilized with a minimum of delay, lighter artillery which remained capable of rapidly reducing stone fortifications – all of these acted to speed up the pace of offensive operations. This was of crucial importance, for conquest delayed could be conquest denied. A campaign that ended with the target region only half occupied was likely to be followed by a strategic riposte which could regain much of the territory that had been lost. Furthermore, and even more importantly, the best way to make large conquests was through mass surrenders. When it became natural to assume that an invading army would be able to carry through many sieges in a single campaigning season, rather than just a few, the result was an exponential increase in the ability of the aggressor to make convincing threats. This in turn meant – even more than in the fourteenth century – that the capture of a town usually cascaded into the surrender of its whole hinterland. The age of the European 'Gunpowder Empires' had arrived.

Within Europe, however, there was only so much room for these expansive states to grow before they ran into one another. When they did, after Charles VIII's invasion of Italy in 1494, a new era began. That new era, however, cannot be understood without reference to the structures and methods of war it inherited from the medieval period.

References

Ayton, A. 1994. 'English Armies in the Fourteenth Century', in *Arms, Armies and Fortifications in the Hundred Years War*, ed. A. Curry and M. Hughes, Woodbridge, 39–68.

Contamine, P. 1972. *Guerre, état et société à la fin du moyen âge. Etudes sur les armées des rois de France, 1337–1494*, Paris.

Cook, W. 1993. 'The Cannon Conquest of Nasrid Spain and the End of the Reconquista', *Journal of Military History*, 57, 43–70.

Grose, F. 1812. *Military Antiquities Respecting a History of the British Army*, vol. 1, London.

Hall, B. 1997. *Weapons and Warfare in Renaissance Europe: Gunpowder, Technology, and Tactics*, Baltimore.

Labarge, M.W. 1980. *Gascony: England's First Colony, 1204–1453*, London.
Mallett, M. 1974. *Mercenaries and their Masters. Warfare in Renaissance Italy*, Totowa.
Morris, J.E. 1914. 'Mounted Infantry in Medieval Warfare', *Transactions of the Royal Historical Society*, 3rd series, 8, 77–102.
Rogers, C.J. 2000. *War Cruel and Sharp: English Strategy under Edward III, 1327–1360*, Woodbridge.
—— 1998. 'The Scottish Invasion of 1346', *Northern History*, 34, 51–69.
—— 1995. 'The Military Revolutions of the Hundred Years War', in *The Military Revolution Debate: Readings on the Military Transformation of Early Modern Europe*, ed. C.J. Rogers, Boulder, 55–94.
Solon, P. 1970. 'Charles VII and the Compagnies d'Ordonnance, 1445–61: A Study in Medieval Reform', doctoral dissertation, Brown University.
Stewart, P.J. 1961. 'The Army of the Catholic Kings: Spanish Military Organization and Administration in the Reign of Ferdinand and Isabella, 1474–1516', doctoral dissertation, University of Illinois.
Vaughan, J.F. 1975. *Valois Burgundy*, Hamden.
Verbruggen, J.F. 1997. *The Art of Warfare in Western Europe during the Middle Ages*, Woodbridge.
Winkler, A.L. 1982. 'The Swiss and War: The Impact of Society on the Swiss Military in the Fourteenth and Fifteenth Centuries', doctoral dissertation, Brigham Young University.

Further reading

Allmand, C.T., ed. 1973. *Society at War: The Experience of England and France during the Hundred Years War*, Edinburgh.
Colloquium. 1997. *From Crecy to Mohacs: Warfare in the Late Middle Ages (1346–1526). Acta of the XXIInd Colloquium of the International Commission of Military History (Vienna, 1996)*, Vienna.
Curry, A. and Hughes, M., eds. 1994. *Arms, Armies and Fortifications in the Hundred Years War*, Woodbridge.
Fowler, K. ed. 1971. *The Hundred Years War*, London.
—— 1967. *The Age of Plantagenet and Valois*, New York.
Hewitt, H.J. 1996. *The Organization of War under Edward III 1338–62*, Manchester.
Heymann, F.G. 1995. *John Zizka and the Hussite Revolution*, Princeton.
Housley, N. 1992. *The Later Crusades, 1274–1580. From Lyons to Alcazar*, Oxford.
Keen, M.H. ed. 1999. *Medieval Warfare*, Oxford.
—— 1984. *Chivalry*, New Haven.
—— 1965. *The Laws of War in the Late Middle Ages*, London.
Newhall, R.A. 1940. *Muster and Review*, Cambridge.
—— 1924. *The Conquest of Normandy, 1416–1424*, New Haven.
Prestwich, M. 1996. *Armies and Warfare in the Middle Ages: The English Experience*, New Haven.
Rogers, C.J. 2002. 'By Fire and Sword: Bellum Hostile and "Civilians" in the Hundred Years War', in *Civilians in the Path of War*, ed. M. Grimsley and C.J. Rogers, Lincoln, 33–78.
Vale, M. 1981. *War and Chivalry*, London.

2
Spanish Military Power and the Military Revolution

Fernando González de León

Introduction

Almost fifty years ago, in a seminal essay, Michael Roberts described the massive modernization of European armies in the sixteenth and seventeenth centuries as a 'military revolution'. This transformation, which according to Roberts began around 1560, involved primarily a substantial increment in the scale and cost of armies and warfare, resulting from the advent of standing armies and of new tactics based on the use of firearms by smaller groups of soldiers instead of massive infantry charges. This was accompanied by a professionalization of military leadership, and a rise in the sophistication and complexity of the government offices that dealt with warfare (Roberts, 1995). Roberts used the Spanish army as a contrast to the allegedly progressive Dutch and other northern European armies, and his successors, scholars such as Maury Feld, Raffaele Puddu and others, have largely accepted this paradigm. The most important exceptions are the work of René Quatrefages and Geoffrey Parker, but even the latter makes important concessions to Roberts's views on this matter. In a monograph with *The Military Revolution* as the first part of its title, Parker gave the Roberts thesis a new lease of life, and included within its parameters the development of new 'Italian design' fortifications and the ocean-going warship (Parker, 1988). Despite some revisionist efforts, the notion that a tactically and structurally retrograde Spanish military contributed to the decline of Spain remains an issue.

More recent explanations of Spanish military decline involve analyses of foreign policy. In 1987 Paul Kennedy opened this debate by arguing for the central role of what he called an 'imperial' or 'strategic overstretch', a surfeit of military commitments that vastly exceeded resources (Kennedy, 1987, pp. 31–59). In 1998 Parker revisited this issue by examining the major features and flaws of what he calls *The Grand Strategy of Philip II*, that is, the coherent set of Spanish military and diplomatic priorities and objectives, denying any significant role to the military revolution in the thwarting of these goals.

Nonetheless the question lingers: did technical backwardness or other factors such as strategy play a more decisive role in the early decline of Spain? What may prove useful at this point in the historiography is to put to the test the traditional image of the Spanish military, and to examine how tactical and strategic factors associated with the military revolution conditioned Spanish expansion in southern Europe and America in the first half of the century, and influenced Spain's later failure in northern Europe.

Early reforms

Early modern Spain was the result of the marriage of Isabella of Castile and Ferdinand of Aragón in 1469. Partly to unite their subjects, the Catholic Monarchs set out to complete the medieval Iberian crusade called the Reconquista, by attacking the last Muslim outpost in western Europe, the kingdom of Granada. Although their realm has often been identified as one of the first modern nation-states in Europe, the armies they led remained quite heterogeneous in almost every way. Close to a thousand *Guardas Reales* or Royal Guards formed the core of the army, but prominent vassals fulfilled their traditional obligations to the crown by fighting in person, along with their retainers; and the three medieval crusading orders of knights, as well as the major cities, also provided considerable numbers of troops. There was also a small international contingent, including Swiss infantry, from whom the Spaniards almost certainly learned how to use the pike and how to maintain deep and tight formations. In weaponry these forces were also rather diverse. Most were foot soldiers armed with crossbows, arquebuses, lances or sword and shield. The mounted branch was similarly heterogeneous, with both light cavalry (*jinetes*) and heavily armoured members of the high aristocracy (McJoynt, 1995, pp. 13–56).

The war in Granada (1483–92) provided useful military experience, and the process of creating a more cohesive army began soon thereafter. This was a period of constant experimentation, and one of the most innovative eras in European military history, an authentic military revolution which has received too little recent scholarly attention. In 1493 the light cavalry was placed under royal administration, and the proportion of arquebusiers in the infantry grew to a quarter of the total by 1500 (Quatrefages, 1996, p. 310). Three years later the monarchs issued the first set of general military ordinances replacing the lance with the Swiss pike and establishing the company as the core unit of their army. An important pioneer, Captain Gonzalo de Ayora, began intensive and *en masse* infantry drilling, and issued a set of instructions for this practice (Historia, 1993, pp. 281–2). By 1509 these companies were gathered in colonelships, and in an expedition to north Africa Pedro Navarro, another prominent innovator, divided them into combat squadrons (Quatrefages, 1996, p. 245).

Since 1494 there had been a sizeable Spanish expeditionary force in Naples, fighting the French for control of that kingdom, and one of the major debates in the historiography of this transformation has been whether reforms originated in Spain, with the likes of Ayora, Alonso de Quintanilla and others, or in Italy under the leadership of Gonzalo Fernández de Córdoba, the Great Captain, Navarro and those who succeeded them. Modernization actually came from both places, structurally and administratively from Spain and strategically and tactically from Naples. The Great Captain did not introduce any significant organizational improvements. His talent was oriented towards combat, and he has been described by Hans Delbrück as the major forerunner of early modern battle tactics (Delbrück, 1990, p. 74). At the same time as the reforms outlined above were being introduced in Spain, Gonzalo de Córdoba was devising ways to profit from them, especially in the use of light cavalry and arquebusiers. He could also rely on the services of one of the most inventive military engineers of his day, Pedro Navarro, a field fortification expert and one of the first to use landmines in sieges (Taylor, 1993, pp. 137–8; Duffy, 1996, pp. 11–12). Under their leadership and that of their successors, pikemen and arquebusiers eventually switched combat roles, as pikes became a way to support shot and not vice versa. The imaginative use of firearms, ambushes and battlefield entrenchments, and the relentless pursuit of the defeated enemy – in other words the aggressive quest for total tactical victory – became hallmarks of their strategy. Such methods were perhaps the most appropriate to a monarchy seeking to expand its holdings, and seemed well tuned to the character of a warrior king like Charles V.

The Italian Wars came at a time when improvements in artillery had rendered medieval fortifications obsolete, which in turn made sieges less important than battles. Tactically, the battles of the Italian Wars are, as Jeremy Black points out, a series of tests 'in which a variety of weapons, weapons systems, and tactics were used in search for a clear margin of military superiority' (Black, 1996, p. 50). The French, despite boasting the most advanced artillery train, often relied on antiquated techniques such as aristocratic heavy cavalry shock tactics and the individual prowess of heroic knights such as the famous Bayard. One scene repeats itself throughout the Italian Wars (1494–1536): the French, with superior artillery and an eager cavalry, favour the offensive, and frequently lose while attempting to storm fortified positions defended by Spanish pikemen and shooters. In April 1503 at Cerignola, which Delbrück called 'the first truly modern battle', the combination of cavalry, arquebusiers and artillery, as well as the use of entrenchment, resulted in a lopsided Spanish victory over their offensive-minded foes that led to the French loss of

Naples (Delbrück, 1990, p. 297). The major French success of the war came nine years later at the battle of Ravenna, where a furious artillery barrage succeeded in ejecting the Spanish infantry from their fortified position. However, they effected an orderly withdrawal under fire, which reduced their losses and suggested the high levels of discipline and morale that structural reforms had fostered (Oman, 1937, pp. 130–50).

During the peace of 1516–21 the proportion of arquebusiers in the Spanish infantry rose to almost a quarter, one of the highest totals in contemporary armies (Taylor, 1993, pp. 47, 50–1). When war with France again broke out, this time over control of Milan, these improvements had an immediate impact. In 1522 at Biccoca the Spanish infantry, led by Don Fernando Dávalos, Marquis of Pescara, routed the famous Swiss foot soldiers who attempted to storm their dug-in positions. On Pescara's instructions, row after row of arquebusiers discharged their weapons, then knelt down to reload while others came from behind to fire, submitting the enemy to an almost continuous and decisive barrage (Oman, 1937, pp. 178–85). It was one of the earliest instances of a manoeuvre known as the countermarch, which Parker, who considers it a crucial element of the military revolution, calls a 'Dutch discovery' of 1594 (Parker, 1988, p. 19). Effective and innovative use of firearms were the keys to several crucial victories in the 1520s, none more important than the battle of Pavia in 1525. On that occasion Pescara's Spanish arquebusiers again maintained a steady rate of fire that routed the Swiss infantry and the French cavalry. The remarkable collaboration between the Imperial infantry, cavalry and artillery, which stood in sharp contrast to the disjointed efforts of the French, led to the capture of the French monarch Francis I, who was eventually forced to yield Milan to Charles V (Oman, 1937, pp. 186–207). In the future, battlefield success would increasingly depend on the disciplined tactical coordination that Pescara and his associates had pioneered.

Expansion in America, 1492–1540

Spanish expansion in the New World in the sixteenth century proceeded at different paces, depending not only on the terrain but on the cultures of the local indigenous population. Small expeditions easily seized most of the major Caribbean islands after Columbus's voyage of 1492, but resistance to coloniza-tion was at least temporarily effective in remote areas where nomadic or semi-nomadic warlike peoples such as the Araucanians of Chile used asymmetrical or guerrilla tactics. However, the conquests of Mexico (1519–21) and Peru (1532–36) were the key to the Hispanization of the Americas, and these two territories became military bases from which Spanish power in the continent inexorably expanded.

To this day the collapse of the Aztec and Inca empires remains puzzling. How did 1600 conquistadors, equipped with a dozen or so light cannon and a few dozen horses and arquebuses, conquer a fierce militaristic civilization such as the Aztec, with dozens if not hundreds of thousands of warriors at its disposal? How could a lightly armed band of at the most three hundred topple a vast and well-organized Inca empire fighting in its home turf? To be sure, the Spaniards counted on the sometimes unreliable support of native allies who resented their overlords, but these allies were insufficient to reach anywhere near numerical parity and, like the Tlascalans of Mexico, they had to be defeated first before agreeing to join the invaders. The influence of another factor, European diseases such as smallpox, to which the Indians had never been exposed and were thus especially vulnerable, seems to have been exaggerated, since again no possible mortality rate could have made this anywhere close to an even match. Moreover the Spaniards were also weakened and killed, not only by the ailments they had brought with them, but also by tropical diseases against which they had no immunity (Hanson, 2001, pp. 213–16).

In addition to factors such as morale and leadership, the primary causes of the quick demise of the Amerindian empires were a number of tactics associated with late medieval European warfare and with the military revolution. The conquistadors defeated their adversaries in every single aspect of contemporary warfare: field battles such as Otumba and others; urban combat, as in Tenochtitlan; urban sieges as in Tenochtitlan again; naval warfare on Lake Texcoco; and fortress defence in Sacsahuaman in Peru. The major battles in the conquest of Mexico and Peru, those encounters that decided the fate of a continent and its millions of inhabitants, share certain features. As their memoirs constantly remind us, the conquistadors, many of whom had fought in Italy, kept to a strict three-corps formation (vanguard, battle and rear) to respond to surprise attacks, minimize the risk of capture and provide mutual support (Hemming, 1970, p. 92). The Amerindians, especially the Aztecs, fought for individual prowess and not in formation. The notion that the Aztecs' primary objective was to seize prisoners for human sacrifice is only partially true. The Aztecs quite often, and the Incas always, fought to kill, as the conquistadors discovered on a number of occasions. The very fury and courage of the Amerindians' massive assaults afforded excellent opportunities for the effective use of arquebus and crossbow volleys. However we should remember that neither of these two weapons was in great abundance in these expeditions, and that they took minutes to load. Obviously the long Spanish pikes were essential to stave off attackers and to provide cover not only for the shooters but also for the swordsmen, who could use the bristling squares as movable fortresses from which they could make sallies. They had already operated in this manner in Italy and earned the admiration of Niccolo Machiavelli (Machiavelli, 1990, p. 51). Native armies equipped with occidian blades fought at a distinct disadvantage.

Another Iberian advantage was cavalry, which the Amerindians lacked. At the battle of Otumba (1521), when 500 Spaniards and a few thousand Tlascalans managed to defeat an Aztec army as much as eighty times their size in open field, Hernán Cortez's forty light horsemen or lancers played a crucial role by charging at pivotal moments and providing the infantry with useful respites. Mounted men had a similar effect under Francisco Pizarro at Cajamarca (1532), where roughly 170 Europeans defeated thousands of the best fighters in the Inca empire and captured the Inca himself, and at Teocajas (1534), where a native army of around 50,000 failed to stop the Spanish advance on Quito. The willingness of the vastly outnumbered Spaniards to use shock tactics disconcerted both Aztecs and Incas, who could not neutralize an armoured rider except by charging him *en masse*, which of course made them more vulnerable to shot. Besides, the natives' unfamiliarity with cavalry allowed the conquistadors to mount effective surprise attacks, especially in Peru (Hemming, 1970, pp. 111–12).

Hanson has recently suggested that the rational and experimental approach to warfare traditional in the western world was a crucial factor in the European victory. Actually the ongoing military revolution in western Europe had accentuated such features at that precise moment. Like Pedro Navarro and others in Italy, Castilian engineers such as Martín López and others demonstrated significant mechanical ingenuity in devising siege engines, portable bridges and other equipment from local materials, which allowed them to survive and eventually succeed in street fighting in canal-laced Tenochtitlan. They even manufactured gunpowder from sulphur found at the Popocatepetl volcano. The crowning touch was López's construction of a flotilla of fourteen brigantines, which he assembled on site from parts he had previously built elsewhere, to help in achieving the submission of Tenochtitlan (Hanson, 2001, pp. 230–2).

Administrative and organizational reforms

By the 1530s Charles V ruled over a vast empire stretching from central Europe to the Pacific coast of the Americas. Many of these lands (Spain, the Netherlands and the Holy Roman Empire) he had inherited. Others such as Milan, Mexico, Peru and places in north Africa his soldiers had conquered outright. In order to manage such a far-flung collection of territories the emperor relied on the highly efficient postal and courier service established by his immediate predecessors, and on the largest ambassadorial network of its day. He also counted on a complex system of government councils, at the top of which stood the Council of State (1522), as well as other regional councils dedicated to local administration of particular states within the monarchy. In the mid-1510s a Council of War had come into being, which worked as a subdivision of the Council of State though with its own secretary (Elliott, 1964, p. 163; Conti, 1998, pp. 26–8). This governing body underwent a variety of changes and transformations of membership and jurisdiction throughout the century, and would eventually became a separate council staffed by military specialists during the reign of Philip II. Later on, in the 1590s, there would emerge additional even more specialized sub-councils or *juntas*, like the *Junta de la Armada del Mar Oceano* or Naval Council, and the *Junta de Guerra de Indias* or Council of American War (Conti, 1998, pp. 225–6).

The adaptation of the Spanish machinery of government to the demands of war could proceed organically and slowly, but the restructuring of the military itself had somewhat greater urgency. By the early 1530s it had become clear to Charles V and his advisers that despite repeated and severe defeats the French king, Francis I, would not readily abandon his territorial objectives in Italy. It was also evident that the most reliable troops under Imperial command came from Spain, especially from Castile. However the emperor had assembled a heterogeneous collection of soldiers from his vast European holdings, including Germans, Italians and Netherlanders, as well as Spaniards, who at the most amounted to about 20 per cent of the total, a ratio that would hold relatively steady for more than a century. Most served in the infantry, as in the 1530s the primarily light cavalry amounted to less than 10 per cent of the army (Oman, 1937, p. 61; Parker, 1990, p. 276).

Charles's armies needed a stable organization to encompass the major tactical and structural changes that had taken place during the first three decades of the Italian Wars. More specifically, his armies required a tactical rank to handle the increasingly complex matter of combat formations. The result was the Genoa Ordinances of 1536, which officially recognized the division of the Spanish infantry into three permanent *tercios* (or regiments), each of roughly three thousand soldiers and divided into specialized companies of pikemen and arquebusiers of around three hundred, led by two new ranks, the *Maestre de Campo* and the sergeant major, in charge of organizing the *tercio* into various fighting or marching formations. The *tercio* thus became one of Europe's largest and most complex tactical and administrative formations since Roman times, the first standing force in early modern European history which would remain continuously in being until the early eighteenth century (Quatrefages, 1996, pp. 314–20).

The new units, named for the states where they usually lodged (Sicily, Naples, Lombardy and eventually Flanders), in addition to occasional and newly recruited units from Spain, soon developed their particular traditions and *esprit de corps* (Parker, 1990, p. 178). The Spaniards' status as the special forces or shock troops of the Empire was evident in the ordinances; though they could occupy ranks in foreign units the *tercios* were their exclusive preserve. The rest of the emperor's soldiers – Germans, Italians and others – remained in colonelships during most of the sixteenth century, but their colonels and the lieutenant-colonels (functionally equivalent to the sergeant major) had always to defer to the *Maestres de Campo*. These soldiers justified their exceptional position in a number of important battles in the middle decades of the century, especially Ceresole (1544), a defeat by the French where they stood firm while Germans and Italians fled, and Mühlberg (1547), in which Spanish arquebusiers were crucial in defeating the Protestant army of the Schmalkaldic League of the Holy Roman Empire and putting an end to the war (Oman, 1937, pp. 249–53).

Charles V's last major reforms concerned artillery. His decree of 1552 standardized the calibres used in that branch, and at mid-century the Imperial army could boast of a specialized and well articulated artillery corps rivalled only by the French (Duffy, 1996, p. 18). In the latter decades of Charles's reign the transformation of the Spanish military from its medieval beginnings was complete, and the structures that would characterize it for most of the early modern period were already in place.

The war in the Low Countries

Exhausted from decades of campaigning, Charles V abdicated in 1556, leaving his son Philip II (1556–98) in control of his hereditary lands other than the Holy Roman Empire. This division should have allowed Philip to avoid direct armed conflict with Protestantism. However in 1567 Protestant riots and political agitation for greater autonomy in the Netherlands drove Philip to re-engage the Protestants militarily by sending north a Spanish army under his best general, Don Fernando Alvarez de Toledo, Duke of Alba.

Upon arrival Alba proceeded to complement the Spanish core of what became known as the Army (or *tercios*) of Flanders with a much larger number of soldiers recruited locally, as well as in Germany. From that point on, Spanish recruits would be sent first to Italy to be trained in the garrisons for roughly two years, and then up the famous Spanish Road – one of early modern Europe's longest and most important military corridors, running from Milan to Luxembourg – to join the veterans of Flanders. Until the early years of the seventeenth century, when the French and the German Protestants closed the Habsburg land access to the Low Countries, this complex training and logistical system, unique in Europe, functioned largely as intended. As an English veteran of the Army of Flanders, Sir Roger Williams, observed: 'For that time, we must confess, none had the school of wars continually but themselves. Their actions show their discipline, which were not amiss for others to follow' (Williams, 1972, p. 15).

The larger factors that prevented the suppression of the Dutch Revolt will be examined later. However it is clear that the failure to obtain a decisive victory in the Netherlands was not the result of tactical backwardness. The importance of the Duke of Alba as a military reformer has yet to be studied, but it became evident when, before marching to Flanders, the duke added fifteen musketeers to each company, whether of pikemen or arquebusiers (Quatrefages, 1983, p. 193). The musket had certain clear advantages over the arquebus: better aim, longer range, and heavier calibre that could penetrate the breastplate of enemy horsemen and help to protect foot soldiers against mounted pistoliers or arquebusiers. It was also more expensive, heavier and more difficult to use, thus requiring a better-trained soldier. Consequently orthodox opinion in the mid-sixteenth century had denied an offensive role to the musket and reserved it primarily for the defence of fortified positions (Smythe, 1964, pp. 59–60).

The sight and sound of musketeer platoons provoked surprise in the Netherlands, and an experienced French captain observed that Alba's muskets 'stunned the Flemings when they felt its noise in their ears'. New muskets were probably the decisive equipment factor in some very one-sided Spanish victories, such as Gheminghen (1568), Mook (1574) and Gembloux (1578), in which thousands of rebel soldiers lost their lives as opposed to only a couple of dozen Spaniards (Quatrefages, 1983, pp. 184, 443–4). These margins of victory resemble incidents in the Spanish conquest of Mexico or Peru more than battles in early modern Europe, and help to underline the *tercios'* 'revolutionary' tactics.

The patent success of the musket in the wars in the Low Countries probably played a major role in its introduction into other European armies in the late sixteenth century. In the meantime the musket gradually became one of the most important weapons in the *tercios*. In 1571, 8 per cent of the Spanish infantry were musketeers versus 20 per cent arquebusiers, but 30 years later there were 20 per cent musketeers and 35 per cent arquebusiers, giving a total of 55 per cent employing firearms, roughly similar to that of the Dutch (Parker, 1990, Appendix B; Smythe, 1964, pp. 60–1; Nickle, 1975, Appendix II). In addition to government design, these trends were probably also self-reinforcing. As Parker indicates, pikemen had the highest mortality rate in the army and musketeers the lowest, and these numbers may suggest that pikemen became fewer because they suffered greater casualties from the increasing proportion of enemy shooters (Parker, 1990, pp. 209–10).

Officers now had to learn new skills of tactical leadership, especially how to coordinate to greatest effect pikemen, arquebusiers and musketeers. To meet this need there sprung up an abundant crop of 'how to' manuals. Works like *Maestro de Campo* Francisco de Valdés's *Espejo y Disciplina Militar* (Brussels, 1589), Bernardino de Mendoza's *Theorica y Practica de la Guerra* (Madrid, 1595) and Diego de Ufano's *Tratado de Artilleria* (Brussels, 1612), to mention only three of the most popular treatises, went through many editions in the major western European languages. The sheer volume and number of the publishing output of the Spanish officer corps has no contemporary parallel, certainly not in the Dutch or Swedish army. In Venice, the hub of military publishing in the sixteenth century, we find 67 works of military science issued between 1492 and 1570, most though not all of which were written by Italians. In contrast there are 45 to 50 first editions of works of military science published in the Low Countries and Spain from 1567 to 1609. A large number of these treatises came from officers of the Army of Flanders, and consequently most of them deal exclusively with land warfare and with infantry (González de León, 1996, pp. 64–5). These writers proposed standards of promotion and reward in the army which directly challenged medieval and early modern notions of the innate military talent of the aristocracy. Armies, they argued, had to be led by technically-trained professional soldiers regardless of class origin, not by aristocratic adventurers without expertise. Some, like Artillery General Cristóbal de Lechuga, went even further, and advocated the foundation of a military academy that would teach ballistics, fortification and their allied sciences to the future officers of the army.

The musket had tactical implications that not even Alba had foreseen, but which military theorists set out to explore in their published technical manuals. Most officers understood that armies equipped primarily with firearms could neither line up nor fight in square formations fifty men deep. The majority of these works of military science published by army commanders deal with the then current debate on the tactical value of each of the three major infantry weapons and the best infantry formation. In his *Espejo y Disciplina Militar* Valdés maintains that victory belongs to the best-formed squadrons, and he recommends one of the staples of the military revolution, a shallow formation (*gran frente*) to accommodate the increasing number of musketeers (Valdés, 1944, pp. 35–8). Another veteran officer, Lieutenant Martin de Eguiluz, in his *Milicia, Discurso y Regla Militar* (written in 1586) described a manoeuvre that was clearly already current in the Spanish army, designed to maintain a steady rate of fire. Platoons of arquebusiers arranged in long, shallow, three-deep rows would emerge from the cover of pikes, shoot, yield their place in the firing line to those behind them, and go back to reload. By rotating these platoons the *tercios* could keep the enemy under constant fire. In other words, here we have in 1586 the theoretical formulation of the essential features of the countermarch described as standard practice, even though scholars have consistently attributed its invention to Maurice of Nassau and the Dutch in 1594 (Eguiluz, 1592, pp. 126–7).

The new firepower also made it possible, and indeed imperative, to reduce the size of the Army of Flanders's tactical units. Not surprisingly, in the late sixteenth century the army witnessed a marked increase in the number of *tercios* and regiments, from 23 in 1573 to 29 in 1594. By then these were not only Spanish, since the Italians had also achieved *tercio* status. The number of officers also went up, from one Spanish officer per 16 men in 1571 to one per 9 in 1601 (Parker, 1990, p. 276). Moreover from 1567 to 1609 the average size of the army's basic tactical units decreased dramatically even as their overall number grew. In 1573 there were 269 infantry companies and a total of 57,500 men, that is an average of more than 200 soldiers per company (Quatrefages, 1983, pp. 502–5). Twenty years later, in 1594, the average was roughly 100 soldiers per company, and this was after a so-called reformation, when understaffed units had been disbanded. In only two decades the average size of the company had been cut in half. Not even the Dutch army after Maurice's reforms had smaller companies, typically numbering 120 to 150 soldiers (Nickle, 1975, p. 140). These changes were hardly accidental. It was in the government's interest to keep the number of *tercios*, companies and officers to a minimum in order to save on pay, so that the army's inspector general kept very close watch on personnel numbers, and reformations took place every few years (Parker, 1990, pp. 207–21). But tactical evolution or revolution demanded these changes, expensive though they were.

Also contributing to mounting costs was the cavalry, which began to rise in importance late in the century, reaching numbers and proportions not seen since the early 1500s. They certainly proved their importance on the field at Gheminghen (1568), Mook (1574) and Gembloux (1578) (Williams, 1972, pp. 26–7; Oman, 1937, pp. 555–7, 561–7). Furthermore light cavalry was, in sharp contrast to the notions prevalent in traditional scholarship, also essential in siege warfare. As a sort of rapid deployment force they were used to cut off an enemy town on the eve of a siege and prevent the entry of reinforcements, as they did during the 1572 siege of Mons (Williams, 1972, p. 40). Infantry was too slow to produce the surprise necessary for an effective encirclement. The royal cavalry's efficient performance of this task often made the difference between a failed or a successful siege, and the Low Countries war had many more sieges than battles. Thus the number of mounted men grew steadily. In 1573 Alba had 35 cavalry companies in the Spanish Netherlands and a total of 4780 riders, of whom 3000 were heavy cavalry (Quatrefages, 1983, p. 505). In 1579 Philip II decreed that at least one-fifth of all light cavalry troops be arquebusiers (12 out of 60 per company) (Clonard, 1851–62, IV, p. 157). His objectives were achieved and surpassed. By 1594 the heavy cavalry had been so completely phased out that it did not even figure in the plans of the high command, but the number of light cavalry had significantly increased – to 57 companies and roughly 5500 soldiers. Most of these units were equipped with firearms. Moreover the same decrease in the number of soldiers per company and increase in the ratio of officers experienced earlier in infantry had taken place in this branch, and for similar reasons: tactical flexibility and the need to prevent backsliding or desertion. Cavalry tactics evolved from the frontal shock employed by late medieval cavalry to spread-out formations of light riders armed mainly with firearms (arquebuses and pistols) and firing coordinated volleys at the enemy's flank in a sort of mounted version of the counter-march (Eltis, 1995, p. 64). In those circumstances it became easier for mounted soldiers to bolt from the battlefield, as indeed happened in July 1600, when the failure of the royal cavalry in the dunes off Niewpoort triggered a major defeat (Oman, 1937, pp. 584–603).

The Army of Flanders's third tactical branch, the artillery, also experienced comprehensive growth and evolution in the first half of the war. As in the Dutch army, cannon calibres and carriage designs became fewer and were standardized in the early 1600s (Barado, 1890, p. 275). The Army of Flanders was almost unique in its day in having a specialized artillery branch with its own set of officers, regulations and bureaucracy. These features only grew more complex during the course of the war. By the turn of the century the army could rely on a sophisticated array of devices, such as artillery trains with gunners, drivers and artillery lieutenants, and engineering corps as well as companies and regiments of sappers, which the *tercios* were also among the first to use. However, in contrast with the Dutch army where even the rank of artillery general sometimes stood vacant, most of these posts were filled by professionals permanently employed by the king, not by civilians under temporary contracts (Nickle, 1975, p. 113).

Command structure was certainly 'revolutionary' in this army, which could count on one of the most complex and modern chains of command of its day. In the Dutch army, for instance, there was only a skeleton high command staffed by a handful of officers, whose duties and responsibilities ended when the campaign was over. Furthermore the infantry and cavalry command were never coordinated, and no one knew who could issue orders to whom. Thus the only connection between the two branches was Maurice of Nassau. The structure of the Dutch high command, like that of many other sixteenth-century armies, was primarily personal. Thus Maurice of Nassau held no formal rank in the army and was able to lead it only through the strength and prestige of his social status in the United Provinces. In other words, even in the midst of its 'military revolution' the Dutch retained a command structure that was more medieval than modern (Nickle, 1975, pp. 101–11). The Army of Flanders, on the other hand, could rely on the services of a permanent staff of *Oficiales Mayores*, arranged in a clear and fixed hierarchical structure and with constant duties and powers that were independent of the charisma or social status of the rank holders (see the flow chart in Parker, 1990, p. 277).

Although these tactical trends offered signs of the continuing vitality of the Spanish military, they represented a growing financial burden for the crown. Musketeers and cavalrymen were the best-paid and best-equipped soldiers of their day, and the increase in their absolute and proportional numbers in royal armies entailed an accompanying rise in the defence budget of nearly a quarter by some calculations (Thompson, 1995, p. 281). The same applied to the increase in the number of officers and the reduction in the average size of units. To this we should add the cost of fortifications, barracks, a military hospital and a pension system for veterans, areas in which the Army of Flanders was also at the forefront of European developments. Not surprisingly, the costs of running this force quadrupled during the reign of Philip II (Parker, 1990, pp. 161–74, 265). Nonetheless Spain might have succeeded in crushing the revolt had the Madrid government been able to focus exclusively on it, but other objectives and interests also had claims on royal funds.

Strategy, technology and the origins of decline

In recent years strategic explanations of the decline of Spain have become more common, especially in the work of Paul Kennedy and, with a technological twist, in that of Geoffrey Parker. What Kennedy calls 'imperial overstretch' began to loom large among the problems of the Spanish monarchy during the reign of Charles V (1516–56), who inherited a vast collection of lands ranging from Iberia to Naples, the Holy Roman Empire and the Netherlands. The conquistadors took his imperial banners to the shores of the southern Pacific Ocean unimpeded by foreign interlopers, so that the government's strategic horizons did not reach much beyond Europe and the Mediterranean, where there were three main enemies: the Protestants in Germany, the French and the Turks. Charles succeeded in driving the French from Italy, but he could not stamp out Protestantism in Germany, or, despite various victories, prevent the Turks from gaining virtual control of the eastern Mediterranean and making significant gains in north Africa. In 1558 the threat to Spain itself became urgent when a Turkish fleet launched a successful attack on Minorca.

Engaged in an expensive war with France, the Madrid government could not direct enough attention and resources to the Turkish problem, except by fits and starts. However events with crucial strategic implications took place in the 1550s. In 1555 Charles V abdicated and separated the Holy Roman Empire from the lands he bequeathed to his son Philip II, thus freeing him from direct involvement in central Europe. And two years later royal forces were victorious over the French at St Quentin (1557) and Gravelines (1558), leading to the signing of the Treaty of Cateau-Cambresis (1559), by which France relinquished all remaining territorial and dynastic claims in Italy (Oman, 1937, pp. 254–66, 274–82). In the 1560s Philip ignored mounting political turmoil in the Netherlands and turned his attention towards his endangered southern flank.

Philip's Mediterranean policy in the 1560s and early 1570s was largely successful. In 1560 the Turks destroyed a Spanish galley fleet in Djerba, near

Tripoli, but it was rapidly rebuilt, reaching the impressive total of 155 vessels in 1574 (Parker, 1979, p. 130). Between 1563 and 1565 Spanish amphibious forces captured the Peñon de Vélez in north Africa and relieved Oran and Malta from Turkish sieges. The outbreak of the Dutch Revolt in 1567 provided a significant short-term diversion of funds and attention. However Alba succeeded in crushing the revolt temporarily, allowing Philip II to concentrate on the south again. In 1568 the Moriscos of Granada revolted, and in 1570 the Turkish fleet again went on the offensive. The Papacy, Venice and Spain reacted by forming a Holy League and launching a leviathan fleet of 200 galleys, 100 auxiliary vessels and 55,000 soldiers, staffed and financed mainly from the resources of the Spanish monarchy. The resulting victory of Lepanto (1571) crushed the Turkish fleet and set the stage for a series of temporary truces which eventually turned into a mutual military disengagement in the Mediterranean.

A clear change in the Spanish monarchy's imperial strategy occurred during the reign of Philip II, from a Mediterranean-focused defence to an Atlantic strategy from 1575 onwards. This was especially so after 1580, when Spain absorbed Portugal and its overseas empire, the second largest in the world, which in Africa and East Asia included much larger holdings than Spain itself had in those areas. This monarchy 'on which the sun never set', the first global empire in history, had new and more dangerous enemies. First among them were the English, who, encouraged by their Protestant queen, Elizabeth I, began to encroach on the Iberian colonial monopoly in the 1560s, stepped up their efforts in the 1570s, and reached a crescendo in the 1580s, with hundreds of raiding expeditions led by Hawkins, Drake and others that resulted in millions of escudos in commercial losses to Spain. The French, who mounted attacks on the Azores in the 1580s, remained a constant threat, and in the 1590s the Dutch joined the anti-Spanish maritime effort, eventually reaching the Portuguese possessions in the East Indies. Viewed as a whole, this nameless conflict was the first global naval war in history.

In the Mediterranean the enemy had been only one, the Ottoman Turk, (although with French help and collaboration). In the Atlantic the situation was a good deal more complex. It involved the English, the Dutch, and later the French, in addition to the irregulars, pirates and corsairs. All of them had a transoceanic, global reach that none of the enemies of Charles V, who were all local powers, had ever enjoyed. In addition they were also commercial rivals, who began outplaying the Iberians at the very mercantilistic colonial game they had pioneered. Furthermore Spain had important allies in its naval duel with its most powerful maritime enemy, the Turks, namely the Catholic princes of the Empire, and the Italian city-states such as Genoa (even Venice and the Papacy, traditional rivals in Italy, participated in Lepanto), as well as Persia. But she was almost alone in the battles of the Atlantic and the Pacific.

Even within the monarchy, as Thompson has pointed out, Mediterranean kingdoms such as Naples and Aragón (including Catalonia) became reluctant to pour in resources to fight such remote enemies (Thompson, 1991, pp. 87–8).

More damaging than geopolitical isolation was the problem of materiel. The new strategy involved the use of very expensive new tools of war often associated with the military revolution. Ocean-going warships were more costly than galleys, particularly in terms of materiel such as guns and ammunition. For instance the most expensive Mediterranean campaign, Lepanto, cost 'only' 1,200,000 escudos, less than 15 per cent of the monarchy's annual revenues. It was, as Parker suggests, not an unbearable expense (Parker, 1979, p. 127), whereas the Armada sent against England in 1588 cost more than ten times that amount and it failed (Parker, 1998, p. 269). In the late sixteenth and early seventeenth centuries the Atlantic galleon fleet cost nearly double what the Mediterranean galley fleet had in the sixteenth (Thompson, 1995, p. 284). Spanish galleons, however, were not specialized warships like those of the English, due to the far-flung nature of Spain's empire and the needs of the convoy system on the Indies run between Spain and America for which they had been designed. Visually imposing, they were slower and less well armed than their counterparts, their guns too cumbersome to engage in prolonged naval shoot-outs. Here too the military revolution seemed to be working to Spain's disadvantage (Parker, 1988, pp. 47–56, 195–225).

On land, the shift to a northern or Atlantic focus of foreign policy centred around the war in the Netherlands, a religious and political conflict in which another major innovation connected with the military revolution became crucial. A new type of fortification developed by Italian engineers earlier in the century had been widely adopted in the cities of the Low Countries, with some 43 kilometres of walls built by 1572 (Parker, 1988, p. 12). Thick and low walls reinforced by a complex network of bastions, ravelins and crownworks bristling with heavy artillery, all designed to keep enemy troops away, absorb their shots and respond in kind when they came near, turned sieges into laborious blockades that consumed thousands of troops and lasted months if not years even when successful, which they often were not. The writing was on the wall as early as 1552, when Charles V failed to take Metz in Lorraine after one of the most massive sieges of the century (Duffy, 1996, pp. 51–2). The Italian Wars had been marked by rapid troop movements and field battles, areas in which tactical innovation, discipline, morale and leadership could make a huge difference. In contrast the new 'Italian' style of defence tied up half the army's personnel in garrison duty, turned campaigns into exercises in manoeuvre warfare, fostered a series of interminable sieges that nullified Spanish advantages in many of the areas cited above, and drained off vast sums of money, almost half of the entire royal budget in any given year (Parker, 1990, pp. 11–12). Only when, as in the early to mid-1580s, the king could channel the necessary resources to the Low Countries, did the Army of Flanders make significant headway. In 1589 Philip deployed the Army of Flanders in support of the Catholics in the French Wars of Religion, a decision instrumental in the preservation of official Catholicism in France but which put the *tercios* on the defensive in the Netherlands.

The cost of installing Italian-design defences in dozens of towns and ports throughout its global empire ruined the finances of the Madrid government. The total military budget (which included deployments of equipment and personnel in Africa, Asia, America and Europe) doubled or even tripled during the reign of Philip II. By the early seventeenth century, expenditure on fortifications had increased fivefold and overall spending was double or triple royal income (Thompson, 1976, p. 34; Parker, 1998, p. 112). Although Spain commanded resources massively greater than those of any other contemporary European state, its revenues, despite an opportune increase in silver income from the Indies in the latter decades of the century, could not keep pace with outlays. The gap had to be bridged with heavy borrowing against future income, leading to four damaging royal bankruptcies during Philip's reign. The usual result of financial and strategic overstretch was temporary paralysis and collapse, state bankruptcies which led to waves of mutiny for pay in the Army of Flanders, like the one that so greatly helped the Dutch in the 1590s (Parker, 1990, pp. 185–206).

Conclusion

The notion of a military revolution, even a tactical one, that began in the Dutch army demands substantial modification or total abandonment, and we need a new model that can encompass all of the significant changes that took place over the entire century, not just those that occurred after 1560. Actually the military revolution of the sixteenth century seems to have occurred in two phases. In the early or southern European phase, when major armed conflicts, even those in America, involved primarily Mediterranean powers, the structure and tactics of the early modern army emerged and the Italian design of fortifications came into being, though too late to have much effect on the Habsburg–Valois struggle. In this period Spanish tactics and organization, and Italian engineering, represented the cutting edge of the military revolution. In the northern European phase during the latter decades of the century the new fortifications spread all over Europe and the world, and the specialized warship became the ultimate weapon in a new globalized warfare. During this era, despite continuing modernization of its land forces, Spain began to fall behind. Ironically the links between the early military decline of Spain and the military revolution are perhaps stronger than have previously been suggested, but not for the reasons alleged. The second phase of the revolution made it possible to devise 'grand strategies' like that of Philip II. Although geopolitical overreaching on the part of the king and his advisers surely played a central role, the failure of Philip II's global designs, which laid the foundation for the eventual decline of Spain in the seventeenth century, was largely connected to the continuing transformation of warfare. In the final analysis the military revolution worked both for and against Spanish military power.

References

Barado, F. 1890. *Literatura Militar Española*, Barcelona.

Black, J.M. 1996. *The Cambridge Illustrated Atlas of Warfare: Renaissance to Revolution*, Cambridge.

Clonard, Conde de (Soto, S.M.) 1851–62. *Historia Orgánica de las Armas de Infantería y Caballería Española*, Madrid.

Conti, F. 1998. *Los Consejos de Estado y Guerra de la Monarquía Hispana en Tiempos de Felipe II (1548–1598)*, Valladolid.

Delbrück, H. 1990. *The Dawn of Modern Warfare. History of the Art of War*, vol. 4, Lincoln.

Duffy, C. 1996. *Siege Warfare. The Fortress in the Early Modern World 1494–1660*, New York.

Eguiluz, M. de. 1592. *Milicia, Discurso y Regla Militar*, Madrid.

Elliott, Sir J.H. 1964. *Imperial Spain 1469–1716*, New York.

Eltis, D. 1995. *The Military Revolution in the Sixteenth Century*, London.

González de León, F. 1996. ' "Doctors of the Military Discipline": Technical Expertise and the Paradigm of the Spanish Soldier in the Early Modern Period', *The Sixteenth Century Journal*, 27, 61–85.

Hanson, V.D. 2001. *Carnage and Culture. Landmark Battles in the Rise of Western Power*, New York.

Hemming, J. 1970. *The Conquest of the Incas*, San Diego.

Historia. 1993. *Historia de la Infantería Española. La Infantería en Torno al Siglo de Oro*, Madrid.

Kennedy, P. 1987. *The Rise and Fall of the Great Powers. Economic Change and Military Conflict from 1500 to 2000*, New York.

Machiavelli, N. 1990. *The Art of War*, New York (first published 1521).

McJoynt, A.D. 1995. Introduction to *The Art of War in Spain. The Conquest of Granada, 1481–1492*, by W.H. Prescott, London.

Nickle, B.H. 1975. 'The Military Reforms of Prince Maurice of Nassau', doctoral dissertation, University of Delaware.

Oman, Sir C. 1937. *A History of the Art of War in the Sixteenth Century*, London.

Parker, G. 1998. *The Grand Strategy of Philip II*, New Haven.

—— 1990. *The Army of Flanders and the Spanish Road, 1567–1659. The Logistics of Spanish Victory and Defeat in the Low Countries' War*, Cambridge.

—— 1988. *The Military Revolution. Military Innovation and the Rise of the West, 1500–1800*, Cambridge.

—— 1979. *Spain and the Netherlands, 1559–1659*, New Jersey.

Quatrefages, R. 1996. *La Revolución Militar Moderna. El Crisol Español*, Madrid.

—— 1983. *Los Tercios*, Madrid.

Roberts, M. 1995. 'The Military Revolution, 1560–1660', in Rogers, 1995, 13–35.

Rodríguez-Salgado, M.J. and Adams, S., eds. 1991. *England, Spain and the Gran Armada, 1585–1604. Essays from the Anglo-Spanish Conferences of London and Madrid 1988*, Savage.

Rogers, C.J., ed. 1995. *The Military Revolution Debate. Readings on the Military Transformation of Early Modern Europe*, Boulder.

Smythe, Sir J. 1964. *Certain Discourses Military*, Ithaca (first published 1590).

Taylor, F.L. 1993. *The Art of War in Italy 1494–1529*, London.

Thompson, I.A.A. 1995. ' "Money, Money, and Yet More Money!" Finance, the Fiscal-State and the Military Revolution: Spain, 1500–1650', in Rogers, 1995, 273–98.

——— 1991. 'The Spanish Armada: Naval Warfare between the Mediterranean and the Atlantic', in Rodríguez-Salgado and Adams, 1991, 70–94.

——— 1976. *War and Government in Habsburg Spain, 1560–1620*, London.

Valdés, F. de. 1944. *Espejo y Disciplina Militar*, Madrid (first published 1589).

Williams, Sir R. 1972. *The Works of Sir Roger Williams*, Oxford.

3
Ottoman Expansion, 1451–1556
I. Consolidation of Regional Power, 1451–1503

Rhoads Murphey

1451–1556: An overview

The discourse on Ottoman military matters has long been dominated by considerations of the Ottomans' readiness for war, especially their ideological readiness, and on their military organization and methods of warfare. This focus on Ottoman weaponry and battlefield tactics gives pre-eminence to debates over the superiority, inferiority or simple parity of Ottoman military methods vis-à-vis the west, with the underlying assumption that the only obstacle to unlimited Ottoman expansion was their ability to overcome their enemies in a purely military sense (Parry, 1975). This emphasis, and the evidence on which it rests, is largely derived from contemporary western sources, which were written at a time when the Ottoman empire was not just a military adversary but also an ideological and political foe.

The present discussion is organized along rather different lines. Alongside resources and technique, or the sinews and science of Ottoman warfare, we will be examining the political and dynastic dimensions of Ottoman expansion. As the starting point we will take it as given that by the late fifteenth century the Ottomans possessed both the means (material) and the motivation (spiritual) to conduct warfare, and that their mastery of the arts of war was at least on a par with their western adversaries, recognizing however that siege warfare techniques, though rapidly advancing, were as yet far from perfected in either the west or the east before 1500. What is significant is that the Ottomans managed to adjust their methods over time so as to keep pace with changing methods of warfare, whereas the so-called 'Gunpowder Empire' historical interpretation, which places heavy emphasis on technical determinants to explain Ottoman expansion, provides only a necessary and not a sufficient cause for this phenomenon.

The first period of Ottoman expansion during the reign of Mehmed II (1451–81) gave them a sufficiently large land base to support plans for further expansion. As a result of Mehmed's efforts at fiscal centralization, taken together with some inherent peculiarities of the Ottoman land tenure system such as the state-controlled *miri* land regime and the *timar* system, which allowed for more efficient extraction of available resources, by the turn of the sixteenth century the Ottomans had gained a distinct advantage over their contemporaries in terms of the speed and efficiency of their mobilization for war. In the second half of our hundred year period (more fully discussed in Chapter 4), beginning around 1503, the southward expansion of the empire and the inclusion of Syria and Egypt tipped the resource balance even more decisively in favour of the Ottomans, thereby providing the financial strength needed to meet the challenge posed by the expansion of the Habsburg empire during the 1520s and 1530s. Yet despite the unprecedented scale of Ottoman accumulation of wealth, power and resources, assessments by contemporary westerners of Ottoman military capabilities in the sixteenth century were neither more nor less exaggerated than they had been in the fifteenth, when apocalyptic fears of an imminent Ottoman invasion gained wide circulation in the west in the aftermath of the fall of Constantinople (Miyamoto, 1993; Murphey, 2000). For their part the Ottomans were realists and knew very well the constraints – material, environmental and fiscal – under which Ottoman military planners had to operate. Taking these realities into full account, our approach to Ottoman military preparedness will focus not so much on the monumental scale of Ottoman resources as their efficiency in managing, allocating and deploying them. As the empire's geographical scope expanded and it began to acquire trans-Mediterranean, supra-Danubian dimensions, the issue of balancing and prioritizing its military involvements became an ever more pressing concern.

This much said about the Ottomans' capacity for war, we can proceed to our account of Ottoman expansion as a realization of alternative choices adopted for the protection (and sometimes opportunistically for the enhancement) of the prestige, power and wealth of the dynasty, working on the assumption that expansion was governed not by overriding religious or ideological concerns, but by pragmatism and dynastic interest. It is self-evident that possession of wealth and resources was useful for promoting the interests of the dynasty, both by giving scope for imperial patronage and by lending credibility to its threatened use of military force, but the path and sequence of events that led to the Ottomans' emergence as a major international power in the period 1450 to 1550 shows that the key to success lay not so much in consistent pursuit of a fixed geopolitical strategy as in adaptability when confronted with changing circumstances.

The first Ottoman experiment in empire had ended abruptly in 1402, when the Ottoman sultan, Beyazid I (the Thunderbolt), was defeated by Timur in a battle near Ankara. The loss of Ottoman prestige thus occasioned very nearly delivered a fatal blow to the fledgling Ottoman polity, and it did not fully recover from the effects until after the removal of the Venetian fleet from Salonica in 1430, bringing an end to their seven-year occupation of the city. The renewed assertion of Ottoman hegemony in the Balkans during the reign of Mehmed II (1451–81) came as a natural, and even expected, part of a longer-term historical evolution that had its roots in the previous century. The shift from a defensive to an offensive mode in Ottoman relations with their immediate Balkan neighbours is readily apparent after Mehmed's accession. But, despite the seemingly limitless energy of the 21-year-old monarch following his prestigious capture of Constantinople in 1453, there was still much to accomplish before the Ottomans were secure in the Balkans, let alone ready to assert credible claims for wider domination. The Ottomans had first to pass through the tedious but indispensable stages of consolidating their regional power base and ensuring the full and final integration of their two principal land masses in Asia (Anatolia) and Europe (the Balkans). This integrative process could now be overseen and orchestrated, both on land and sea, from their new imperial capital Istanbul, but 1453 was more a new beginning than the culmination of the previous century-and-a-half of imperial growth.

Undeniably the fall of Constantinople marks a turning point in Ottoman history, but an event of arguably equal importance for the full restoration of the dynasty's military reputation occurred in 1473, 22 years after Mehmed's accession to the throne. The decisive victory by Mehmed's standing armed troops, supplemented but no longer dominated by the volunteers and self-sustaining mounted raiders of the frontier zone, over the tribally based army of his rival Uzun Hasan in the east, put to rest once and for all questions about the leadership status of the Ottoman dynasty. The rival independent Turkmen dynastic formations of Anatolia, who gained a new lease of life after Beyazid's defeat by Timur in 1402, only really lost their credibility and viability as potential alternatives to Ottoman leadership once Mehmed had triumphed over them on their own home ground. Mehmed's success in 1453 was unquestionably significant in enhancing the international prestige of the dynasty, but his victory at Bashkent in 1473 won him admiration among his native subjects, especially in Anatolia, allowing him to accumulate power, respect and authority to a degree unheard of by his predecessors on the Ottoman throne.

Before 1450, and to a considerable degree even during the first two decades of Mehmed's reign, the real position of Ottoman dynastic power vis-à-vis both internal challengers and regional competitors ruled out any realistic ambitions for domination in the wider Mediterranean sphere. On the contrary, the first decade-and-a-half of Beyazid II's reign, until the death in exile of the pretender Cem Sultan in February 1495, saw the resumption of a credible threat that the empire might return to its former position as a regionally divided state, as had occurred between 1402 and 1413. Hence Ottoman expansion between about 1450 and 1550 can be viewed not as a continuum, but as divisible into two symmetrical although rather disproportionate halves, one covering the years 1451–1503 and the other 1503–56.

During the first period the empire's main task was the reunification of the Balkan lands and Anatolia, and the reassertion of Ottoman claims as a regional power, while the second period witnessed the rapid transformation of the empire from a regional to an international power. The impetus that drove expansion in the second period was in part the emergence of a new contender for regional power. The creation of the Safavid state in Iran with the accession of Shah Ismail in 1501, and especially his expansionist programme against territories in eastern Anatolia, threatened to reopen the question of leadership in the Muslim world. The contentious three-way dynastic rivalry with the Safavids and Mamluks based in Syria and Egypt elicited a strong response from the Ottomans, the end result of which was a doubling of their territory in the east over the five-year period 1514–18. Ottoman holdings in Asia increased from 176,000 to 412,000 square miles, transforming their power base and raising their prestige in the Muslim world to unprecedented heights (Pitcher, 1972, pp. 134–5). However the greater challenge to Ottoman dynastic interests came from the mounting power of the Habsburgs, whose accumulation of territories in Europe already impinged on the Ottoman sphere of influence in the west. With the accession of the brothers Charles V in Madrid in 1516 and Ferdinand I in Vienna in 1522, the Habsburg menace increased, as new initiatives, even when incompletely coordinated between them, threatened to engulf key Ottoman strategic positions. The simultaneity of these threats and the scale of the Ottoman responses to them determined that the character and scope of Ottoman expansion in the second period would be markedly different from the first. What is striking about the Ottomans in the period after 1503 is their ubiquity and their activism in a wider arena, stretching from the Mediterranean to the Red Sea and from the Caucasus to the gates of Vienna. This marked not so much a change of emphasis or degree in Ottoman conquest and expansion as the creation of an empire of a different species altogether.

1451–1503: Reassertion of leadership and consolidation of regional power

A series of dramatic military victories achieved at key stages of the reign of Mehmed II (1451–81) contributed to the decisive restoration of the Ottomans' position of primacy within their core zone of strategic interest. None of these taken singly was enough to achieve permanency of control over this region, and much of Mehmed's reign was devoted to a painstaking and piecemeal absorption of small territorial enclaves of independent authority which still persisted after 1453. That the protection of this core strategic zone, and in particular of key points in the immediate vicinity of his newly declared capital Istanbul, was paramount in his thoughts is made clear by his behaviour in the immediate aftermath of the city's fall. 'The Conqueror' was seemingly acutely aware both of his short-term vulnerability to counter-attack and the loss of his prize capture, and of the fact that in the longer term an effective Ottoman assertion of rights of succession to both Seljukid and Byzantine imperial rule would require a skilful combination of military force and the arts of persuasion through cooperation and alliance-making. It is the mutually reinforcing success of the Ottomans in the spheres of war and diplomacy that explains the dynasty's ability, within a few decades of the Conqueror's death in 1481, to include within its key areas of strategic concern both Cairo, which was targeted and won in 1517, and Vienna, which was subjected to a two-week siege in 1529.

Our treatment of Ottoman territorial expansion in the early period, between about 1450 and 1500, will be based on the premise that state behaviour was governed by the ruler's calculations of dynastic self-interest and by his sensitivity to issues relating to dynastic pride. Ottoman expansion in this period is best understood not as a determined pursuit of the goal of universal sovereignty based on the infinite expansion of the *Dar ul Islam* (Abode of Islam) at the expense of all other religions, but rather as the gradual reassembling and reunification of the Ottomans' territorial base in the Balkans and Anatolia on the one hand, and a defence of their core strategic interests as a regional power in the Aegean on the other. The Ottoman mission in this period is fully intelligible according to the accepted norms and traditions of inter-state relations in the late Renaissance era, which placed a high priority on the sovereign's responsibility to defend dynastic dignity and honour, and to extend the scope of dynastic power.

Immediately after the fall of Constantinople in May 1453 one of Mehmed's first acts was to renew the trading concession of the resident Genoese commercial colony in Galata, on the same terms granted by his predecessors, the emperors of Byzantium (Inalcik, 1988, pp. 275 ff.). This conciliatory approach, and the young ruler's intention to rely on a combination of war and diplomacy to secure his imperial interests, was confirmed during his first year on the throne, when Mehmed signed no fewer than eleven agreements with a range of Ottoman vassals, tributaries and foreign powers to acquire their cooperation or in some cases to ensure their neutrality.

Diplomacy continued to be important in the period after 1453. In the two-year period after the fall of Constantinople Mehmed entered into or renewed agreements with a further eighteen partners (Hammer, 1827–35, IX, 282, nos 74–91). Some agreements, such as those with the Genoese and the

Dubrovnikans (Biegman, 1967), had a mostly commercial character, while others (for example Moldavia and Wallachia) had a more explicit military, strategic and political purpose. The essential point was that each contributed in some way to a strengthening of the sultan's position by allowing him scope to initiate military strikes against his enemies when they had been divided and weakened, or otherwise isolated, by his diplomatic initiatives.

The pacification and neutralization of Venice during the eleven-year period from the transfer of his capital to Istanbul until the commencement of the Veneto-Ottoman 'Long War' in July 1463 gave Mehmed a vital breathing space in which to build up his resources and improve his defences, so that when conflict was no longer avoidable he could confront his adversaries with confidence. During the early phases of the war (1463 to around 1468) he faced a three-cornered military alliance, with Venice and Hungary combining against him in the west, and the rival central Anatolian dynasty of the Karamanids, in loose cooperation with Venice, opening a seriously distracting second front in the east. Mehmed's success in countering such coalitions was due partly to his own alliance-making, and in the latter and concluding phases of the war, between 1474 and 1479, Venice was reduced to its own devices, supported only by a dwindling number of former followers of the dead Albanian leader Iskandar Beg (alias George Castriota).

At the beginning of his reign in 1451 Mehmed was fully aware that his empire was not yet ready for an all-fronts confrontation with the dynasty's many rivals and potential opponents. During the first years after his establishment in Istanbul he pursued a policy of cautious expansion balanced with conciliation. He was determined to avoid the unwanted consequences of ill-timed or ill-prepared military interventions, as the scale of his preparations for the capture of the relatively modestly defended harbour of Trabzon in 1461 shows. He was concerned – sometimes almost to a pathological degree – not to spoil his record of military success and his imperial image as 'Conqueror' acquired in 1453, and he chose military targets carefully, ensuring that they were both strategically important and at the same time reducible with the means at his disposal (Murphey, 2000). Only at the very end of his reign can Mehmed be observed ignoring this logic, when in the summer of 1480 he launched simultaneous naval expeditions against Otranto in Apulia and the heavily fortified island of Rhodes. The result of this over-commitment of forces was that the diversionary attack on the Italian front succeeded but proved unsustainable, while the more strategic objective of capturing the headquarters of the Knights of Saint John and imposing full Ottoman control over navigation in their own territorial waters failed.

Apart from the aberration of 1480 Mehmed pursued an astute programme of achievable and sustainable intervention, which by the end of his reign secured Ottoman hegemony in a zone stretching from the Euphrates in the east to the shores of the Adriatic in the west, a land base similar to the former Eastern Roman Empire. Extending the empire along the east–west axis of the *Via Egnatia* to the terminal point at Vlore in southern Albania was completed by 1479, when, at the conclusion of the Veneto-Ottoman war, Ottoman control over both parts of Albania was consolidated. Along the north–south route of the former *Via Militaris*, whose terminal point was Belgrade, Mehmed had made substantial progress early in his reign by his annexation of those parts of Serbia (excluding Belgrade) which lay outside the zone of Hungarian border military control. These gains were substantial, and in historical terms they constituted a natural evolution, since the limits of earlier empires had always coincided with the same natural frontiers (rivers, mountains and sea coasts) that now shaped the zone of undisputed Ottoman imperial control. Still it would be risky to conclude that this accumulation of territory yet presaged Ottoman aims for universal sovereignty, or signalled their mounting of a serious campaign aimed at the reunification of the eastern and western halves of the former Roman Empire or a permanent extension of Ottoman rule to the Italian peninsula. On the contrary, it was the need to counter such neo-Caesarian claims on the part of the Habsburg Holy Roman Emperor Charles V that prompted Ottoman activism at the western margins of their empire after 1520.

The pattern and scope of Mehmed's conquests during the early part of his reign show the essentially defensive logic that governed his prioritization of the various military options that confronted him. Moreover conquests in this period were not always as definitive or final as the word suggests. The Ottoman capture of Corinth in 1458 was followed by a spirited defence against a determined Venetian counter-offensive in 1463. While the Ottomans' eventual success brought about the permanent closure of Venice's front-door access to the Ottoman mainland, it was not until Mehmed's successor Beyazid closed off the Aetolian back door by his victory at Lepanto (Naupaktos) in 1499 that the Ottomans could claim unqualified control of all of their Balkan lands and their principal adjacent seaways. The Ottomans acquired mastery over the waters that linked their land possessions in Asia and Europe only gradually. The most significant gains came in the latter part of Mehmed's reign, with the Ottoman naval victory at Negreponte (Euboea) in 1470 constituting a turning point in the Aegean, followed soon after by effective closure of the Black Sea with the capture of Caffa in 1475.

Mehmed's principal and overriding concern after the capture of Istanbul was to restrict the access of enemy fleets to the immediate precincts of the capital, whether from the Black Sea or the Aegean. It is clear that in the early days of his reign he gave the highest priority to erecting a secure barrier guarding the maritime approaches to Istanbul from the south. One of his earliest conquests was the harbour of Enez (Ainos) in 1456, close to the mouth of the Maritza river, and the offshore islands guarding the entrance to the

Dardanelles followed soon after. Even earlier Mehmed had set about reinforcing the shore-based defences called the 'Sultan's Fortress' (*Kale-yi Sultaniyye*) and the 'Lock of the Sea' (*Kilid Bahr*). Two authoritative Ottoman sources agree that the first efforts to erect a defensive shield at the entry to the Dardanelles date from 1454, the year immediately following Mehmed's installation in Istanbul. Tursun Beg's account relates that 'the Conqueror placed awesome guns in the two newly-erected castles after which not even a bird could pass into the Straits without first asking permission of the castle wardens' (Tursun Beg, 1978, folio 60b, ll. 5–11). Significantly, the same passage speaks of the Conqueror's rebuilding of Istanbul's defensive walls as part of his comprehensive plans for the city's reconstruction. Another authoritative, though less immediately contemporary, Ottoman source dates the fortification of the Dardanelles to the same period (Kemalpashazade, VIII, 1997, folio 100, ll. 5–12). Likewise Kritovoulos's contemporary account of the Conqueror's reign gives a clear indication that the feverish pace of construction under way at the mouth of the Dardanelles in 1464 was intended to complete the work started ten years earlier (Kritovoulos, 1954, pp. 197–8). Later on, as Mehmed was completing his preparations for the joint land and sea expedition against Trabzon in 1461, he developed an auxiliary shipbuilding facility in the capital, which seems to have taken shape over the period between 1459 and 1461 (Inalcik, 1973, p. 230). This transfer of part of the fleet's docking capacity from Gallipoli to a place more secure against enemy attack was also partly motivated by defensive concerns.

On the whole, Mehmed's conquests were systematically planned and executed operations designed to achieve two key objectives. The primary objective was to create a security zone as well as a supply and free market exchange area around Istanbul. This required strict Ottoman monitoring and control of navigation within their home territorial waters of the northern Aegean, Marmara and the Black Sea, which gave access to the empire's extensive hinterlands both in the eastern Balkans and Anatolia. A second objective was to remove territorial enclaves which might be used as bases by hostile foreign powers. The removal of the independent duchies and despotates of the Peleponnese, nominally accomplished over the three-year period 1458–60, can be seen to have been motivated not so much by Ottoman land hunger or desire to increase their resource base, as by strategic concerns that Venice might seek to widen its already entrenched position as a Levantine empire-builder in its own right if the Ottomans hesitated to fill the power vacuum created by the fall of Byzantium.

Mehmed was aware of Venice's considerable strength, and at first he wisely pursued a defensive strategy until he was better equipped to match it and in a position to exploit its strategic vulnerabilities. The reality of his position throughout the 1460s was that he had two weak internal fronts, one in the recently annexed Morea and the second along the still unpacified eastern Anatolian frontier. Thus whenever he absented himself for expansionist wars on remote fronts such as Bosnia he exposed the empire to attack by the Karamanids, alone or in alliance with either the Mamluks or the Turcoman Akkoyunlu. The full incorporation of Karamanid territories in the east hence remained a top priority not just during the 1460s, but until after the victory at Bashkent in 1473.

The tenuity of the Ottomans' initial position in the Morea is indicated by the fact that key strategic points such as Corinth tended to become focal points for resistance to Ottoman rule and had to be reconquered. The year after the Ottomans captured Lesbos, with its strongly fortified harbour Mytilene, in 1462, both Corinth and Mytilene became the targets of Venetian-led offensives, whose object was to dislodge the Ottoman garrisons. In 1463, while the sultan's armies were engaged in Bosnia, the Venetian siege of Corinth was already well under way before relief forces led by Grand Vezier Mahmud Pasha arrived, and the successful defence was due almost entirely to the efforts of the local commander Elvan Beg-oghlu Sinan Beg (Kemalpashazade, VII, 1954, pp. 257–8; Babinger, 1978, p. 227). Mahmud Pasha's forces, consisting of an estimated ten to fifteen thousand irregulars, were employed not to engage the enemy but to carry out a mop-up campaign, whose main purpose was to frighten the local inhabitants and discourage any future collaboration with Venice.

After the successful defence of Corinth the fortifications at the isthmus were destroyed, forcing a permanent Venetian retreat from that sector (Kemalpashazade, VII, 1954, p. 256; Tursun Beg, 1978, pp. 52–3). However in the following year, 1464, Ottoman campaign plans against Bosnia were again disrupted by the need to carry out an Aegean rescue operation, this time of the fortress of Mytilene, which the Ottomans had only taken two years earlier. The sultan again dispatched his Grand Vezier to relieve the garrison and to carry out urgent repairs to the fortifications, before proceeding to the front in Bosnia with the sultan himself and the main body of the army, a delay which led to logistical and seasonally related campaigning difficulties and inconclusive results.

From the rather haphazard pattern of Ottoman deployments in the 1460s we gain a sense of the military realities early in Mehmed's reign. Despite the undoubted boost to his reputation as a military commander resulting from his capture of Istanbul, and a growing anxiety in the west about his intentions against Europe, these realities dictated that Mehmed was still forced to choose between the mutually exclusive options of protecting recent conquests in his core territories in the southern Balkans and Anatolia, or expanding his frontiers in the northern Balkans. As noted above, the turning point after which he was able to dictate the course of events and escape the reactive pattern of his military commitments came not in 1453 but in 1473, after the battle of Bashkent.

An authoritative Ottoman source expresses Mehmed's dilemma in the summer of 1464 as follows:

> It is preferable and of the highest priority according to both reason and precedence that before rushing to the capture of fortresses such as Jajce [on the Bosnia-Hungary frontier] currently in the hands of the Infidel, attention should be paid to relief of the beleaguered Muslims who are now desperately defending the fortress of Mytilene. To rid the home territories of Islam from the menace posed by all types of idolaters must take precedence over plans for the removal of the obstinate unbelievers from the lands of the infidels.
>
> (Kemalpashazade, VII, 1954, p. 261)

Another zone of Ottoman activism in the middle part of Mehmed's reign was central Anatolia, whose incomplete integration into the empire was still a continuing source of irritation that prevented the full assertion of his imperial authority and also had resource and strategic implications. A secure base in Anatolia was essential before he could undertake the next phase of expansion, which envisaged an extension of imperial control to the northern shore of the Black Sea. This would bring the vast supply potential of the northern economies within the purview of a unified redistributive and market authority based at Istanbul. To achieve this key objective Mehmed called a temporary halt to his prolonged conflict with Venice on several occasions, as in 1467–68, enabling him to concentrate his forces against Karaman, and again in 1471–72, when Ottoman peace proposals were tabled, allowing him to concentrate his forces in the east in the lead-up to his confrontation with Uzun Hasan in 1473. The final elimination of the second-front syndrome, which throughout the earlier part of his reign had hampered both his Balkan and his Black Sea expansion plans, gave Mehmed a new lease of life that he was quick to capitalize on during the remaining years of his reign.

The crowning achievement of Mehmed's efforts at creating a strategically secure and economically cohesive empire in the core zone, defined by the Black Sea, Marmara and Aegean transportation, communications and market exchange nexus, was his annexation of the Genoese colonies (principally Caffa) on the coastal perimeter of the Crimean peninsula. This was accomplished during 1475 and in a follow-up naval campaign in 1479. In a linked development, he also succeeded in forming a cooperative alliance-cum-client relationship with the Tatar dynasty of the Giray hans, who ruled in northern Crimea and the adjoining steppe regions. At the time the Girays were represented by the formidable warrior Mengli Han, who ruled, with two brief interruptions, between 1466 and 1514. Conforming to a long-standing pattern in relations with distant provinces at the margins of their empire, Ottoman conquest was balanced and stabilized through concessions to local ruling elites, thus ensuring their loyalty and cooperation in the longer term. In exchange for their alignment with Ottoman interests, the Giray family and associated leading members of the tribal aristocracy retained a relatively full measure of administrative autonomy and even sovereign dignity. On their part the Ottomans guaranteed that a representative of the 'royal' Giray clan would always succeed to authority in the hanate. This represented perhaps an even greater concession of power than in the case of the Christian tributary states of trans-Danubia, to whom the Ottomans' main concession was the granting of freedom of religion within the territorial boundaries of their voyvodates. Furthermore in the Crimean case the partnership was based on sharing the gains from military cooperation in the form of livestock and human captives. By making their vassals stakeholders in the Ottoman enterprise, in many ways the Ottomans strengthened their position more than by acquiring direct control over resources through annexation.

After the campaigns against Moldavia in 1475 and 1476 Mehmed's northern vassals on the shores of the Black Sea were rendered fully compliant (for details and an account of the participation by his Tatar auxiliaries see Ureche, 1878, pp. 125–53). With the final piece of his territorial acquisitions also in place Mehmed was at last in a position to make good the claim traditionally associated with the period immediately following the fall of Constantinople, that he was 'Lord of the Two Continents and of the Two Seas' (Hammer, 1827–35, I, p. 88; Inalcik, 1988, p. 415). As his reign drew to a close, the empire over which he ruled could legitimately claim to have reoccupied the historical region that once belonged to his Byzantine predecessors, with the exception that the extension of Ottoman control east of the Euphrates (apart from Trabzon) was still to come (Engel, 1970, p. 70; Pitcher, 1972, map xvii). The Ottomans now possessed the body as well as the head of the former Byzantine empire.

The extension of the Ottomans' imperial reach beyond the historical region of the Balkans, Black Sea and Aegean home region in the late fifteenth century faced a further obstacle whose limiting influence cannot be ignored. Advances in the fields of siege techniques, pyrotechnics and artillery use, though enthusiastically embraced by the Ottomans, were still relatively recent developments. Gunpowder technology was rapidly introduced after the 1440s, but perfecting the new techniques took rather longer, and before the end of the fifteenth century firearms by no means yielded the decisive and impressive results that they later achieved. It is an indisputable fact of the first period of Ottoman expansion that, in this field at least, the Ottomans met as many setbacks and disappointments as they achieved successes. Counterbalancing the breaching of the walls of Constantinople in 1453 was the failure of the siege of Belgrade in 1456 and the repeated failure of Ottoman assaults against the heavily fortified Albanian fortress of Croia (Kruje). In addition to the two failed sieges during Murad II's reign in 1448 and 1449, Mehmed himself met success only on his fourth attempt, which took place in 1478, and even on that occasion the fortress was not actually taken by force, but yielded due to lack of supplies after a year of blockade. These failures cannot be explained by a lack of Ottoman expertise. The simple fact is that the weaponry was not sufficiently developed to yield consistent results, nor was it easy to keep the powder dry during transport over rough terrain. The Ottomans managed to devise strategies for overcoming such technical and supply difficulties, but in the final analysis it was patience, perseverance and human ingenuity, rather than the sophistication of the means employed, that made the telling difference in Ottoman military enterprise during the late fifteenth century.

Ottoman success in pacifying Albania, as elsewhere in the Balkans, was achieved through a combination of defensive warfare and their ability to attract support among military and administrative elites of the regions targeted for incorporation. They offered extensive concessions and rich rewards in return for rather basic levels of military cooperation. Their use of Christians as grooms, attendants, frontier guards, scouts and occasionally even as combatants, is well documented in both Ottoman and contemporary western accounts (Mihailovic, 1975, pp. 43–4).

By the conclusion of their sixteen-year war with Venice in 1479, the Ottomans had reduced a power that at the beginning of the war had represented a formidable contender for dominance in the Aegean and the western Balkans to a vestigial position, confined to small number of offshore bases on the Dalmatian coast in the north and a few outposts at the extreme southern end of the Peloponnese. Venice was forced to agree unconditionally to the Ottoman terms by which it secured the reactivation of its life-sustaining Levantine trade. Thereafter it took a much more conciliatory stance in its diplomatic relations with the empire. Though the republic had lost the war and retained its remaining Aegean colonies only as tributaries of the Ottoman state, through its resident *bailo* in Istanbul Venice became the principal broker and often beneficiary of the complex commercial and diplomatic arrangements that began to typify Ottoman relations with the west in the sixteenth century.

The scope of Ottoman conquest in the Balkans during the reign of Mehmed II was not radically different from that achieved by his great-grandfather Beyazid I (d. 1402), and defined in a strictly territorial sense it was more a catching up with the past than a significant expansion of the zone of Ottoman control. Throughout the medieval period the Ottomans' imperial horizons were formed by the lands of the conventional 'seven kings' of Europe, the Roman emperor and the kings of Bosnia, Serbia, Wallachia, Moldavia, Hungary and Poland (Redhouse, 1890, p. 1443). Before the close of the fourteenth century both Serbia and Wallachia had joined the Ottoman imperial system as loyal vassals and buffer states facing Hungary, the most inveterate of the Ottomans' imperial adversaries throughout that and most of the following century, and by 1429 the southern parts of Bosnia assumed a parallel position as Ottoman tributaries. Mehmed II widened the scope of these standing arrangements only by the inclusion of Moldavia, whose leader the voyvoda Petru Aron accepted Ottoman terms of subordination imposed in a treaty of 1455 (Babinger, 1978, p. 137). Thus far the scope of Ottoman foreign relations remained firmly within the bounds defined by the medieval context of the 'seven kingdoms'. The realignment of real power relations was also a much more gradual process than the stark wording of treaties and other formal diplomatic instruments would suggest. Aron's successor Stephan ('the Great', 1457–1504) was not brought into full compliance with Ottoman overlordship until the sultan himself presided over a punitive raid in 1476, and the full fruits of Moldavian–Ottoman military cooperation were not realized until the reign of Mehmed's successor Beyazid, when Stephen's non-participation in the Polish invasion of 1497 proved his loyalty, or at least demonstrated his unwillingness to openly thwart his imperial overlords.

The supersession of the geographical bounds of the Ottomans' regional empire in the Balkans, as defined by the seven kingdoms, came only after a prolonged process of conquest and reconquest, subordination and re-subordination. There is no reliable indication that this point had been reached before the middle of Beyazid's three-decade reign, around the year 1503, or if we regard Moldavia as the key, the end of Stephen's term of office in 1504.

The early part of the reign of Beyazid II (1481–1512) witnessed the consolidation and completion of his immediate predecessor's plans for the creation of a new, revitalized Ottoman empire, materially self-sufficient and undisputed master of its own extensive maritime domain in the Black Sea and Aegean region. One unfinished task of capital importance was the imposition of full Ottoman control over the internal circulation of goods within the empire's core regions. Beyazid's bold stroke against the Moldavian port cities of Kilia and Akkerman in 1484 gave the Ottomans unqualified control over navigation throughout the Black Sea, and direct access not only to the raw materials but also to the markets of both eastern and central Europe, while at the same time providing a narrow but strategically significant land link to their Crimean allies in the east. Ottoman military planning in this period focused on targets with potential for promoting the fuller integration of the empire's economic regions, and Beyazid paid particular attention to enhancing Ottoman naval capacity. It was essential for the cohesion of their existing territory, let alone sustainable further expansion, that the Ottomans should have the ability to project their power and presence across both the Black Sea and the Mediterranean, and during the course of Beyazid's prolonged, but in the end rather inconclusive, campaigns against Egypt between 1485 and 1491 Ottoman naval vessels were deployed for the first time in an offensive capacity outside the confines of the northern Aegean.

Beyazid was not uniformly successful in his maritime ventures. However the scope of his activities clearly demonstrates the wider range of Ottoman imperial intentions, and reveals that they had at least begun to think globally. The high-profile Ottoman naval presence in the Black Sea and the eastern Mediterranean during the early years of Beyazid's reign indicates that the empire had finally come of age, and was already taking the first, albeit tentative, steps towards developing its capacity for activism in the wider Mediterranean sphere.

Beyazid's conflict with the Mamluk ruler Kayit Bay (1468–96) provides an instructive example of how, whether in a conflict between Muslim and Christian rulers or in a confrontation between two Muslim sovereigns, dynastic politics operated on multiple levels. On one level such challenges served the purpose of preserving and enhancing the honour, prestige and reputation of opposing ruling houses, even when after fighting to a stand-off the material interests of neither was served. Already well before Beyazid's majority and accession to the throne, Ottoman intentions to extend their sphere of influence against the Mamluks on the southern Anatolian border of Cilicia had been signalled. In 1468 his father had arranged the young prince's marriage to the Zulkadrid princess Aisha, daughter of the ruler of the principality, and from the 1470s onwards the real issue of contention between the Mamluk and Ottoman dynasties was their competition for political influence over the tiny Zulkadrid principality wedged between their two sprawling empires. The contest was carried out mostly indirectly, each side lending its support to a rival candidate for the succession when the throne fell empty, or engineering successive *coups d'état* to create opportunities for their respective protégés. For at least a generation before Beyazid's open declaration of war on Egypt in 1485 – a serious step and one difficult for a leading Muslim monarch to square with public opinion – both Mamluks and Ottomans had been engaged in clandestine operations in Zulkadria. The most serious rift in relations had occurred in 1472, when the Ottoman protégé Shehsuvar was forcibly deposed, taken to Cairo and publicly executed.

When at the close of the Moldavian campaign in 1484 Beyazid summoned up the courage to declare war on Kayit Bay he made no reference to the long-standing competition over Zulkadria or to opposing territorial claims, but cited only three deliberate Mamluk diplomatic affronts of more recent vintage. In addition to Kayit Bay's offer of hospitality in Egypt to Prince Cem, Beyazid's rival for the succession to the Ottoman throne, Kemalpashazade cites the Mamluk's detention of an Ottoman envoy to the court of the Bahmanid Sultan Shams al-Din Muhammad III, and Kayit Bay's neglect of the customary practice of offering 'condolences and congratulations' (*taziye ve tehniye*), to mark the death of Mehmed II in 1481 on the one hand and the succession of his son Beyazid on the other (Kemalpashazade, VIII, 1997, folio 36b). The current rules governing international relations determined that the avenging of deliberate acts giving rise to *lèse majesté* was of itself sufficient to justify the commencement of hostilities, in the west as well as in the east, and Kemalpashazade's account of the outbreak of war between the Mamluks and Ottomans in 1485 makes it clear that calculated assaults on the sovereign dignity delivered by foreign powers were not taken lightly. Left unavenged such seemingly harmless gestures had a corrosive influence and could seriously undermine the sultan's position at home. Thus even without the still unresolved questions of dynastic influence and geopolitical advantage bound up in the continuing struggle for precedence in Zulkadria, the clash of imperial wills in 1480–81 had already made the outbreak of an Ottoman–Mamluk war a near certainty. In the fixed trinity of dynastic priorities concerned with the accumulation of power, prestige and wealth, the middle element was by no means the least important, nor can it be dismissed as a trivial or transitory concern for the leading dynastic figure.

The conflict with the Mamluks between 1485 and 1491 – even if it brought little in the way of tangible results – still served a dual purpose in salvaging Beyazid's honour, and at the same time providing an opportunity for the Ottoman navy to test its capabilities on the high seas, far from its main bases in Istanbul and Gallipoli. Beyazid's next initiatives, undertaken with an unprecedented combination of well-coordinated offensive forces on land and sea, decisively demonstrated that the empire had reached a stage of development where, in addition to its proven capability for defending its regional security interests, it stood ready to assume a leading position in the international arena. In one sense Beyazid's assault on Lepanto in 1499 and his capture of Venice's last Peloponnesian strongholds at Moron, Koron and Navarino in the following summer can be characterized as a completion of his father Mehmed's unfinished business. Beyazid's conquests completed Mehmed's campaign to force the withdrawal of all the Latin occupiers from their mainland positions, whether on the northern shores of the Gulf of Corinth or in the Morea. But, in contrast to Mehmed's 'Long War', undertaken with the same objective some three decades earlier, Beyazid's war with Venice and its sometime ally France was both short (1499–1503) and decisive. In 1501 the Ottomans managed to drive off a determined enemy attack on the fortress of Mitylene on the island of Lesbos, carried out this time by a joint Franco-Venetian team (Vatin, 1991). But the difference in this war was that the Ottomans repeatedly demonstrated their ability to seize the offensive initiative, as happened in the principally naval campaigns of 1499 and 1500.

These Ottoman tactical successes, while impressive, were not sufficient to claim clear naval superiority over Venice. Nonetheless they had convincingly shown their ability to defend the inner Aegean shores of their empire and the sea routes which led to them. Furthermore the excursion north into the Ionian Sea suggested future possibilities for a greater Ottoman naval presence in the Adriatic on the far shore of their Balkan provinces. Apart from having established Ottoman competence to defend its interests with its own naval forces, Venice's position as a supplicant had been reconfirmed. Henceforth the republic fully understood that it would preserve its licence to trade in the Ottoman lands only by maintaining its non-aligned status and by shunning future calls to participate in anti-Ottoman coalitions. In the period that followed the end of the war, confirmed by the Venetian senate in January 1503, Venetian neutrality would be of inestimable value to the Ottomans as they were exposed to the heightened threat of Habsburg expansion in the ensuing decades. Thus in a diplomatic sense too the year 1503 represents the closing of one era and the beginning of another.

A further indication of the Ottomans' coming of age as an empire is provided by changes in fiscal practice, engendered by the need for supplementary funds to support the naval construction programme undertaken in the year of the siege of Mytilene. The extraordinary levy called *avariz* introduced in 1501, while seemingly first envisaged as a special subvention for the navy, soon became a permanent, and later a very prominent, feature of general Ottoman state finances (Kâtib Chelebi, 1913, p. 20). By this time the toll of fighting on a wide front on both land and sea had begun to tell. This implied that future plans for imperial expansion would have to be assessed under the strict discipline of careful cost–benefit, risk–reward calculations and resource assessments. The fact that the Ottomans managed to project their direct presence and indirect influence in an ever-widening arc, stretching from the western Mediterranean (Algiers) to the Persian Gulf (Basra) in the south, and across the previously unexplored expanses of central and eastern Europe in the north, during the coming decades of the sixteenth century testifies to their success in the acquisition and management of resources on the one hand, and their self-discipline in the balancing of commitments on the other.

References

Primary texts

Kâtib Chelebi. 1913. *Tuhfet ül-Kibar fi Esfar ül-Bihar*, Istanbul.

Kemalpashazade, VII. 1954. *Tevarih-i Al-i Osman: VII Defter*, facsimile published by Ş. Turan, Ankara.

Kemalpashazade, VIII. 1997. *Tevarih-i Al-i Osman: VIII Defter*, ed. A. Uğur, Ankara.

Kritovoulos. 1954. *History of Mehmed the Conqueror by Kritovoulos*, trans. C. Riggs, Princeton.

Mihailovic, K. 1975. *Memoirs of a Janissary*, trans. B. Stolz, Ann Arbor.

Tursun Beg. 1978. *History of Mehmed the Conqueror by Tursun Beg*, trans. H. Inalcik and R. Murphey, Chicago.

Ureche. 1878. *Chronique de Moldavie depuis le milieu du XIVe siècle jusqu'a l'an 1594*, trans. E. Picot, Paris.

Secondary sources

Babinger, F. 1978. *Mehmed the Conqueror and his Time*, Princeton.

Biegman, N. 1967. *The Turco-Ragusan Relationship*, The Hague.

Engel, J., ed. 1970. *Grosser Historische Weltatlas: Zweiter Teil – Mittelalter*, Munich.

Hammer, J. 1827–35. *Geschichte des Osmanischen Reiches*, Budapest.

Inalcik, H. 1988. *Essays in Ottoman History*, Istanbul.

—— 1973. 'Istanbul', in *The Encyclopaedia of Islam*, vol. 4, Leiden, 224–48.

Miyamoto, Y. 1993. 'The Influence of Medieval Prophecies on Views of the Turks, Islam and Apocalyptism in the Sixteenth Century', *Journal of Turkish Studies*, 17, 125–45.

Murphey, R. 2000. 'External Expansion and Internal Growth of the Ottoman Empire under Mehmed II: A Brief Discussion of Some Controversial and Contradictory Aspects of the Conqueror's Legacy', in *The Great Ottoman-Turkish Civilization*, vol. 1, ed. K. Çiçek, Ankara, 155–63.

Parry, V. 1975. 'Manière de Combattre', in *War, Technology and Society in the Middle East*, ed. V. Parry and M. Yapp, London, 215–56.

Pitcher, D. 1972. *An Historical Geography of the Ottoman Empire*, Leiden.

Redhouse, J. 1890. *A Turkish and English Lexicon*, Constantinople.

Vatin, N. 1991. 'La siège de Mytilène (1501)', *Turcica*, 21–23, 437–61.

4
Ottoman Expansion, 1451–1556
II. Dynastic Interest and International
Power Status, 1503–56

Rhoads Murphey

Syria, Egypt and a tri-continental empire

The year 1503 marks a watershed in the evolution of the Ottoman empire from regional giant to superpower status. In that year a peace treaty was concluded with Venice at the end of the war of 1499–1503, the terms of which represented a de facto recognition by the latter of Ottoman dominance in the region. In the same year they also reached limited truce agreements with Hungary and Poland, the two strongest states among the 'seven kingdoms' which formed the traditional group of Ottoman adversaries (the others being the Holy Roman Empire, Bosnia, Serbia, Wallachia and Moldavia). In time-honoured fashion Sultan Beyazid II (1481–1512) thereby secured peace in the north and west to allow him to turn to a serious crisis that was brewing in the east. This year also marked the commencement of the race for succession between three of his sons, Korkud, Ahmed and the eventual victor Selim. These developments were typical of Ottoman experience in both the international and domestic spheres during the preceding two centuries. What was different about the events of 1503 is that Ottoman domestic politics was becoming increasingly and inextricably entwined with rivalries in the international sphere. The challenge from the south emanating from Egypt was now intensified by a new contender, Shah Ismail, the dynamic founder of a new dynastic order in Iran. In the case of this Safavid challenge, not only was the Ottomans' geopolitical position of pre-eminence in the Near East put at risk, but their spiritual leadership was also called into question. At the same time the inherent weaknesses in the Egyptian Mamluk state made the latter's position in southern Anatolia a target for a three-way dynastic struggle for regional dominance, while the Mamluk state itself was also at risk of invasion or even conquest by the rising Iberian powers. This highly volatile situation threatened to undermine the Ottomans' geopolitical position and security on multiple fronts.

In 1492 the Mediterranean balance of power had been seriously upset by the fall of Granada, and the subsequent expulsions of Jews and Muslims from Spain only made matters worse. While Beyazid's success in the 1499–1503 war with Venice demonstrated Ottoman resolve, this was by no means a full response to the scale of the wider threat. The Mediterranean situation deteriorated when Pedro Navarro's troops landed on the north African coast at Oran in 1509, and proceeded to carry out massacres and deportations of the native Muslim population. At the same time the northward press of Portugal's viceroy of the Indes, Alfonso D'Albuquerque, was beginning to be felt at the entrance to the Red Sea after his naval victory off Diu earlier the same year. In the years 1510 to 1516 which preceded the Ottoman decision to launch an attack on Egypt, the Muslim world faced the very real threat of encirclement from the Spanish advance along the African coast and the increasing Portuguese penetration into the Red Sea, especially after their attack on Aden in 1513. It was fully realized by Ottoman military planners, even before Sultan Selim's accession in 1512, that meeting this challenge would require full-scale Ottoman assistance, or in the longer term an Ottoman assumption of leadership in place of the Mamluks.

The power struggle between Ottomans, Mamluks and Safavids was resolved in the Ottomans' favour by Selim's unhesitating approach. Selim did not flinch from causing a potentially destructive rift in the Muslim world by his aggressive assertion of Ottoman leadership at a time of general crisis. His military success in eastern Anatolia during 1514 and 1515, and his later triumphs on the Syrian front, were tempered by his conciliatory and non-confiscatory approach to post-conquest administration. Although he pursued a hard line against 'heretics' and the *kizilbash* supporters of Shah Ismail's political cause, on the whole the fiscal regime in the east was markedly lenient. From the outset the Ottoman administration signalled its intent to leave the hereditary tribal leadership, mostly Kurdish and in some places Arab, in place to serve as a stabilizing element in the border districts. In the Morea they had pursued a determinedly incorporative approach, in which the goal was the complete removal of enclaves of local control and a rapid transition to direct Ottoman rule through the imposition of the *timar* system, direct taxation and other aspects of the central administrative apparatus. The contrasting gradualist attitude to their eastern provinces is reflected in the descriptive phrase used to designate the tax-exempt enclaves created by the Ottomans east of the Euphrates, held to be 'set aside from the revenue assessors' pen and cut off from the government inspectors' feet'.

Revenue figures for 1528 show that eastern Anatolia represented less than 3 per cent of the Ottoman provincial tax base excluding *timar* (Barkan, 1953–54,

p. 277). Although the stabilization of the eastern frontier was not fully achieved until the Treaty of Amasya in 1555, the cause of consolidating Ottoman rule was greatly advanced by a consistent policy of fiscal leniency and a permissive attitude towards the creation of semi-autonomous zones under tribal jurisdiction, so that acceptance of Ottoman rule did not require a quantum leap of faith or imply the loss of significant material interests on the part of indigenous populations.

Selim's conquests in Syria and Egypt represented the most ambitious expansion the Ottomans had yet attempted. The distance between this sector and the territories in the core region, or the mostly heavily defended frontiers in the east and north, was enormous. The creation of a tri-continental empire was no great challenge from the purely technical point of view, as the Ottoman military machine possessed clear superiority over its Mamluk counterpart, but the long-term survival of the empire required that at least one front remain relatively quiet. In the end it was the southern sector which performed this vital stabilizing role. The measured quality of the Ottomans' response to the Portuguese threat from the Red Sea provides evidence of an empire which showed its greatness not by the extent of its further expansion, but by its restraint. This enabled it to defend its vital interests through a sensible balancing of its imperial priorities, and a careful avoidance of the obvious risks associated with over-extension.

In sum, Selim's intervention in Egypt was prompted by a particular convergence of shorter-term concerns and the over-arching influence of longer-term Ottoman goals. The rapid deterioration of the general strategic situation in the eastern Mediterranean after 1509 had given rise to concerns of a geopolitical nature, and Selim was able to exploit the shift in domestic Ottoman public opinion which had discredited his father's non-interventionist approach. He had made use of these changing sympathies during his bid for his father's throne in 1512, but after his accession he had to deliver on his promises. Finally, though this was unrelated to the timing of Selim's intervention in 1517, the Ottomans had for some time envisaged the incorporation of Egypt as part of their master plan for the economic integration of the eastern Mediterranean region, animated by what one scholar has called 'commercial intentionality' (Brummett, 1994, p. 20).

Throughout the Syria–Egypt campaign Selim was acutely aware of the constraints under which the Ottoman army and navy were forced to operate, and the lessons from this experience were not soon forgotten. In the event it was not until 1525, nine years after the fall of Cairo, that a serious Ottoman offensive to dislodge the Portuguese fleets from the Red Sea was mounted, and even then the commitment of forces was relatively small-scale and involved only eighteen ships. Not until 1538 was a fleet with serious offensive capabilities deployed in that sector, with the aim of conclusively establishing the

Ottomans at Aden in order to control shipping through the Bab al Mandab Straits. The eventual extension of Ottoman rule to the south beyond Egypt had the clear purpose of containment, rather than the opening up of new frontiers for expansion. This is indicated by the fact that the sector remained relatively quiet compared with the Mediterranean and central Europe.

West of Egypt in the Maghrib, the Ottoman response to Spanish aggression was quite limited and took some time to gather intensity. Despite the fact that by 1529 Algiers had been transformed into a secure Ottoman base, initially they relied mostly on local initiative and manpower. It was only after the 1547 peace agreement between Ferdinand I of Austria and Selim's successor Suleyman that the Ottomans felt prepared to mount a full-scale response to the long-standing threat on the north African front, which after the fall of Tunis in 1535 pressed ominously against Ottoman Egypt itself. Only in 1551, fully three decades after the fall of Cairo, was an Ottoman fleet mobilization on a scale sufficient to assert control over Tripoli organized. This represented only the first stage of a repositioning of Ottoman forces, whose ultimate aim was to dislodge the Spanish from their entrenched position at La Goletta in the Bay of Tunis. Because of distance, the full integration of Ottoman conquests in north Africa into the imperial system was in any case problematic, and to the degree that it was ever achieved it was only very gradually.

Selim's Syria–Egypt campaign journal, kept by his secretary Hayder Chelebi, provides eloquent testimony to the commander's anxieties about Ottoman vulnerabilities on the home front in the Aegean and other parts of the northern Mediterranean during his absence on campaign. In particular the fleet of the Knights of St John, based at Rhodes until 1522, occupied his thoughts as he planned each successive phase of the campaign over the thirty-month period between June 1516 and his return to Istanbul in December 1518. Due to outfitting delays and weather problems his own armada contributed nothing, not even logistical support, to his victories on land. Selim had defeated the Mamluk army near Aleppo in August 1516 and taken Cairo in January 1517 before the armada caught up with him. In fact, according to the admiral Cafer Beg's letter dated 26 March 1517, it did not leave Istanbul until the early spring of 1517 (Cafer Beg, 1938, document 13). The diarist records the sultan's inspection of the fleet in Alexandria in May, but almost immediately upon its arrival it was ordered to return to base. This decision was seemingly prompted by Selim's worries about Ottoman vulnerability in the northern Mediterranean, and their exposure to attack either by the Knights of St John or by a coalition of western fleets seeking to take advantage of the prolonged absence of the Ottoman navy in the southern Mediterranean. In a further precautionary move, during his march back to Istanbul in spring 1518 Selim ordered the recall of Selman Reis, his naval officer responsible for defending the Red Sea against the Portuguese advance. This deliberate Ottoman de-escalation in the

Red Sea was balanced by the heightened priority Selim gave to homeland defence, as can be sensed from his near-simultaneous orders to organize the repair and improvement of the fortifications at Foca on the Aegean coast (Hayder Chelebi, 1858, pp. 489, 491, 498).

Selim's chief focus following his conquests in eastern Anatolia, Syria and the Nile Delta was defence, and his next offensive, planned for the spring of 1519, was the island of Rhodes, which straddled the main sea route to Egypt (Hayder Chelebi, 1858, p. 499). There can be no doubt about the wisdom of Selim's policy of restraint in the face of temptations to further extend Ottoman imperial expansion. Sustaining Ottoman activism in the eastern Mediterranean and its other core regions following the annexation of Egypt and Syria in 1518 required careful management of resources and the political wisdom to avoid over-commitment to issues of secondary importance. Later Ottoman advances, to Aden in 1538 and Basra in 1546, were undertaken more to close frontiers and protect against the threat of encirclement by the Portuguese in the Indian Ocean than in pursuit of dreams of empire east of Suez. The balance of Ottoman strategic concerns after Selim's expansion is apparent from the relative size of the fleets deployed to the Adriatic and the Indian Ocean in 1538. Barbarossa's fleet, which defeated a powerful western alliance at the battle of Preveze, was at least three times the size of the seventy-ship armada of Hadim Suleyman Pasha's search and reconnaissance mission to the Indian Ocean in the same year (Setton, 1984, p. 446).

The final phase of Ottoman expansion

During the reign of Sultan Suleyman ('the Magnificent', 1520–66), the Ottoman empire was exceptionally well positioned to meet the greatest challenge it had yet faced in the international arena. This strong position arose partly from the resource contribution made by its recently acquired Arab provinces and partly from its balanced approach in the allocation of those resources. After 1520 the context of Ottoman relations with the west was no longer confined to the relatively familiar shape and manageable proportions of the league of the seven kings. The empire's ultimately successful confrontation with Habsburg imperialism would require not only the full deployment of its resources, but also an ingenuity and flexibility in devising non-military ways of combating its rivals.

Increasing Ottoman engagement across a widened zone, which by the mid-sixteenth century encompassed both the central Mediterranean and central Europe, came about in response to specific events and provocations whose full scope we can only hint at here. Nonetheless the event-driven character of Ottoman expansion in this period seems clear, both from the halting pace of Suleyman's advance into Europe after his devastation of the Hungarian army at Mohacs in 1526, and from the inescapable residual demands imposed by the need to protect and defend the borders in the east created by Selim's extensive conquests.

A key feature of Ottoman success in the sixteenth century was the widened scope and enhanced effectiveness of its diplomacy. Not only did they strengthen existing alliances, in particular with their own vassals and with neutral states like Venice, but they also entered into new alignments aimed at further isolating their most powerful enemies. The Ottomans in this period proved particularly adept at creating communities of interest both with un-expected new partners and with more familiar ones which, in the not so distant past, had faced them in a confrontational posture. One example of the new spirit of accommodation was Poland, which in 1533 agreed to an external peace with the Ottomans (Kolodziejczyk, 2000, pp. 70, 117–19). After the con-quest of Syria and Egypt the Ottomans gained considerable leverage in regu-lating their foreign relations, especially with maritime powers with strong commercial interests such as Venice, because the stakes involved in gaining or losing most-favoured nation status had been incalculably raised. The Ottomans were now able to use the offer, or the threat of withdrawal, of capit-ulations ensuring unrestricted access to Ottoman markets to attract new allies, and to modify or soften the political stance of its existing trading partners. In 1537 Venice was tempted to escape this commercial tutelage by cooperating with Pope Paul III's plans for an anti-Ottoman crusade, but after the western defeat at Preveze it sought re-confirmation of Ottoman capitulations on the standard terms. By this stage in their imperial growth not only did the Ottomans have less to fear than ever before, even from their most powerful and determined European enemies, but they also had more than ever before to offer in the way of consolation and reward to those who cooperated with them. Such mutually beneficial arrangements, by effectively preventing the formation of lasting coalitions of anti-Ottoman forces, greatly enhanced their strategic position during the heightened confrontation with the Habsburgs in central Europe after 1540.

The final phase of Ottoman expansion in Europe came about under the particular, sometimes peculiar, influence of recurring crises in relations with the Viennese branch of the Habsburgs under Charles V's younger brother Ferdinand I. Into the complex matrix of intersecting spheres of Ottoman and Habsburg influence and competition for position in the Mediterranean was added the further complication of a self-divided Habsburg empire. Following the territorial division agreed by the brothers at the Treaty of Brussels in 1522, reading Habsburg intentions and judging the appropriate Ottoman response was not always an easy matter for Suleyman and his advisers.

With the capture of Belgrade in 1521 Suleyman secured the Danube water-way and completed the communications, transport and defence requirements of the sub-Danubian and broader Black Sea region of his empire. His capture of Rhodes in the following year secured the sea routes between the Anatolian provinces, and linked Istanbul with the main centres of commerce in the southern Mediterranean. At this juncture the empire was ready to enter an age of unprecedented economic prosperity, commonly referred to as the *Pax Ottomanica* and characterized by domestic plenty, a stable monetary system and budgets providing enough revenue to contribute to steadily-mounting reserves. Suleyman had an ambitious programme of domestic building and urban renovation and he made generous disbursements, not just for the beautification of his capital, but also in the provinces. Between 1537 and 1540 the ramparts of Jerusalem were repaired and extended on a deliberately impressive scale, but their purpose was more symbolic than practical since the risk of attack was remote (Northedge, 1997, p. 882). It is clear that conducting war was only one of the resource-demanding activities on which Suleyman intended to stake his reputation as sovereign, and certainly conquests alone would never have earned him the appelation 'magificent' by which he was known in the west. Although the Ottomans were by now capable of sustaining an all-fronts war with the Habsburgs on both land and sea, from Suleyman's point of view such an eventuality would represent an unwanted distraction.

In the years between 1526 and 1540, following the dramatic victory at Mohacs, Suleyman was not massing his forces in preparation for an invasion of Europe but investing in an ambitious programme of ship construction and naval enhancements which would yield results only in the longer term. At the same time he was planning to extend Ottoman rule to Iraq at the expense of the Safavids. The main significance of this lay not in its strategic importance but in its potential for the enhancement of Ottoman imperial prestige. By his capture of Baghdad in 1535 Suleyman acquired the triple crown by adding the former seat of the Abbasid Caliphs to the Umayyad capital Damascus (occupied by Selim in 1516) and the Mamluk capital Cairo.

The shifting of Ottoman priorities in Europe from land to naval warfare is apparent from the year 1532, when Spanish invasion of the Morea resulted in a brief occupation of the strategic fortress of Koron, captured by the Ottomans three decades earlier from the Venetians. In the same year Charles V and Suleyman embarked on potentially intersecting itineraries – Charles attending the Imperial Diet at Regensburg while less than 300 miles to the south-east Suleyman was besieging Koszeg – but it seems that neither was disposed to cross the line from brinkmanship to confrontation. Thus by the time Charles made his triumphal entry into Vienna Suleyman was already making his way back to winter quarters in Istanbul.

This missed land encounter has to be analysed in the context of the urgent and repeated pleas by Ferdinand for Charles to lend support to his claim to the crown of Hungary, disputed since 1526 by the Ottoman-backed contender

John Zapolya. From Charles's point of view, risking the dynasty's reputation and squandering his resources on the doubtful prospect of forcing the Ottomans to yield over Hungary – a strategic region whose surrender they would fight hard to prevent – was ill advised. Furthermore in 1532 Charles had other worries, and the resources required for a decisive victory against the Ottomans in the Danube basin were unavailable unless and until he disengaged in Italy or Flanders, while his own plans for taking on the Ottomans involved not Hungary but the Mediterranean.

For their part the Ottomans had for some time, even as early as the reign of Mehmed II, been engaged in military and administrative centralization. As part of this they had sought to erode the power and influence of, as well as the state's military dependence on, the fiercely independent, self-financing light cavalry warrior class of the *akindji* raiders. Throughout the Middle Ages the Danube frontier had served both as their breeding ground and source of sustenance, but since 1475 the availability of unlimited numbers of Tatar raiders through their Crimean vassals had rendered this indigenous Ottoman group largely superfluous. Suleyman's desire to further pacify the northern frontier, and to encourage the expansion of trade through the Black Sea to destinations in central and eastern Europe, is confirmed by his diplomatic moves, while he also made an effort to rein in his Crimean vassals and make them more subservient to Ottoman military needs and foreign relations priorities.

Sahib Giray, who assumed control of the Crimean hanate in 1532 and reigned for a relatively undisturbed two decades until 1551, had served a prolonged period as guest-cum-hostage at the Ottoman court during his minority. As part of his training to assume the burdens of leadership he had accompanied Suleyman on campaign and fought at the siege of Koszeg in 1532. Later he also participated, as his sovereign's respected but at the same time scrupulously loyal and subservient vassal, during the campaign against Moldavia in 1538 (Murphey, 2001a). Apart from the dispute over the Hungarian crown, by 1538 the outline of the Ottomans' general policy of stabilization of their northern borders to accommodate the southward shift of the centre of gravity of their empire to the Mediterranean was in place.

Until 1540 the Ottomans' policy concerning Zapolya had been to support him as independent king of Hungary in his own right. Since 1526 the objective had been to prevent Zapolya's loss of sovereignty and Ferdinand's assertion of the right of annexation of a reunited kingdom of Hungary to the already adjacent Habsburg territories in Austria (Makkai, 1946, p. 156). This alliance with John Zapolya was superseded suddenly in 1541 by an Ottoman occupation of central Hungary and the setting up of an Ottoman protectorate in eastern Hungary, managed along similar lines to the vassal states established in 1395 (Wallachia) and 1455 (Moldavia). This came about in response to unforeseen circumstances caused by Zapolya's premature death in July

1540, which left the kingdom in the hands of his widow, as regent for his infant son. It was this rather than a fundamental change in Suleyman's policy that prompted Ottoman intervention. The goal of preventing Ferdinand's possession of territory that would make the Ottoman and Habsburg empires coterminous – thus seriously destabilizing the Ottomans' northern frontiers – remained unchanged, but the appropriate means for achieving it had to be adjusted to accommodate altered circumstances. Justifying war by using the need to defend the *Pax Ottomanica* might seem a contradiction in terms, but in view of Ferdinand's intransigence Suleyman was left with no other viable option. He certainly had no intention of standing idly by to witness the realization of Ferdinand's dream of empire, the inevitable consequence of which would be a resumption of the battle for the Balkans. The inelegant and in many ways less than desirable solution of a three-way division of Hungary gave him some breathing space to attend to other imperatives, notably the Mediterranean and north Africa, where the threat from Charles was more pressing than in trans-Danubia.

The enforcement of the Ottoman solution for Hungary required one more serious intervention in 1551, when Ferdinand decided to renew his claims, this time not by means of a direct attack on the Ottomans' position in central Hungary, but by attempting to destabilize, and ultimately to eliminate, the Ottoman protectorate in Transylvania. This represented not just a threat to Ottoman material interests, but also an open challenge to their dynastic prestige, since it repudiated the terms of the Ottoman–Habsburg peace treaty of 1547. Although Suleyman and Ferdinand had agreed to a temporary truce in 1533, the 1547 agreement was ground-breaking in that the emperor Charles himself had endorsed it. Ferdinand's decision to occupy Transylvania in the summer of 1551 was thus not just flouting his brother's authority, but also his way of throwing down the gauntlet to the Ottomans (Barta, 1994, p. 257). As a measure of the ultimate success of Suleyman's policy of stabilizing and pacifying the northern frontiers of his empire, it is significant that the reinstallation of Zapolya's son John II (Sigismund) in Transylvania was achieved not through the sultan's own direct intervention, but accomplished through Ottoman clients in the north, the voyvodas of Moldavia and Wallachia. Suleyman, ever the master of the pragmatic solution, had devised a means of controlling one set of allies or vassals by using another group, more reliable or more thoroughly subordinated, as his enforcers.

Suleyman's solution for the stabilization of his eastern Anatolian borders with Safavid Iran had similar overtones to his solution of the Hungary quandary. Although he presided over three campaigns against Shah Tahmasp (1524–76), only one of these mobilizations, the first aimed against Baghdad in 1535, had the clear purpose of Ottoman territorial extension. After the capture of Baghdad there was no clear dynastic imperative to be served by extending

Ottoman rule further to the east. His excursions in 1548–49 and 1551–53, both confined to the Azeri–Anatolian corridor, were meant to consolidate control over regions that were already nominally in Ottoman possession at the conclusion of the first campaign in 1536. Suleyman used the opportunity in 1548 to oversee the upgrading of the key strategic region around Van to the rank of *beylerbeyilik*, or fully-fledged Ottoman province, and by thus making his intentions in the region firmly known to the Safavids he prompted them to transfer their capital to Kazvin in the interior.

After 1536, stabilizing the eastern frontier and reaching mutually acceptable terms for a permanent accommodation with Tahmasp were Suleyman's main concerns. It would not be overstatement to claim that Suleyman's excursion in 1553–54 to Nahcivan, the capital city of the sub-Caucasian province of Karabagh, was intended more as a show of force to coax the Safavids to the bargaining table (which is what eventually transpired at Amasya in 1555) than as a serious bid to extend the Ottoman frontier to the shores of the Caspian. Between Suleyman's arrival at the border town of Kars in July 1554 and his dismissal of the troops for the winter season at Erzerum five weeks later, there was barely enough time to deliver more than a warning shot across the bows of his sovereign opponent's ship of state. The permanent retention of an Ottoman extension to the shores of the Caspian would have required an investment in the creation of a heavily-fortified frontier zone in the east on a par with that already established in the 1540s in western Hungary. The latter was necessary to counter a serious threat to key Ottoman security interests, whereas no such claim could be made for the Caucasian region. Even the seemingly limitless resources of the Ottoman state under Suleyman would not support unnecessary expenditure on such a scale. In the end Tahmasp decided not to call Suleyman's bluff and the two sides reached terms for a settlement of their differences. Though sometimes disposed to spend, even extravagantly, on gesture, the fundamental rationality of both polities must be presumed, and it is clear that neither was willing to incur bankruptcy for the sake of empty gestures.

Unlike his father Selim, who had pursued an unwavering hard-line approach against Shah Ismail, the founder of the new Safavid dynastic order, and had even imposed a mutually damaging trade embargo in a vain attempt to force Ismail's compliance, Suleyman was determined not to allow either ideological enmity or sectarian difference to undermine the carefully laid foundations of his *Pax Ottomanica* (Murphey, 1993). It is a telling indication of the sensible and sustainable basis of the territorial compromise hammered out between Suleyman and Tahmasp that the essential configuration of the border between the Ottoman empire and the Safavid (later Kadjar) state in Iran remained essentially unchanged for centuries. All this was achieved by Suleyman at minimal cost to Ottoman central treasury coffers and without demanding local contributions or raising the tax obligations expected from his eastern provinces.

The empire reaches maturity

It seems clear that from the 1530s onwards, the Ottomans increasingly – in Iran, Iraq, the Persian Gulf and the Red Sea on one side of their empire, and in the wider Mediterranean world and the Danube basin on the other – began to face a guns versus guns in addition to the classical guns versus butter dilemma. They had to decide what parts of their empire required deployments in maximum strength, and where a minimal military presence would suffice to maintain the status quo. They were fortunate in that, after an initial period of coming to terms with Ottoman rule, the inhabitants of the vast territories in Asia won from the Mamluks and contested with the Safavids did not regard Ottoman sovereignty as fundamentally problematic. On their part the Ottomans refrained from imposing harsh conditions of inclusion and from straining the loyalty of their Muslim subjects in the Arab and Kurdish areas. Quite soon the issue of Ottoman rule ceased to be a contentious one. By calling a halt to further expansion in the east after the Iraq campaign of 1535–36 Suleyman had effectively resolved at least the first of the two dilemmas associated with imperial growth. Yet some have seen this solution as problematic, and regard Suleyman's seeming indecision about the direction of expansion after the mid-1530s as the sign of a crisis of orientation, and a failure by the Ottomans to realize their full potential as a world power (Labib, 1979). Realistically however, by the mid-1530s the Ottoman empire had already reached the fullest extent that was manageable, sustainable and defendable. The Ottomans' final imperial extension into Hungary in 1541 was undertaken not to augment Ottoman wealth and resources, or even to improve their strategic position, but to counter the serious and persistent threat posed by Habsburg imperialism, and then only after all other means had been tried and proved unworkable. From a resource point of view possession of Hungary was a net loss to the Ottoman treasury, and the costs of defending the newly acquired province were heavily subsidized by revenue surpluses from elsewhere, particularly the Arab lands. Analysed in the light of a presumption of Ottoman state rationality, and discarding ideology or acquisitiveness as credible explanations for their behaviour – in other words stripped down to its bare essentials – the only reasonable explanation for the decision to occupy a strip of territory north of the Danube in 1541 (as opposed to 1526, when it was less well defended and to all intents and purposes theirs for the asking) is as part of an offensive defence. Their aim was to place a barrier, in the form of a protective border zone, in the way of an Austrian *Drang nach Osten* that might place their sub-Danubian Balkan provinces at risk and destroy the tranquillity of core regions of their empire.

When the scope for defending Ottoman dynastic interest through indirect means by lending support to the Zapolya family failed in 1540, the Ottomans were left with no viable option other than direct intervention. The point of diminishing returns in Ottoman expansion had been reached before 1541, with the capture of the regional stronghold of Belgrade and the annexation of Hungarian-controlled regions to the west in Srem and northern Bosnia, which formed an integral part of the Sava-Drava-Danube communications nexus. The best way of explaining Ottoman behaviour in 1541 is not their supposedly pre-meditated expansionist aims, but compliance with the logic of action–reaction and stimulus–response that governs the behaviour of states under pressure in volatile situations. From their behaviour in building and maintaining empire in other spheres – for instance in north Africa during the rise of the Algiers-based Barbarossa brothers around 1515 to 1535 – it appears that the Ottomans generally avoided direct intervention when the desired strategic ends could be achieved through reliable intermediaries (Murphey, 2001b).

Analysis of Ottoman troop commitments over the first three decades of their rule in central Hungary shows their concern for maintaining military provision at a level appropriate for each phase of development, from occupation and initial militarization to successive degrees of stabilization. The following numbers of Ottoman garrison forces stationed at three main Hungarian fortresses shows the pattern of gradual de-escalation clearly enough:

	1543	*1549*	*1569*
Buda	2965	1898	1636
Estergom	2875	1887	1317
Istolni-Belgrad	3000	n/a	1400

(Kaldy-Nagy, 1974, pp. 27, 43; David, 1997, p. 920)

The scaled-down Ottoman military presence in Hungary during the late 1560s was demanding enough financially, and commitments in other competing spheres had to be adjusted and sometimes curtailed to sustain even this reduced level of remittances to Hungary to fund pay for the troops.

One of the characteristics of the administrative system developed during the reign of Suleyman was its efficiency in identifying and extracting resources. It had the advantage over its Habsburg rivals – with territories and resources of roughly equal extent (Issawi, 1993) – of greater centralization of power on the one hand, and the contiguous nature of its territorial holdings on the other. The Ottoman empire was favoured by geography and the natural cohesion of its territories, linked by the continuous waterway formed by the Black Sea and the Marmara, Aegean, Ionian and eastern Adriatic seas, most of which – after Suleyman's expulsion of the Knights of St John from Rhodes in 1522, and their forced relocation in Malta – the Ottomans could credibly claim formed

part of their own *mare nostrum*. To this the Ottomans added their own bureaucratic efficiency, which allowed them to project their influence throughout
their tri-continental empire from a single political centre at Istanbul, a devolution of power to trusted elements in each of the empire's respective regions
notwithstanding. Geographical constraints dictated that certain regional
enclaves were never very fully integrated into the imperial system, and such
areas survived, both in the sixteenth century and later, as refuges for forces
resisting Ottoman rule. But on the whole by the mid-1530s the Ottomans had
created an extensive zone of imperial control, whose natural riches and
regional resources they could draw on at will and redistribute according to
centrally-determined priorities. Thus it was not only the size nor even the
configuration of Ottoman territories at the conclusion of their period of rapid
expansion that mattered most, but their exceptionally unhampered ability
(for pre-modern states) to extract and reassign the resource potential of those
territories.

Experts have long debated whether it is more correct to regard the Ottoman
empire in the sixteenth century as part of an emerging world system created
by the west, or as a self-contained 'world economic system' in its own right.
In terms of size, shape and successful integration of territory the Ottoman
empire was not just large, but in a systems sense also advanced for its time.
Citing Giovani Botero's travel account of 1591, Braudel noted the 'planetary
dimensions' of the Ottoman empire, while at the same time commenting on
the advantages it derived from being a 'single-pieced' entity (Braudel, 1984,
p. 467). From a systems as opposed to size perspective, Veinstein judged that
the Ottoman empire in the sixteenth century had indeed gained the status of
'une "économie-monde" sous le contrôle de l'état' (Veinstein, 1989, p. 210).

In the light of constraints imposed by relatively primitive transport and
communication in an age dominated by animal and sail power, it is certainly
difficult to imagine how the Ottoman empire could have been much bigger. If
anything, Botero's judgement concerning the 'planetary' proportions of the
empire understates the reality. Based on measurements derived from modern
political boundaries, the Ottomans' tri-continental empire had roughly 14,000
miles of coastline requiring lesser and greater levels of monitoring and over-
sight (Random House, 1973). Given such scale, it almost seems a quibble to
argue whether or not the Ottomans achieved stature as a world power in the
sixteenth century.

Another dimension of the debate on world systems centres around the significance of the multi-centric distribution of Ottoman economic activity.
According to Faroqhi, despite the fact that the Ottomans successfully created a
vast unified market and supply system, where free inter-regional exchange was
unhampered by internal customs barriers, the persistence of a north–south
divide between the imperial economy of Istanbul and subsidiary commodities

exchange systems based in Cairo impeded full economic integration (Faroqhi, 1994, pp. 478–9). On the other hand Brummett points out that it was partly because of the vitality of the unsubordinated regional trade networks of the southern Mediterranean that the empire was successful in fighting off successive bids by the Venetians, Portuguese and other maritime commercial powers of the western Mediterranean to challenge Ottoman trade hegemony in the Mediterranean after the fall of Egypt (Brummett, 1999, p. 245). A further factor in the longer-term prospering of the Ottoman economic system was the permissiveness, even liberalism, of the Ottomans in decisions about widening access to Ottoman markets through international trade agreements in the period after 1569.

A final test of Ottoman imperial success rooted in a combination of territorial expansion and systems management improvements lies in the sphere of fiscal administration. While detailed assessment is outside the scope of this chapter, it does appear that sixteenth-century Ottoman emperors not only succeeded in accumulating resources on a massive scale, but perhaps even more importantly they managed to contribute regularly to the accumulation of treasury reserves. There is also evidence that budget-deficit provinces and regions were being heavily subsidized by budget-surplus regions, and that some regions were being deliberately privileged by under-taxation. This shows that Ottoman fiscal administration, based on a centralized system of revenue transfers and reallocations, was working effectively, thus allowing the needs of all regions to be met and the foundations of the *Pax Ottomanica* to be supported, while at the same time allowing planners of imperial ventures (including military campaigns) generous discretionary funds to work with.

The slowing of Ottoman expansion towards the end of Suleyman's reign marks the beginning of a new era of stable frontiers. Although Ottoman relations with Europe were hardly uniformly peaceful in the ensuing period, the Ottoman empire continued to thrive for 250 years, until the national separatist movements of the early nineteenth century, and it survived for another 100 years after that. This durability in the face of many challenges is partly a legacy of Suleyman's recognition of the rational limits beyond which the costs of expansion and defence of new territorial acquisitions would have begun to outweigh the benefits deriving from further extensions of imperial rule.

Beginning in Suleyman's reign, the Ottomans developed new methods of extending their sphere of influence, not by direct rule or acquisition of new territory but by mapping out areas of mutual interest with new international partners. This new pattern of diplomacy, which saw the formation of multilateral international partnerships – initially in strategic alliances with Habsburg opponents like France, and later widening to include Protestant powers such as England (1580) and Holland (1612) – increasingly supplanted the older pattern of confrontation dating from the period of competition for regional dominance among the seven Balkan kingdoms. Already in the Ottoman–Polish treaty of 1553 we observe the invocation by Suleyman of a principle which became a feature of Ottoman multilateralism after the mid-sixteenth century, namely the expectation that Ottoman allies should be 'friends to our friends, enemies to our enemies' (Kolodziejcyzk, 2000, pp. 236, 240). From this date onwards, and certainly after the signing of formal capitulations with France in 1569, the era of permissiveness and widened use of trade incentives with an ever-expanding international clientele can be said to have begun. By this time the Ottomans had definitively shifted their emphasis in the international arena to winning friends with the carrot rather than expecting always to beat their opponents into submission with the stick.

A recent assessment (Inalcik and Quataert, 1994, p. 6) holds that Ottoman trade liberalism emerged as a key feature of imperial strategy only in the post-classical era, commonly held to begin after 1600, and yet Suleyman seems to have understood the benefits of this foreign policy orientation and its potential for sustaining the *Pax Ottomanica* in the mid-sixteenth century. The tendency to credit Suleyman, the most 'magnificent' of all the Ottoman sultans, with the highest levels of achievement in all spheres of endeavour is not always justi-fied. Yet to give credit where credit is due, the legacy of multilateralism firmly rooted in Suleyman's innovations at the height of the so-called classical era enabled the Ottomans to emerge as major players on the world stage in the mid-sixteenth century, remaining there for centuries, not just as conquerors but also as masters of persuasion and diplomacy. In this respect, if not in all others, Suleyman did manage to break the mould. His successors inherited an empire which, unlike the first empire, which foundered immediately after the death of its warrior-founder Beyazid ('the Thunderbolt') in 1402, was built to last.

The basis of Ottoman military strength

Nevertheless the ultimate decisive factor underpinning the expansion of the Ottoman empire described in this and the previous chapter was military power, and this gives rise in conclusion to the question as to what gave the Ottomans the competitive edge in warfare during the sixteenth century, and indeed beyond this period.

Military historians have long debated the transformatory effects of the introduction of gunpowder technology on the conduct of war in the sixteenth century, rightly identifying the growing importance of musket-bearing infantry forces in the military provision of all states with expansionist ambitions, as well as their increasingly important role in homeland defence. Because of the universal and rapid spread of the new methods based on diffusion of small arms, only those states which consistently managed to equip and deploy large numbers of these new-style forces could hope to defend their places in the existing world order. Hence acceptance of these new realities was as immediate and universal as the spread of the new pyrotechnic weapons themselves. The difference between states lay more in their natural geographical positions, and in the inherent adaptability and elasticity of their institutional structures to respond on a scale adequate to meet the demands imposed by the spread of the new technology. Lynn has suggested that as an alternative to the standard interpretative framework focusing on changes in weaponry and battlefield tactics – long thought to form the key dimension of the military revolution – historians should focus more attention on the evolving state of military institutions and forms of military recruitment, factors which he believes provide a more satisfactory explanation of the distinguishing characteristics of the various military systems encountered in early modern Europe and the Ottoman world (Lynn, 1996, pp. 509, 536ff.). Without adopting the extreme position of denying the importance of technological and tactical changes in warfare, Lynn's rebalancing of emphasis opens up new possibilities for assessing technological change within its wider fiscal, administrative and regionally-specific environmental context.

A comparison of western and Ottoman military provision in the age of the gunpowder revolution reveals that perhaps the most important distinctions between the Ottomans and their contemporaries lay on the one hand in disparities in the scale and ease of their access to the essential raw materials needed to wage war, and on the other in the more advanced evolutionary state of the Ottoman central bureaucratic apparatus, which allowed them to extract resources of men, materials and money more efficiently than their European counterparts. These main distinguishing features can be sub-divided for discussion into weaponry and raw materials, war finance, and military and bureaucratic systems.

The reliable projection of military power based on gunpowder technology depended first and foremost on the state's direct access to and control over large quantities of high-quality gunpowder. In the case of the Spanish army under Philip II (1556–98) Thompson's detailed study has revealed that this generally acknowledged paradigm infantry force of the mid to late sixteenth century continued to rely on a decentralized system of gunpowder distribution supplied from a variety of domestic contractors, while becoming increasingly dependent on imported raw materials to supply those producers. Thompson concluded that despite Philip's valiant attempts at administrative reform and centralization Spain's munitions industry remained inadequate, in terms of both quantity and quality, for the task of meeting the rising demand for key supplies to fuel his wars on multiple fronts (Thompson, 1976, pp. 234ff.). Spain's vulnerability in its preparedness for war arose not from technological deficiencies or constraints, but from the lack of adequate infrastructural and institutional development to support an efficient state-run munitions industry. In contrast to Spain's situation, the Ottomans possessed more than adequate domestic sources of the raw materials for gunpowder production, distributed across a wide territorial base from Egypt to Macedonia and at several locations in its core province of Asia Minor. Perhaps even more important, it was able to impose a closer degree of control over the production, storage and distribution of these supplies, since they were organized and run under the direct administrative aegis of the state. The imperial cannon foundry and gunpowder works in the capital Istanbul was at the heart of a highly centralized distribution system, employing sea, river and overland transport networks, which could quickly and efficiently supply the most distant fronts, as well as the Ottoman navy, with an ease that held the empire's European counterparts in awe. Although the issue of gunpowder's quality and reliability was not fully resolved by any sixteenth-century state, shortage of supply was never an issue for the Ottomans, as it was for many of their contemporaries, and since production took place almost exclusively in state-administered ateliers they were able to impose a closer scrutiny and control over the manufacturing process than most.

Perhaps the most serious vulnerability faced by the west in its efforts to maintain military provision at a level sufficient to counter sixteenth-century Ottoman expansion lay in the area of resource control and management. The Ottomans' main competitors in the west ruled over territories where they could exert only partial jurisdictional control, and where they had only indirect access to the sources of manpower recruitment and, perhaps most importantly, revenue extraction. Over the course of the sixteenth century Charles V and his successors managed to increase the level of contributions from provincial sources coming into the central treasury to an impressive degree, but with the escalating costs associated with warfare these newly-added resources still proved inadequate, so that the state faced a chronic shortage of funds and a steadily mounting balance of payments problem. Hence while Castile's annual revenue stream quadrupled from one to four million ducats between 1522 and 1560, Charles's reckless borrowing from a series of private lenders in the years preceding his abdication in 1556 forced his son and successor Philip II to suspend payments to the state's creditors in 1557 and 1560, and to declare state bankruptcy in 1575 (Muto, 1995, pp. 242–6). As a result, during the last quarter of the century Philip possessed neither the internal cash flow nor the external credit to be reliably able to deploy his state-of-the art *tercio* regiments, which were often needed on multiple fronts. Furthermore the Spanish system of limiting service contracts to the five to seven months needed to complete a single season of campaigning and to return home restricted the effective range of their deployment to contiguous territories and nearby fronts (Tracy, 2002, pp. 196–7).

Comparison of the resource position of the Spanish and Ottoman empires in the 1560s and 1570s provides a striking contrast. Philip inherited an accumulated budget deficit of 30 million ducats from his father in 1556, but his decision to embark on an ambitious naval construction programme and his participation in the great sea battle of Lepanto in 1571 doubled this level of debt to 60 million (Thompson, 1976, p. 72). Conversely Suleyman bequeathed a treasury surplus to his son Selim II in 1566, so that even after the customary cash distribution to his household troops and others at the time of his accession the credit balance in the Ottoman treasury in 1568 had risen to 127 million silver akçes, or approximately two million ducats (Barkan, 1957–58, p. 291). This reserve fund allowed the sultan to order the immediate rebuilding of his own fleet, so that in each of the three years immediately following the defeat at Lepanto sizeable Ottoman fleets reappeared in the Mediterranean. In 1574 the last of these succeeded in forcing the permanent evacuation of the Spanish garrison at La Goletta, which had been established after Charles's attack on Tunis in 1535. Clearly all that the combined efforts of the international maritime coalition at Lepanto had accomplished was to cut off one of the heads of the Ottoman hydra.

Throughout most of the sixteenth and on into the seventeenth century the Ottomans were better positioned than any of their potential adversaries to endure the steady drain of resources needed to win multi-seasonal conflicts and to wage prolonged wars of attrition. The differing pattern of Ottoman and western investment in military provision in this period resembles in some ways the American–Soviet confrontation during the Cold War era of the second half of the twentieth century. In the end what secured the triumph of the Americans was not superior military technology, but superior spending power and the potential of their economy to absorb the rising costs associated with a prolonged arms race without collapsing.

As regards military systems, the Ottomans were ahead of any of their contemporaries in the development of a full-scale standing army with its own institutional traditions and standards of service. Though the Janissary infantrymen are best known, it should not be forgotten that the sultan also had at his personal disposal six permanent regiments of mounted household troops who constituted a trained and experienced force numbering some five to six thousand by the mid-sixteenth century. Thus the sultan was able to project Ottoman military power at short notice in any direction he chose, and to react quickly to developments on any front, and this was yet more the case when he commanded even a portion of his vast internal *timariot* reserves, whose mobilization required greater forethought but who were equally at his disposal. This ability to concentrate military power rapidly from his own independent resources gave the sultan a considerable strategic advantage over his western contemporaries, who all relied to a greater or lesser extent on forces supplied through third-party contractual arrangements. Parker has used the term 'military devolution' to describe the prevailing pattern of state dependency on private contractors associated in the west with the latter part of the sixteenth and the first decades of the seventeenth centuries, noting that in his view this impeded the progress of military standardization and professionalization of army service (Parker, 1988, pp. 64–7). The training and discipline of the troops mustered internally by the Ottomans was bound to be more consistent and reliable than that of those who served in the armies assembled by their counter-parts in the west, which was the case until the mid-seventeenth century (give or take a decade or two), when, according to the view now prevailing among military historians, western armies definitively abandoned the system of troops assembled through third-party contract arrangements in favour of state-commissioned armies (Lynn, 1996, pp. 518, 544–5). Until this transition had been completed in the west the Ottomans were alone in their possession of a military system that relied predominantly on its own internal resources, organized in accordance with expected and universally known standards of service, and supported by a bureaucratic regime that provided both pre-dictability and an unquestioned and centralized chain of command leading all the way to the sultan himself. The problems associated with multiple armies, multiple musters and multiple (and competing) commands could not be avoided entirely in an empire which drew its recruits from a tri-continental land base, but compared to their European adversaries in the era of 'military devolution' the Ottomans managed to keep the difficulties arising from con-flicting military cultures to a minimum.

The overall picture for the sixteenth century indicates that the most decisive factor allowing the Ottomans to maintain the competitive edge over their European contemporaries was not weaponry or tactics, but rather the central-ized bureaucratic structure which gave them the ability to mobilize men, money and materials for war more effectively than their opponents. By 1547 the military and organizational might of the Ottoman empire, supported by its financial independence and its seemingly inexhaustible supply of raw materials, had already convinced Charles V that a partition of Hungary leav-ing the lion's share to the Ottomans was inevitable (Setton, 1984, p. 485). He had also, though more regretfully, come to accept the need for a permanent revision of his grand strategy in the Mediterranean, and a reassessment of his ambitious plans aimed at uniting both its halves under Habsburg dominion. By mid-century the limits of the possible for Europe's sixteenth-century super-power had clearly been reached and exceeded, as Charles's abdication and division of his empire's territories acknowledged a few years later in 1556. For the next hundred years and more, until the commencement of the pan-European anti-Ottoman counter-offensives of the late 1680s, which were sus-tained by heavy Papal subsidies, the Ottomans retained the military initiative and held their own against all but the most determined international collations of forces.

References

Primary texts

Cafer Beg. 1938. Text of letter to Selim I, in *Topkapı Sarayı Arşivi Kilavuzu*, ed. T. Öz, Istanbul, document 13.
Hayder Chelebi. 1858. 'Ruzname', in *Münşeat ül-Selatin*, vol. 1, by A. Feridun, Istanbul, 435–500.

Secondary sources

Barkan, O. 1957–58. 'H. 954–955 (1547–1548) Mali yılına ait bir bütçe örneği', *Istanbul Üniversitesi Iktisat Fakültesi Mecmuası*, 19, 219–332.
——**1953–54**. 'H. 933–934 (M. 1527–1528) Malî yılına ait bir bütçe örneği', *Istanbul Üniversitesi Iktisat Fakültesi Mecmuası*, 15, 251–329.
Barta, G. 1994. 'The Emergence of the Principality and its First Crises (1526–1606)', in *History of Transylvania*, G. Barta and others, Budapest, 247–300.
Braudel, F. 1984. *Civilisation and Capitalism, 15th–18th Century*, vol. 3, London.
Brummet, P. 1999. 'The Ottoman Empire, Venice and the Question of Ending Rivalries', in *Great Power Rivalries*, ed. W. Thompson, Columbia, 225–53.
——**1994**. *Ottoman Seapower and Levantine Diplomacy in the Age of Discovery*, Albany.
David, G. 1997. 'Istolni Belgrad', in *The Encyclopaedia of Islam*, vol. 9, Leiden, 920.
Faroqhi, S. 1994. 'Crisis and Change, 1590–1699', in *An Economic and Social History of the Ottoman Empire, 1300–1914*, ed. H. Inalcik and D. Quataert, Cambridge, 413–636.
Inalcik, H. and Quataert, D., eds. 1994. *An Economic and Social History of the Ottoman Empire, 1300–1914*, Cambridge.
Issawi, C. 1993. 'The Ottoman-Habsburg Balance of Forces', in *Süleyman the Second (i.e. the First) and his Time*, ed. H. Inalcik and C. Kafadar, Istanbul, 145–51.
Kaldy-Nagy, G. 1974. *Macaristan'da 16. Yüzyılda Türk Yönetimi*, Budapest.
Kolodziejczyk, D. 2000. *Ottoman–Polish Diplomatic Relations, 15th–18th Century*, Leiden.
Labib, S. 1979. 'The Era of Suleyman the Magnificent: Crisis of Orientation', *International Journal of Middle East Studies*, 10, 435–51.
Lynn, J.A. 1996. 'The Evolution of Army Style in the Modern West, 800–2000', *International History Review*, 18, 505–45.
Makkai, L. 1946. *Histoire de la Transylvanie*, Paris.
Murphey, R. 2001a. 'Süleyman I and the Conquest of Hungary: Ottoman Manifest Destiny or a Delayed Reaction to Charles V's Universalist Vision', *Journal of Early Modern History*, 5, 197–221.
——**2001b**. 'Seyyid Muradi's Prose Biography of Hizr ibn Yakub, alias Hayreddin Barbarossa', *Acta Orientalia Acadamiae Scientarum Hungaricae*, 54, 523–36.
——**1993**. 'Süleyman's Eastern Policy', in *Süleyman the Second (i.e. the First) and his Time*, ed. H. Inalcik and C. Kafadar, Istanbul, 229–48.
Muto, G. 1995. 'The Spanish System: Centre and Periphery', in *Economic Systems and State Finance*, ed. R. Bonney, Oxford, 231–59.
Northedge, A. 1997. 'Sur', in *The Encyclopaedia of Islam*, vol. 9, Leiden, 882–5.
Parker, G. 1988. *The Military Revolution. Military Innovation and the Rise of the West, 1500–1800*, Cambridge.

Random House. 1973. 'Coastline Measurements of the World', in *The Random House Dictionary of the English Language*, New York, 1947–8.

Setton, K.M. 1984. *The Papacy and the Levant, 1204–1571. Vol. 3: The Sixteenth Century to the Reign of Julius III*, Philadelphia.

Thompson, I.A.A. 1976. *War and Government in Habsburg Spain, 1560–1620*, London.

Tracy, J. 2002. *Emperor Charles V, Impresario of War: Campaign Strategy, International Finance, and Domestic Politics*, Cambridge.

Veinstein, G. 1989. 'L'empire dans sa grandeur (XVIe siècle)', in *Histoire de l'Empire Ottoman*, ed. R. Mantran and others, Paris, 159–226.

5

Naval Power, 1450–1650: The Formative Age

Jan Glete

Early modern sea power and historiography

The sea both separates and connects land. Efficient shipping increases trade and specialization of production, and makes cultural contacts between people easier. Maritime lines of communication are, however, also vulnerable to violence, and they can be used for transportation of military forces. Sea power, the ability to control the sea with armed force, is therefore important for rulers and societies connected with the sea.

From the mid-fifteenth to the mid-seventeenth century, European sea power developed from a medieval setting into an early modern framework. Up to the late fifteenth century wars at sea were fought with infantry weapons and with cargo-carriers temporarily armed for war, or with galleys that could be built quickly when a war began. This was changed by the introduction of guns, specialized warships, permanent navies controlled by states, and by maritime expansion outside Europe. Naval power organized by territorial states was gradually separated from mercantile power and city oligarchies. The centre of maritime activities and warfare at sea shifted from the Mediterranean to western and northern Europe. The driving forces behind these changes and their results are important parts of the transformation of Europe.

Many of our ideas about early modern political and naval history were formed by studies made in the nineteenth and early twentieth centuries, when the nation-state had its heyday. The modern state was seen as the self-evident outcome of historical change. Its army and navy were regarded as instruments of national political interests and policies. Navies were evaluated as the more efficient the more they adhered to nineteenth and early twentieth-century ideas about operational doctrines, professional officers, naval administration and the primacy of the gun-armed battle fleet. With that perspective the large sailing battle fleets of the period 1650–1850 became classic examples of what the nation-state could achieve through a systematic long-term policy.

They were important in struggles between great powers, they protected trade and attacked enemy shipping, and they were key instruments for the spreading of European power around the world. The American sea officer Alfred Mahan is the best known of several naval historians who placed navies in this historical context (Mahan, 1890).

Warfare at sea before the mid-seventeenth century fitted less well into this picture. Navies were smaller or non-existent, and operational fleets often consisted of temporarily armed merchantmen. Warships were smaller than in the age of the battle fleet. Galleys were still important, a fact which was interpreted as conservatism. Naval tactics and strategy looked primitive or subordinated to privateering interests of plunder. Naval commanders were often aristocrats and gentlemen rather than professional officers, and naval policy was regarded as undeveloped and short-sighted compared to later standards.

Earlier generations of naval historians often assumed that early sailing warships and guns had approximately the same technical capabilities as their better-known eighteenth-century descendants. That made it difficult to understand why the early navies did not achieve the same level of operational efficiency. Historians of naval technology, on the other hand, emphasized the primitive state of the art in an age when ships were designed without the support of advanced theory, and usually even without drawings which showed the shape of the hulls. European naval history was also written as national histories. Comparative studies of naval policy, administration, technology and operations were rare. Without at least approximate benchmarks for comparison, various legends and entrenched ideas about pioneering efforts or backwardness, efficiency, neglect or lack of naval policy became long-lived parts of naval historiography.

More recent historical research has attempted to place the pre-1650 European navies in other perspectives (Guilmartin, 1974; Bruijn, 1993; Rodger, 1997; Glete, 2000; Hattendorf and Unger, 2003). Naval development was an important part of the transformation of Europe from a continuum of small autonomous cities and societies with power confined to local elites, into a continent of territorial states with an effective monopoly of violence. From this state-formation perspective early navies are interpreted as instruments of ambitious rulers and rising elites rather than of nascent nation-states. Princes and leaders of republican regimes often had to fight for their survival in an age when rebellions and civil wars were common. The future of the rulers was often at stake, and this stimulated the search for innovations which might strengthen their power in relation to competitors.

Technologically this period was an age of path-breaking innovation and bold experiment, while the following two centuries saw an evolutionary and increasingly path-dependent process of refinement, until a new period of innovation radically changed navies in the nineteenth century. Historians today have a better awareness of the political, financial, organizational and technological constraints on early modern sea power, and they see efforts to handle these problems as interesting questions for study. There are good opportunities for future studies of the interaction between political culture, policy, administration, technology and operations, which can increase our understanding of how early modern sea power actually worked.

Navies, state formation and economy

State formation is the process of rulers and elites creating organizations and social institutions in order to regulate behaviour in societies and to draw increased volumes of resources from it. This process is usually based on some kind of bargaining between rulers and various interest groups (Tilly, 1990, pp. 16–33). From this perspective navies are the result both of ambitions from above to regulate society and of demands from society for better control of violence at sea. Sea power could be used for protecting trade and coasts, and if rulers found innovative forms of organizing such protection their power in society became more legitimate. Their subjects were less likely to revolt, obstruct taxation or resist political and administrative control if they were protected from something worse. Sea power was, however, also important for political control of territories dependent on maritime trade or threatened by seaborne invasion. If rulers controlled the sea they could also control contacts between their subjects and outside power-holders. This made it easier to suppress and prevent the rebellions and political coalitions across borders which had been typical of medieval societies (Glete, 2002, pp. 16–41).

Naval power before 1650 often grew dramatically as a result of domestic rather than international conflicts. The establishment of the Tudor, Oldenburg and Vasa dynasties and their navies in England, Denmark-Norway and Sweden after long periods of civil war illustrates the point. During the Wars of the Roses (1455–85) and the many inter-Scandinavian conflicts between 1448 and 1536, pretenders to thrones or one party in a conflict had frequently received support from across the sea, not least from the German Hanse (Fudge, 1995). Navies became political instruments whereby rulers could cut off such contacts and curb mercantile sea power. Other examples are the development of Dutch naval power during the revolt against Philip II, the growth of Swedish naval power during the domestic conflict of the 1590s, Richelieu's foundation of a French navy during the civil war in the 1620s, and the drastic expansion of the English navy during the civil war in the 1640s (Glete, 1993, pp. 123–58).

Europe is a large peninsula with several smaller peninsulas and large islands, and many major cities are ports. Trade routes often pass through narrows at sea which are easy to control, primarily the Dardanelles-Bosphorus, the entrance to the Adriatic Sea, the Straits of Gibraltar, the Channel and the Sound. This geographical configuration made interaction between sea power and state formation important. Maritime cities often acted independently of territorial princes if the latter did not enforce effective control of the sea. Some states were dependent on the sea for internal communications, and sea power made it possible to control and protect wide territories and seas from a centre of political, naval and military power. Cities like Constantinople, Venice, Seville/Cadiz, Lisbon, London, Amsterdam, Copenhagen and Stockholm were major ports which became naval bases and centres for economic, political and administrative control of states and maritime-oriented empires.

Does this mean that the early modern state was important for trade and economic change? Economic historians, of whom Fernand Braudel has been the most influential, have often answered this question with no. Trade followed its own economic logic and avoided regulations, blockades and wars with various subterfuges, and war and navies are not regarded as important for the economy except as burdens on it (Braudel, 1981–84). Other scholars have concluded that lower protection costs, reduced violence and improved property rights were important for increased productivity in maritime transportation (Lane, 1979; North, 1981, pp. 144–57). Immanuel Wallerstein has argued that world systems of trade and political influence required a strong and well-armed state at the core (Wallerstein, 1974, p. 38). Jonathan Israel has identified the seventeenth-century Dutch republic, which used its navy to protect and promote Dutch trade in an age of endemic wars, as a particularly effective state of that type (Israel, 1989, pp. 405–15).

The fact that permanent navies (and armies) hardly existed in Europe before 1500 but were the normal form of armed force two centuries later is remarkable and calls for explanation. As a social phenomenon they won in competition with alternative forms of protection and violence-control at sea. In economic theory organizations with structures and identities of their own are the results of attempts of societies to use scarce resources in a rational way. Organizations divide labour, reduce transaction costs, process large volumes of information, and develop systems for control. Sea power became increasingly dependent on long-term planning, on advanced technology in shipbuilding and gun-founding, on specialized skills in handling warships and guns, and on systems for large-scale mobilization of seamen and concentration of stores. All this favoured the development of permanent structures, and early modern navies are often described as the most complex organizations of their age. Their hierarchical structure and dependence on external resources raised by political power-holders made them into obedient instruments of those who controlled them from the top (Glete, 2002, esp. pp. 51–66).

Once the early modern state had started to develop organizations it began to have an advantage over earlier private and temporary forms of sea power.

The process was slow and far from straightforward across Europe, although rapid in some states. Private interests also developed new technologies and skills in warfare at sea, and private investments in guns and armed ships were often a considerable part of the total sea power of a nation. When warships were few these resources were a valuable additional asset in emergencies. Operational fleets with armed merchantmen and temporarily commissioned officers did not become obsolete until after 1650, when stronger states radically increased the size of navies and warships; while privateering lasted until the nineteenth century, although it became strictly controlled by the states (Glete, 1993).

Naval technology

The main technological elements of the transformation of sea power were the development of specialized sailing warships and of dependable guns powerful enough to damage wooden hulls, rigs, crew, and targets on land. Innovations in ship design, gunpowder and metallurgy made it possible to bring large amounts – by early modern standards – of firepower to sea, and to deploy it in any part of the world (Lavery, 1987; Glete, 1993, pp. 22–65; Conway, 1994; Conway, 1995). It was a Eurocentric form of warfare. Gunpowder technology, the ability to build ocean-going ships, and centralized states did exist in Asia, especially in China, Korea and Japan, but they were not combined and developed in the same way as in Europe (Cipolla, 1965).

Primitive gunpowder weapons were used at sea in the fourteenth century, but it was only in the late fifteenth century that they became important for sea power. Heavy guns had been developed for breaking fortress walls and they were originally often mounted on ships for the same purpose. Early guns were thin tubes made of wrought iron, which could fire large-calibre stone shot to good effect. Round stone shot was, however, expensive to make. During the latter half of the fifteenth century thick-walled guns cast in bronze (copper alloyed with tin), which could fire iron shot of up to about 40 to 50 pounds with large powder charges, became operational. Bronze artillery was reliable and durable, and wrought-iron guns and stone shot were phased out during the sixteenth century. However bronze was expensive, and this was a limit to mass production of heavy guns for warships (Guilmartin, 1974, pp. 135–75).

Cast iron was a cheaper alternative but the metallurgical problems were difficult. Cast-iron guns were produced in England from the 1540s and the technology slowly spread to the Netherlands and Sweden, and in the early seventeenth century to Spain. This technology was imperfect and unreliable, and was mainly used for small guns, typically 3 to 12-pounders. Cast-iron guns could be produced at much lower cost than bronze guns, and it became economically possible to arm merchantmen with a considerable number of guns. From the mid-seventeenth century dependable cast-iron guns of large calibres could be produced. They replaced bronze guns and made it possible to mass-produce guns for large warships, which was one economic precondition for the growth of large battle fleets.

The oared galley was the traditional specialized warship, primarily in the Mediterranean, where light winds made them especially useful. Large crews made them dependent on almost weekly contact with land for supply of water and provisions (Pryor, 1988). Galleys were technologically mature before 1450 and guns only caused an increase in their average size. Older naval historiography believed that galleys became obsolete when heavy guns were introduced at sea. Actually the new weapon gave them a new viability as long as guns were expensive and scarce. One heavy gun could easily be mounted in the bow of a galley and aimed with accuracy against ships or fortress walls. A galley could normally escape from a sailing warship by rowing against the wind and its low hull was difficult to hit. The great expansion of permanent galley navies took place after the introduction of heavy guns at sea. The galley was a key instrument for making the new weapon operational and mobile in the Mediterranean, where the sea connects people while coasts are often mountainous or barren deserts (Guilmartin, 1974).

Improved sailing ships were one of the great technical achievements of the fifteenth and sixteenth centuries. The three-mast rig and sophisticated sailing technology were of mercantile origin but they made it easier to develop gun-armed sailing warships. Improved manoeuvrability and better ability to sail close to the wind and to stay at sea under unfavourable weather conditions made efficient warfare under sail possible. These qualities were essential in a warship to enable it to stay close to lee coasts in bad weather, to gain the weather gauge of the enemy and to manoeuvre rapidly during combat, for example by tacking.

Heavy guns on ships also required changes to the structure of the hull. Earlier a merchant ship could be converted into a temporary warship by adding high but light superstructures fore and aft for infantry armed with missile weapons (Unger, 1980). An efficient gun-carrying ship had to be designed as such. The reduced importance of infantry made it possible to minimize the high superstructures but guns offered new technical challenges. The lowest gun deck had to be at a sufficient height above the waterline, the internal structure of the hull had to be strong enough to carry heavy loads high in the ship, and weight had to be distributed carefully in order to make the ship stiff and stable under sail. The hull also had to be built strongly enough to resist enemy gunfire. Some early gun-armed warships were large, with displacements of up to 2000 tonnes or more, but smaller and more flexible ships could also carry a limited number of heavy guns. Before 1650 warships of 300 to 1000 tonnes dominated navies (Glete, 1993).

The combination of heavy guns with sailing ships started a long process of evolution in which the armament increased from a few widely-spaced heavy guns, often primarily mounted fore and aft (Rodger, 1996), to continuous broadsides of densely-placed guns on one, two or three decks. The weight of the armament rose from 1 or 2 per cent of the displacement of a warship around 1500 to 7 or 8 per cent on ships of the line in the latter half of the seventeenth century. This was a remarkable achievement of early modern naval architecture. Naval historians have often discussed when and where heavy guns ('ship-killers') were first used at sea. No pioneering region or state has been found. In the decades around 1500 heavy guns appeared on sailing ships in the Mediterranean, in the Portuguese overseas expansion, in the Channel and in the Baltic. Specialized warships with armament weights of about 3 per cent of the displacement became common in western and northern Europe in the latter half of the sixteenth century. Sailing technology was still deficient in several respects and up to the mid-sixteenth century galleys and sailing warships with auxiliary oars (galeasses) were still useful in western and northern Europe.

In the latter half of the century English naval architecture led in the further development of more heavily armed sailing warships (Parker, 1996) which were also fast and manoeuvrable. This technology spread to the Netherlands, Denmark and Sweden in the decades around 1600 and to France in the 1620s. Spain and Portugal followed the same path but at a slower pace. From around 1600, Habsburg shipbuilders in the southern Netherlands became skilled at building heavily armed but fast ships with sharp, long and low hulls (called frigates) for trade warfare. The evolution of specialized gun-armed warships from 1450 to 1650 has often been described as the development of certain ship types, primarily the carrack, the caravel, the galleon and the frigate. Actually these names were used for widely different types of ships and hardly used at all in large parts of Europe where the process took place.

The combat value of large cargo-carriers with infantry and only a few guns declined sharply during the sixteenth century. The Spanish Armada of 1588 was the last major fleet with a large number of merchantmen intended to fight with infantry rather than guns (Casado Soto, 1988). However privately owned ships remained essential in warfare. A new type of merchantman with a rather low hull and built to carry a substantial number of guns, usually of cast iron, was developed in the Channel area. The English and the Dutch learned to trade and fight with such ships in waters dominated by the Iberian powers or non-European seafarers, particularly the Mediterranean, the West Indies and the East Indies. Gun-armed merchantmen could serve as auxiliary warships in European fleets even if they were too lightly built and armed to fight major warships with success. During the seventeenth century they were frequently hired by states. Venice refrained from building sailing warships until around 1670 but hired whole fleets of armed merchantmen with their crews from the Netherlands and England (Glete, 1993). Much warfare at sea during the seventeenth century was fought with gun-armed merchantmen.

Strategy, operations and tactics

Schematically, sea power is used for four levels of strategic ambitions, which can be differentiated by the degree of operational freedom which they create at sea and on land, and the degree to which they deny this freedom to the enemy. Firstly command of the sea is reached if the enemy's fleet is destroyed or effectively blockaded and unable to interfere with operations or trade. The inferior side correspondingly tries to avoid this paralysis by keeping his fleet in being and strong enough to tie up enemy resources in operations which limit the superior fleet's ability to exercise command of the sea. Secondly sea control has the aim of protecting strategically and economically important sea lines of communication, typically with convoys. A third strategic level is sea denial, where the navy (or privateers authorized by states) attacks enemy shipping without any ambition to protect friendly shipping. Finally there is coastal defence, with the limited aim of making enemy activity close to the coast difficult.

Operationally, navies can be used as concentrated battle forces for command of the sea or for fleet-in-being strategies, as dispersed sea control or sea denial cruiser forces protecting or attacking shipping, as the naval part of amphibious forces, or as coastal defence forces. Concentrated battle fleets are typically formed to create mobile strategic positions in areas where control of the sea might be decisive for both naval operations and operations on land. In ambitious battle-fleet strategies such positions are established far from the main base in order to influence political and economic activities at long distance by naval means.

These strategies and operational patterns of sea power were in use from 1450 to 1650, but the differences compared to later centuries are so marked that it may be best to focus a brief analysis on them rather than on the similarities. First, most warfare at sea was fought in geographically limited regions. A navy could achieve command of the sea close to its own base and control regions like the Adriatic, the Aegean, the northern or the southern Baltic Sea, the Channel or the Malabar (western) coast of India without having any influence on the rest of the oceans. Economic blockade of an enemy by local control of a passage like the Channel or the Sound was easy to achieve and difficult to break. If the region or the passage was important it might attract foreign navies, but it was normally very difficult to establish effective strategic positions and enforce or break blockades far from the base. Operational fleets were too small and logistical support too undeveloped for that. Well-organized limited forces could operate with limited goals – trade warfare or an attack on an island or town – at very long distances, for example from Europe to America (Hoffman, 1980). However major operations outside Europe required local bases or colonies.

Politically, this made navies useful for defence and control of home waters and narrow passages. The change from infantry weapons to artillery as the main weapon at sea also meant that defensive strategies for territories could be changed. Earlier the fighting power of a fleet carrying an invading army was the army itself. A defender could organize his own naval force and send it to sea with soldiers in order to stop the invasion, but if the invader had a superior army the best defensive strategy was to allow the enemy to land and then fight a decisive battle when he had over-stretched his supply lines. With gun-armed warships a defender with an inferior army might prefer to meet the enemy at sea with his fleet and try to defeat the invader when the superior army could not act. Even states with inferior fleets were seldom invaded from the sea after the introduction of guns, as army commanders were reluctant to commit their soldiers across a sea which was not fully secured.

These preconditions explain why there were few fleet combats and very few long-distance operations with concentrated battle fleets before 1650. The exception was the Baltic, where the naval centres of Lübeck, Copenhagen and Stockholm were close enough to allow concentrated fleets to operate in the enemy's home waters, and to attempt to fight decisive battles and attack and blockade enemy bases. This occurred repeatedly during the wars of 1509–12, 1517–24, 1534–36, 1563–70, 1611–13 and 1643–45, making the Baltic into an unusually battle-intense region in this age. In the Atlantic the most spectacular attempts to change a strategic situation by long-distance deployment of a concentrated fleet were the Spanish attempts to gain control of the Channel in 1588 and 1639. Both ended in catastrophe, which shows how difficult such a strategy was with the technical and logistical constraints of this age.

Gun-armed sailing warships and gun-armed merchantmen did however give their owners a new and useful ability to deploy a limited amount of sea power at very long distances or for a long period of time. Manpower (infantry and oarsmen) was replaced by capital (guns and improved rigs), and this made sea power much less dependent on a continuous supply of food and water. Limited naval forces could be sent anywhere in the world to establish local bases and gradually extend these to colonial possessions, which could in turn support extended sea power outside Europe. Before 1650, Portugal, Spain and the Dutch did this on a large scale in Asia, America and Africa. The new type of ship was also useful for attack on or defence of trade at long distances. Convoys with state-owned warships were seldom organized by navies before 1650. The major exceptions were the Spanish convoys between Seville and the West Indies, and the extensive Dutch system of convoys during the war period

1621–48. It is characteristic that these convoys were run by state institutions, the *Casa de Contratación* in Seville and the Dutch Admiralties, in which merchant interests were influential.

Trade really needed protection. Gun-armed ships were much used for attacks on merchantmen, and trade warfare was an important strategy in this period. It did not require a navy, however. Privateers were effective for this purpose and they frequently operated in naval fashion, with squadrons and chains of command. North African corsairs fighting Christians, English privateers fighting Spain, and Flemish privateers fighting the Dutch often behaved like naval forces, and they frequently cooperated with their states in naval operations. In the Mediterranean private entrepreneurs in galley warfare were common, especially in Italy. The Dutch East India Company (founded in 1602) and the West India Company (1621) were corporations created for both trade and warfare, and were financed by many shareholders. Privateers, entrepreneurs and leaders of armed company forces were frequently the best sea commanders of their age. Men like Hayreddin Barbarossa (d. 1546), Andrea Doria (d. 1560), Francis Drake (d. 1596) and Piet Hein (d. 1629) reached the top of the naval hierarchies in the Ottoman empire, Spain, England and the Dutch republic respectively.

Naval tactics were shaped by various concepts to combine firepower, protection, mobility and coordination of ships. Fleets might be organized for centralized and formalized tactics or for tactics which emphasized individual initiative. Galleys were easy to form into line abreast, which was an offensive formation, and galley tactics were sophisticated in a formal sense and founded on a long tradition. Sailing warships could not move forward against an enemy and make full use of broadside firepower at the same time. This was an inherent limit on their potential for offensive tactics, but early sailing warships were often not broadside-armed but had as many guns as possible directed forward and aft (Rodger, 1996). Warships could be formed into line abreast or line ahead, or into wedges or columns, but with little homogeneity in training and ship design battles were usually decided by duels between ships or small groups of ships, where the skill and determination of the commander and crew, and the quality of ships and guns, were decisive.

Soldiers and infantry weapons were never entirely abolished in sailing warships. Close-range combat with muskets and even boarding frequently occurred in decisive battles, but gun-armed warships with good sailing qualities could avoid closing the range and choose to fight a stand-off combat with guns. Frequently one side tried to fight at close range and board while the other tried to avoid that. Early gunfights were sometimes duels between small groups of ships, which manoeuvred in order to hit and avoid being hit. Relatively few shots were fired, although often by skilled gunners who achieved many hits. When more capital was invested in broadside gunnery the incentive to make this the centrepiece of tactical thinking became stronger. By 1650 this had reached the stage where the line of battle, with ships formed up in line ahead and firing massive broadsides at the shortest possible interval, became the preferred naval tactic. This was necessary for a battle fleet which tried to enforce a command-of-the-sea strategy against a strong enemy.

The Mediterranean

In 1450 there was only one major permanent navy in Europe, the Venetian galley navy, which had been developed over centuries for control of a mercantile empire in the Levant. Venice was the final victor in a series of wars with Genoa, the leading maritime city in the western Mediterranean. Up to 1580 the Mediterranean was the scene of continuous warfare and naval growth, which radically centralized the power structure. The region experienced a combination of wars between great powers and widespread local violence at sea, primarily against trade and exposed coasts.

War about imperial control started between Venice and the rising Ottoman empire, which from 1453 made Constantinople the base for maritime conquests with galley fleets and amphibious expeditions. In 1463–79 and 1499–1502 these powers fought over control of Greece, where Venice had a network of fortified positions as galley bases. The Ottomans developed their naval skills and finally won the contest, most decisively in the naval battle of Zonchio (western Greece) in 1499 (Lane, 1973). Venice was left in control only of the Adriatic. Venetian trade with the Levant was dependent on neutrality in conflicts between the Ottomans and Christian powers. The Ottoman navy was important for logistical support of the conquest of Egypt in 1517, and for the voluntary submissions of the north African cities to the sultan. The capture of Rhodes from the Order of St John in 1522 eliminated the last Christian naval stronghold in the eastern Mediterranean. In the early sixteenth century the Ottoman empire had the largest navy in the world, and it had gained a strategically central position in Europe, Asia and Africa, facing both the Mediterranean and the Indian Ocean. It remained, however, tied to galley technology, which was a handicap for long-distance power projection and competition with the Portuguese, who had reached the Indian Ocean at the same time (Hess, 1970; Imber, 1980; Brummett, 1994).

The unification of Spain in the late fifteenth century and the Mediterranean ambitions of France resulted in several wars, usually called the Italian Wars (1494–1559). In these, navies and transport fleets were important for logistics, support of the armies' flanks, sieges of ports, and protection of the sea lanes between Spain and Italy. Both France and Spain developed permanent galley navies to fight these wars. The Spanish monarchy won control over much of Italy and its naval resources, not least the Genoese experience of galley warfare. From 1530 the new Spanish–Italian galley navy directed its main efforts against the Ottomans and their belligerent allies in Algiers, Tunis and Tripoli, who attacked Christian trade and coasts. The order of St John was given a new home in Malta, which became a well-fortified naval base for warfare against the Muslims. Emperor Charles V led expeditions of conquest against Tunis in 1535 and Algiers in 1541, the latter failing after a gale in which many vessels were lost.

The Ottomans had by then already started an offensive against the Spanish–Italian empire, a policy which up to 1559 periodically made the French and Ottoman fleets allies. In 1537 the Ottomans attacked Venetian Corfu. Spain and Venice joined forces but their fleet was defeated at Prevesa (western Greece) in 1538. Venice left the war and the Spanish–Italian fleet could no longer operate east of Italy. When peace with France was concluded in 1559, Philip II of Spain initiated a counter-offensive, but it ended in a disaster at the galley battle of Djerba (southern Tunisia) in 1560. A decade of frenetic expansion of the Spanish–Italian and Ottoman navies followed. When the Ottomans occupied Venetian Cyprus in 1570 an alliance of Spain, Venice and the smaller Italian states was formed. In 1571 about 500 galleys with a total crew of possibly 150,000 men fought the famous battle of Lepanto (western Greece), which in terms of manpower was the greatest contest in Europe before the late seventeenth century. Lepanto was a crushing Christian victory but its strategic consequences were limited. It marked the end of a long period of Ottoman conquests but it did not give the victors command of the eastern Mediterranean. A truce between Spain and the Ottomans was concluded in 1580. Galley navies existed even after 1650 but large-scale galley warfare was never resumed (Braudel, 1972–73; Guilmartin, 1974).

What were the interconnections between the formation of the Mediterranean empires and galley warfare? Traditionally the Mediterranean world had been controlled from fortified cities and strongholds. Heavy guns made thin walls vulnerable, especially to attacks from the sea, where heavy siege guns could be transported easily. A concentrated force could conquer one town or fortress after another. Local defence declined in efficiency while defence and deterrence by mobile forces became more efficient (Hook, 1977, p. 373). This favoured the empire-builders who could provide the large and mobile galley forces which the situation required. Nearly all coastal areas around the great sea were subordinated in one way or another to an empire which acted as their protector. The limits of these empires were primarily determined by the operational range of their galley forces. It thus seems clear that the introduction of guns on galleys made it easier to create great empires in the Mediterranean (Glete, 2000, pp. 93–111).

Large galley fleets had inherent limits, however. In terms of manpower (including chained oarsmen) and requirements for provisions they were the largest concentrated military forces of the sixteenth century. Logistical problems made them more sluggish in operation the larger they grew, and this made long-distance offensive warfare with galleys uneconomical. When guns became cheaper, sailing warships could fight off galleys with much larger crews and this opened the Mediterranean for armed merchantmen from western Europe (Guilmartin, 1974, pp. 253–73). These ships also frequently acted as predators on competitors, not least the previously dominant Venetian mercantile marine (Tenenti, 1967). The Mediterranean remained an important region for trade but uncertain conditions made shipping expensive, and this probably contributed to its relative decline in comparison to western and northern Europe. Galleys remained useful as coastguard vessels and as troop transports but they were increasingly unable to control even limited areas of the sea (Anderson, 1952; Hanlon, 1998, pp. 9–46).

The Baltic

In the early modern period the Baltic Sea became an important economic and political crossroads between western, eastern and northern Europe. Consequently sea power became important for control of the sea. From a western point of view the Baltic was essential as a source for naval stores for the growing navies and mercantile marines (Rystad, 1994). For early modern rulers in northern Europe it was the scene for operations connected with state formation, empire building and customs from trade flowing through the sea. Naval and military operations in this enclosed sea were interconnected. Naval control of the sea gave an army considerable leverage and operational freedom. The army could be concentrated in a decisive area where it could be logistically supported from the sea, it could be released from defensive tasks along coasts for offensives, and it could be sent across the sea in amphibious attacks (Glete, 2003).

In the Middle Ages power in the Baltic was closely connected with maritime trade. The leading sea power was the German Hanse, and its informal capital Lübeck was the largest medieval city on the Baltic (Dollinger, 1970). With many large cargo-carriers and concentrated financial resources for arming them, the Hanse could exercise much influence in an area where maritime lines of communication were crucial for trade and power projection. The development of two separate but centralized Nordic territorial states with permanent navies changed this. This may look paradoxical, as Denmark, Sweden and Norway had formed a union in the late fourteenth century, not least in order to improve defences against German penetration. The union began with royal ambitions to raise taxes and customs for warfare, especially the Sound toll, which was introduced in 1429. This policy foundered on internal opposition in Sweden and Denmark, and the union did not develop into a state with permanent armed forces.

This is in marked contrast to the results of similar policies followed by the Nordic rulers from the late fifteenth and early sixteenth centuries, when the union broke up and two monarchic states with permanent navies, Denmark-Norway and Sweden, emerged. This is a sign that technical change may have mattered in politics. The early fifteenth-century union rulers had an ambitious naval policy but no heavy guns or gun-armed warships. The Oldenburg and Vasa dynasties could use these new instruments of power and they understood their importance. Both dynasties became naval-minded, probably more than their contemporaries in the Nordic elites, who accepted rather than supported the development of permanent navies (Glete, 2003).

The Nordic navies were originally developed in competition with each other, but the two new dynastic states were not inevitably enemies. They shared a common concern with Lübeck's habit of interfering in Nordic politics and supporting internal opposition. In 1534–36 both Lübeck and Sweden intervened in a Danish civil war. Lübeck was defeated at sea in 1535 and was thereafter unable to act as a major sea power on the same level as the two kingdoms. Both Nordic kings used their navies for political control of their territories, which to a large extent were interconnected by the sea. This con-tributed to the marked centralization of power which took place in these pre-viously decentralized kingdoms. In the last Nordic civil war, between King Sigismund of Sweden (and Poland) and his uncle Duke Charles (later King Charles IX) in 1597–1600, the latter gained control of the largest naval forces. This enabled him to divide enemy army forces and defeat them in detail in Sweden, Finland and Estonia.

The policy of using sea power for political control was extended to a claim that the kings had a shared dominion over the Baltic Sea. This implied that they were the only rulers who had the right to use sea power in the Baltic, that they undertook to protect seafarers from all countries in this sea, and that they had the right to raise customs and sell trading licences to finance this protection. It is remarkable that this ambitious policy became accepted and successfully enforced. Traditional piratical and semi-legal interference with shipping ceased, the Hanse cities refrained from using violence as a mean of competition against western seafarers, and few efforts were made to create competing navies. The Baltic Sea became the first region in Europe where long-distance trade could rely on unarmed cargo-carriers with small crews, which could buy efficient protection from rulers. The best source of income was the Sound toll, which provided the Oldenburg kings with much of the funds they needed to maintain the Danish navy (Glete, 1993, pp. 110–14).

From the mid-sixteenth century Sweden showed an interest in raising similar customs in the northern and eastern Baltic, where several of Europe's largest rivers have their estuaries. This was a driving force behind the expansion which from 1561 to 1660 brought large parts of the eastern Baltic and northern

Germany into a Swedish empire (Attman, 1979). This policy was possible because none of the territorial powers in these regions had much sea power. The two Nordic states kept their navies partly as deterrence against each other, but they were not normally open enemies. They clashed in conflicts in 1563–70, 1611–13 and 1643–45, wars which to a considerable extent were fought and decided at sea. The first of these wars in particular saw many battles and determined attempts to gain command of the sea with the new technology (Glete, 2003). During the sixteenth century the Baltic changed from a region with undeveloped naval policies to a region with advanced technical, strategic and tactical concepts in naval warfare.

Western Europe and the oceans

During the sixteenth century, control of the sea lanes along Europe's Atlantic coast, and from there to America, Africa and Asia, grew in economic and political importance. This also increased the importance of sea power. Most of the permanent Atlantic sailing navies, however, had their origin in regional power struggles rather than in an awareness of the new potential of transoceanic sea power. England and France (originally the Dukedom of Brittany) developed navies for control of the Channel in the decades around 1500, the Dutch navy was initially a force for control of waters around Holland and Zeeland during the revolt against Philip II, and Castile made its largest naval efforts in order to gain control over the Channel during the wars with the English and the Dutch. Portugal was the major exception, as its navy was developed for control of the sea routes, first to western Africa and, from around 1500, to India. After the Portuguese conquest of Goa and other places around the Indian Ocean a Portuguese naval presence in this ocean became permanent. Castile conquered the Caribbean, Mexico and Peru with maritime expeditions but without naval power. That power was gradually developed during the sixteenth century in order to defend the American trade and colonies from French, English and Dutch attacks.

It is striking that those who controlled the centres of maritime trade – Castile, Holland, Zeeland and the north German cities – were slow to develop modern naval power with specialized sailing warships. Regions with many large cargo-carriers had traditionally been strong sea powers, as these ships could carry large infantry crews. The innovations were introduced in the late fourteenth century by princes in countries with few major cargo-carriers, notably England, France and Portugal. These rulers had to build their own great ships if they wished to be powerful at sea. As they also acquired heavy guns as instruments of power on land it was relatively easy to combine the two systems into one. Such experiments did not immediately eliminate gun-armed galleys (another innovation) or the numerous armed cargo-carriers as instruments of sea power. The new warships were, however, indispensable for the Portuguese policy of controlling the profitable spice trade with India, and this evidently stimulated Portuguese naval growth.

There were several wars in western Europe from the 1480s to the 1550s. Spain and the Netherlands were usually allied with England against France and Scotland. Naval operations during these wars were shaped within a largely medieval strategic mentality, involving transport of troops, devastation of coastal areas, and more or less controlled warfare against trade. English intervention in Brittany around 1489, and large-scale troop transports to France (usually through English-controlled Calais) in 1475, 1492, 1512, 1513, 1523 and 1544 did not lead to any contests at sea. An army at sea was still regarded as invincible if not met by a superior army. In 1545 France prepared to invade England across the Channel. English naval power was important in preventing this, but repeated attempts to bring the two fleets into serious combat were frustrated by winds and the difficulties of tactical cooperation between sailing ships and galleys. In the next confrontation in the Channel, in the 1550s, France concentrated its naval efforts on attacks on Dutch–Spanish trade. During the civil wars which started in France in 1562 French sea power totally disappeared until the 1620s.

The Habsburgs, who since 1516 had ruled both Spain and the Netherlands, with their large mercantile marines, showed only sporadic interest in a permanent sailing navy (Sicking, 1998). Lack of modern naval power proved disastrous for Philip II at an early stage of the Dutch revolt (around 1570), when he lost control of the sea lanes to Dutch ports and Dutch inland waterways. He never regained it, and the Dutch were able to build up local naval strength to keep their ports open for shipping, destroy Spanish trade with northern Europe, and give support to their army against the powerful Army of Flanders. English naval control of the Channel made it possible to make military interventions in the Netherlands and France against Spain during the Anglo-Spanish War of 1585–1603.

Philip II had, however, gained control over Portugal and its navy in 1580 and begun to create a Castilian navy. Their first major combined campaign in 1588 became a famous disaster. The Armada campaign was planned as a traditional invasion by a transport fleet, not as an attempt to defeat the English at sea. The Armada carried an army and it passed through the Channel with only limited losses to English gunfire. The combination with the Army of Flanders failed due to faulty planning by Philip II, and the fleet was scattered by a fire-ship attack and severely mauled by English gunfire. Great losses were suffered on the return voyage as the fleet was too exhausted and damaged to face North Atlantic gales (Martin and Parker, 1988; Rodríguez-Salgado, 1988). However, 1588 was not the end of such efforts. New attempts were made in the autumns of 1596 and 1597 but were frustrated by gales. An English attempt to invade Portugal in 1589 was also a failure and revealed weaknesses in the ability to organize large overseas expeditions. An Anglo-Dutch attack on Cadiz in 1596 was a success but it was not repeated.

Long-distance strategies could be sophisticated without involving concentrated battle fleets, decisive battles, attacks on bases or close blockades. During the 1590s English squadrons cruised in the waters between Cadiz and Lisbon, and between the Azores and the Canaries. Spanish silver fleets from America and Portuguese ships with spices from India had to sail in these waters and ran the risk of being captured. The number of prizes taken was small, but this strategy complicated and delayed the important Spanish and Portuguese oceanic trade and increased the cost of protection. The more spectacular attacks on towns and trade in the Caribbean were seldom equally rewarding, except sometimes for the individuals who made them.

The Dutch continued the war with Spain up to 1648. They took the long-distance strategy one step further by establishing local bases in the East and West Indies and Brazil, from which they both developed trade and fought Spain and Portugal. This strategy was commercial as much as naval, and it was implemented by two private companies. Dutch–Spanish naval warfare in Europe was also intense, although the two contenders only once met in a battle-fleet confrontation. That was in 1639, when a Spanish leadership which was both over-confident and desperate (the Count-Duke of Olivares and Philip IV) sent all available naval forces to the Channel in an attempt to turn the tide of war by defeating the Dutch naval forces before they could concentrate. This failed, and the Dutch gathered their forces and inflicted a crushing defeat on Spain at the battle of the Downs, off south-eastern England. This contributed to the Portuguese revolt against Philip IV in 1640, and to the downfall of Olivares's policy of maintaining a Spanish hegemony in western Europe (Alcalá-Zamora, 1975).

This was an exception, however. At sea Spain and the Dutch primarily fought a trade war from 1621 to 1648 (Bruijn, 1993; Goodman, 1997; Rahn Phillips, 1986). Spanish warships and privateers, most efficiently the Armada of Flanders (Stradling, 1992), attacked Dutch shipping around the European coasts. Losses were substantial, and it has been common to describe this as a result of Dutch naval inefficiency (van Vliet, 1998). Actually the Dutch navy was the first in Europe to organize a comprehensive system of convoys, and there are no signs that Spain ever came close to its aim of ruining the Dutch by embargoes on trade and large-scale destruction of shipping. Instead Spain, together with Italy, suffered economically from its own embargoes, and Dutch naval supremacy made it impossible for Spain to protect its shipping in western and northern Europe (Israel, 1982; Israel, 1989, pp. 121–96). Trade with America continued with strong naval escorts, but the most striking feature of this large maritime conflict was Spanish and Portuguese inability to defend their global maritime interests against a small but belligerent and economically efficient nation on the North Sea (Boyajian, 1993).

From 1635 France joined the war against Spain. The French navy had been re-created in the 1620s, after the civil wars during which the central state had lost control of the maritime regions of the country (Castagnos, 1989). The Spanish–French confrontation became the first contest between sailing battle fleets in the Mediterranean. The fleets fought to support their armies along the coasts and for control of the sea between Spain and Italy. France supported the revolt in Catalonia from 1640, and tried to use the navy for offensives in Italy which hopefully might stir up revolts against Spain. These operations led to several battles where the two sides showed approximately equal ability to fight (Anderson, 1969–70). They are little known in naval history, even in Spain and France, but they are interesting as early cases of battle-fleet strategies aiming at command of the sea.

By 1650 the states along the Atlantic coast had sailing navies which had proved useful as concentrated fleets in regional conflicts and in long-distance trade warfare. However none of them were large enough to be used as a long-distance battle fleet in European great power politics. They could not continuously enforce blockades and dominate the seas far from their bases, except in areas outside Europe where small naval forces might be decisive. It is not meaningful to look for a European balance of power at sea before 1650. This changed rapidly during the following decades. The English Civil War started a cycle of naval expansion in western Europe, as the new English republic rapidly expanded its navy in efforts to secure its domestic and international position and to promote trade (Brenner, 1993). This escalated into an Anglo-Dutch naval war (1652–54) which caused a major expansion of the Dutch navy. The age of the great battle fleets had begun.

References

Alcalá-Zamora y Queipo de Llano, J. 1975. *España, Flandes y el Mar del Norte, 1618–1639*, Barcelona.

Anderson, R.C. 1969–70. 'The Thirty Years War in the Mediterranean', *Mariner's Mirror*, 55, 435–51; 56, 41–57.

——1952. *Naval Wars in the Levant, 1559–1853*, Liverpool.

Attman, A. 1979. *The Struggle for Baltic Markets: Powers in Conflict, 1558–1618*, Gothenburg.

Boyajian, J.C. 1993. *Portuguese Trade in Asia under the Habsburgs, 1580–1640*, Baltimore.

Braudel, F. 1981–84. *Civilization and Capitalism, 15th–18th Centuries*, London.

——1972–73. *The Mediterranean and the Mediterranean World in the Age of Philip II*, London.

Brenner, R. 1993. *Merchants and Revolution: Commercial Change, Political Conflict, and London Overseas Traders, 1550–1653*, Cambridge.

Bruijn, J.R. 1993. *The Dutch Navy of the Seventeenth and Eighteenth Centuries*, Columbia.

Brummett, P. 1994. *Ottoman Seapower and Levantine Diplomacy in the Age of Discovery*, Albany.

Casado Soto, J.L. 1988. *Los barcos españoles del siglo XVI y la Gran Armada de 1588*, Madrid.

Castagnos, P. 1989. *Richelieu face à la mer*, Rennes.

Cipolla, C. 1965. *Guns and Sails in the Early Phase of European Expansion*, London.

Conway. 1995. *Conway's History of the Ship: The Age of the Galley: Mediterranean Oared Vessels since Pre-Classical Times*, London.

——**1994.** *Conway's History of the Ship: Cogs, Caravels and Galleons: The Sailing Ship 1000–1650*, London.

Dollinger, P. 1970. *The German Hansa*, London.

Fudge, J.D. 1995. *Cargoes, Embargoes, and Emissaries: The Commercial and Political Interaction of England and the German Hanse, 1450–1510*, Toronto.

Glete, J. 2003. 'Naval Power and Control of the Seas in the Baltic in the 16th Century', in Hattendorf and Unger, 2003, 217–32.

——**2002.** *War and the State in Early Modern Europe: Spain, the Dutch Republic and Sweden as Fiscal-Military States, 1500–1660*, London.

——**2000.** *Warfare at Sea, 1500–1650: Maritime Conflicts and the Transformation of Europe*, London.

——**1993.** *Navies and Nations: Warships, Navies and State Building in Europe and America, 1500–1860*, Stockholm.

Goodman, D. 1997. *Spanish Naval Power, 1589–1665: Reconstruction and Defeat*, Cambridge.

Guilmartin, J.F. Jr. 1974. *Gunpowder and Galleys: Changing Technology and Mediterranean Warfare at Sea in the Sixteenth Century*, Cambridge.

Hanlon, G. 1998. *The Twilight of a Military Tradition: Italian Aristocrats and European Conflicts, 1560–1800*, London.

Hattendorf, J.B. and Unger, R.W., eds. 2003. *War at Sea in the Middle Ages and Renaissance*, Woodbridge.

Hess, A.C. 1970. 'The Evolution of the Ottoman Seaborne Empire in the Age of the Oceanic Discoveries, 1453–1525', *American Historical Review*, 75, 1892–1919.

Hoffman, P.E. 1980. *The Spanish Crown and the Defense of the Caribbean, 1535–1585: Precedent, Patrimonialism and Royal Parsimony*, Baton Rouge.

Hook, J. 1977. 'Fortifications and the End of the Sienese State', *History*, 62, 372–87.

Imber, C.H. 1980. 'The Navy of Süleyman the Magnificent', *Archivum Ottomanicum*, 6, 211–82.

Israel, J.I. 1989. *Dutch Primacy in World Trade*, Oxford.

——**1982.** *The Dutch Republic and the Hispanic World, 1606–1661*, Oxford.

Lane, F.C. 1979. *Profits from Power: Readings in Protection Rent and Violence-Controlled Enterprise*, Albany.

——**1973.** 'Naval Actions and Fleet Organization, 1499–1502', in *Renaissance Venice*, ed. J.R. Hale, Totowa, 146–73.

Lavery, B. 1987. *The Arming and Fitting of English Ships of War, 1600–1815*, London.

Mahan, A.T. 1890. *The Influence of Seapower upon History, 1660–1783*, Boston.

Martin, C. and Parker, G. 1988. *The Spanish Armada*, London.

North, D.C. 1981. *Structure and Change in Economic History*, New York.

Parker, G. 1996. 'The Dreadnought Revolution of Tudor England', *Mariner's Mirror*, 82, 269–300.

Pryor, J.H. 1988. *Geography, Technology and War: Studies in the Maritime History of the Mediterranean, 649–1571*, Cambridge.

Rahn Phillips, C. 1986. *Six Galleons for the King of Spain: Imperial Defense in the Early Seventeenth Century*, Baltimore.

Rodger, N.A.M. 1997. *The Safeguard of the Sea: A Naval History of Britain, Vol. 1, 660–1649*, London.

—— 1996. 'The Development of Broadside Gunnery, 1450–1650', *Mariner's Mirror*, 82, 301–24.

Rodríguez-Salgado, M.J. et al. 1988. *Armada 1588–1988*, London.

Rystad, G., Böhme, K.-R. and Carlgren, W.M., eds. 1994. *In Quest of Trade and Security: the Baltic in Power Politics, 1500–1990, Vol. I, 1500–1890*, Lund.

Sicking, L. 1998. *Zeemacht en onmacht: Maritieme politiek in de Nederlanden, 1488–1558*, Amsterdam.

Stradling, R.A. 1992. *The Armada of Flanders: Spanish Maritime Policy and European War, 1568–1665*, Cambridge.

Tenenti, A. 1967. *Piracy and the Decline of Venice, 1580–1615*, Berkeley.

Tilly, C. 1990. *Coercion, Capital, and European States, AD 990–1990*, Oxford.

Unger, R.W. 1980. *The Ship in the Medieval Economy, 600–1600*, London.

van Vliet, A.P. 1998. 'Foundation, Organization and Effects of the Dutch Navy', in *Exercise of Arms: Warfare in the Netherlands, 1568–1648*, ed. M. van der Hoeven, Leiden, 152–73.

Wallerstein, I. 1974. *The Modern World-System*, vol. 1, New York.

6

War by Contract, Credit and Contribution: The Thirty Years War

Geoff Mortimer

Asked to list the great powers of the day, an informed European in the mid-1600s would undoubtedly have named Sweden, if not first at least in the first breath, along with France, Spain and the Holy Roman Empire. This surprising fact arises from Sweden's intervention in the Thirty Years War in 1630, and her central role in the conflict during the following 18 years. Although the war had no clear winner, Sweden emerged as the main gainer at the Treaty of Westphalia in 1648, securing large territories on the German Baltic coast and a huge cash indemnity for her war expenses. This did not seem a likely outcome in 1630, at which time the Imperialist side did not perceive a significant Swedish threat, and Gustavus Adolphus himself invaded Germany equipped with maps only for a limited war in the north (Roberts, 1992, p. 138). In the event he took Munich two years later, and although there were many setbacks his successors later threatened Vienna, while at the end of the war almost half of the 250,000 troops estimated to be on active service within the Empire territories were in Swedish units (Parker, 1988, p. 303).

By any realistic standard waging war on this scale was beyond the capacity of Sweden, a poor northern country with limited natural resources and a population estimated at no more than 1.3 million (Roberts, 1992, p. 13). That she nevertheless did so illustrates the far-reaching effects of three developments in the organization of early modern warfare, which in combination not only enabled Sweden to achieve disproportionate military strength, but also sustained all the principal participants in the largest and longest war in Europe up to that time. These were the system of military contracting, which allowed princes (and other rulers or states) to engage large numbers of mercenary troops quickly and easily, the availability of sources of credit, which enabled them to put armies in the field having barely paid a deposit on them, and the so-called contributions, which forced the populations of occupied territories to bear the main costs of war.

When Gustavus Adolphus landed in Germany in July 1630 he had an invasion army of about 13,000 men and a further 4000 from the Stralsund garrison (Roberts, 1958, p. 442). These were mainly native Swedish and Finnish troops levied through a system of conscription the king himself had devised some years earlier, and the Swedish chancellor Oxenstierna noted that only 3200 were mercenaries (Krüger, 1988, p. 284). At the time the term 'mercenary' meant simply a soldier hired for pay, and probably at least in theory a volunteer, as opposed to one conscripted under some form of quasi-feudal service obligation, and princes enlisted men from among their own subjects by either or both methods, as well as recruiting mercenaries more widely when necessary. Conscripts had the advantage of being cheap, as they could be paid little, but they were also often thought to be less effective soldiers than professionals, causing Christian IV of Denmark to reject them as 'worse than cattle' (Krüger, 1988, p. 278). Nevertheless they served Gustavus Adolphus well, but at a high cost to their homeland. From the population of around 1.3 million, at least 50,000 men died in the Swedish wars of 1621–31, while the total up to 1648 may have been over 150,000 (Roberts, 1992, p. 124; Parker, 1988, pp. 304–5). Native manpower resources were pushed to the limit, but in no way sufficed to meet Gustavus's needs in Germany. Mercenary recruitment had to fill the gap.

The Swedish army in Germany expanded at a startling rate, trebling in size to 42,000 by November 1630, doubling from that to 83,000 in December 1631, and almost doubling again to a peak of 149,000 in November 1632, the largest force thus far seen in early modern Europe. The overwhelming majority of the additions were non-Swedish mercenaries, who by this time comprised five-sixths of the army (Roberts, 1992, p. 109). Gustavus received some limited help from allied German princes, and his Protestant cause and spectacular victories drew men to the colours, but nevertheless recruitment on this scale and at this speed required the net to be cast widely, with large numbers coming from Scotland, Ireland and elsewhere to supplement those from Germany itself. Moreover it was both an immense administrative task and a huge financial undertaking, for which Sweden had neither an established bureaucracy nor the necessary cash. The answer was, as it had been for earlier participants in the Thirty Years War, to contract the problem out to the men Redlich calls military enterprisers. Redlich's definitive work on this subject has never been surpassed, and is the basis for the following description (Redlich, 1964–65).

Military contracting

The origins of seventeenth-century military contracting can be traced back to the late Middle Ages, to the Hundred Years War and the wars in Italy, but on a relatively small scale and as the exception rather than the rule. At that time any troops raised by individual lords or leaders were usually incorporated directly into the army of the warring prince, and paid by him, for a single campaign only, during which their recruiter would command them and would share in the spoils of war as his main remuneration. Other mercenaries, such as the Swiss pikemen of the later fifteenth century, hired themselves out in bands, but overt individual entrepreneurship only developed in the sixteenth century. The major difference lay in the provision of credit by the contractor in raising troops for a prince at his own initial expense, and thereby investing in a force which he subsequently led and maintained as a separate entity, with the specific object of making a profit from payments for the services of the men he had recruited. The first such entrepreneurs used their own money or borrowed locally against their own lands, but later in the sixteenth century merchant bankers such as the Fuggers began to see them and their business as acceptable risks, and to provide loans. Military contracting in the form which later became prevalent probably developed in the wars in Hungary and the Low Countries, while by the early seventeenth century many princes and cities in Germany retained officers to raise and lead troops for them as and when the need arose. Thus by the time the Thirty Years War broke out in 1618, there existed both an established system of military contracting, and a pool of experienced entrepreneurs, to facilitate the creation of the armies required by the warring parties.

The key figure in the system was the colonel, who upon receiving a commission from a prince would raise a regiment for him, of cavalry or foot as agreed, and would present it at the appointed time and place for mustering before being incorporated into the army. To do this he would send out recruiting agents into promising areas, which might be local to the war zone or in the colonel's own possibly quite distant homeland, and he might also subcontract by commissioning a number of captains to raise companies of men. In the past, princes had normally had to find significant amounts of money to finance recruiting, which involved payments to induce men to enlist, as well as for their subsistence and expenses in getting to the muster place, often with a long lead time before they became an effective military unit. By the beginning of the Thirty Years War, however, a presumption had developed that the colonel would provide or arrange this finance, possibly passing part of this responsibility on to his captains, as in the case of the English mercenary Sydnam Poyntz, who recorded that 'I beeing come to this height got to bee by Count Butlers favour Sergeant Major of a Troop of 200 horse but I was to raise them at my owne charge ... for I had then 3000£ which I carried into the field with mee' (Mortimer, 2002, p. 31). When the Bohemian entrepreneur Wallenstein raised a large army for the emperor in 1625, he wrote this provision of credit explicitly into his colonels' contracts, and these officers of course expected not only to recover such outlays in due course, but also to make a substantial profit on them, commensurate with the risk involved in financing war. Hence the investment gave a colonel a major personal interest in the regiment he had raised, a form of ownership which by the late seventeenth century developed into a clear property right.

The scale upon which this system was used in the Thirty Years War is indicated by Redlich's estimate that over the period some 1500 individuals owned regiments, and that at any one time during the early years of Swedish involvement, 1631–34, the various armies employed around 300 such military enterprisers (Redlich, 1964–65, pp. 170–1). Granted that numbers, both of contractors and of men in their regiments, are far from certain, it is nevertheless clear that the great majority of the Swedish and Imperialist troops were raised and managed in this way, and while the French and Spanish deployed more traditionally based armies, they too supplemented them by using military contractors to raise mercenaries. This approach effectively delegated the massive administrative problem of raising large numbers of men quickly, and concentrating them into an army, and to an extent also the management of them thereafter, as the colonel would usually be responsible for paying the soldiers, recruiting replacements, and quite possibly also for providing some of their weapons and supplies. Such advantages had of course to be paid for, and although the colonel provided very valuable initial credit to the prince during the recruiting period, and often thereafter, he was also in a position to make considerable profits, in large part at the prince's ultimate expense. This he could do both legitimately, from the hire, equipping and provisioning of his regiment, as well as from his own salary, and fraudulently, by drawing pay for an overstated number of men or siphoning off contributions collected from the population, not to mention extortion on his own account and the right to a handsome share of the spoils of war. Although there were risks in a business of this nature, to add to the hazards of a soldier's life, military contractors did well enough as a class to ensure that plenty came forward, and that they either had or could raise the necessary funds. Some, indeed, owned more than one regiment, employing lieutenant-colonels to command in the field, while generals took care to retain their personal regiments as investments and managed them in the same way.

Sources of credit

The second structural feature which contributed to the developing ability to raise large armies quickly in this period was credit. Wars have commonly been fought on credit of some form, with medieval monarchs and modern governments employing a range of means to the same end, that of raising funds to spend on armies and armaments today while ultimately paying for them with the revenues to be collected at some point in the future. In medieval and early modern times warfare often consumed the bulk of the income of the state or prince, so that in most cases wars could only be financed by borrowing, to spread the cost over intervening years of peace, and military potential was ultimately limited by the prince's creditworthiness. The Dutch United Provinces, with a successful trading economy, had a good track record, and were able not only to raise funds in this period but to do so at favourable rates of interest. They, however, were the exception. Their Spanish opponents had several times been forced to impose revised terms on their creditors, effectively a form of bankruptcy, and hence they found loans much harder to come by, and interest rates often prohibitive, while lenders tended to view rulers of smaller principalities even less favourably as risks for military financing. The problem was compounded when wars were of long duration, with few or no intervening years of peace in which to pay down loans, precisely the situation faced by participants in the Thirty Years War.

Two new or much expanded sources of credit at this time were the military contractors and the soldiers themselves. The latter are often overlooked in this context, although it is regularly noted that they were frequently unpaid or underpaid. The relationship is simple. Pay was by far the largest part of the cost of maintaining an army, and hence, to the extent that the men went unpaid, that largest part was effectively financed by a forced loan, that of the soldiers ultimately to the prince. The point was clear to contemporaries such as Sir James Turner, who noted the practice of both sides in the Thirty Years War, of making small advances or 'lendings' instead of paying the men regularly in full, 'but', he added, 'the poorest witted Souldier knows well enough, that his Pay-masters, under the notion of lending them a third part, borrow from them to a very long day, all the rest of their Pay' (Turner, 1683, p. 199). This factor became increasingly significant around the late sixteenth and early seventeenth centuries, when Emperor Rudolf II, Maurice of Orange, and others, began to keep mercenary armies together for the duration of longer wars, rather than recruiting and disbanding on a yearly basis. This involved putting troops into winter quarters instead of paying them off at the end of the campaigning season, the saving in re-recruiting costs largely offsetting their subsistence over the winter, the burden of which was in any case increasingly being imposed on the civilian population. There was also an immediate cash saving, as overdue wages were traditionally settled up on discharge, partly from a contemporary sense of probity, but also to avoid disturbances or deterring men from enlisting the following year. If the men were not discharged they did not need to be paid in full, and the arrears could be rolled forward from year to year.

This became standard practice during the Thirty Years War. Often the soldiers received some rations from the army, the cost of which was offset against the wages they were due, and from time to time they were given modest advances in cash, but the remainder of their pay accumulated as arrears.

Usually there was no alternative, because neither the military contractors nor the princes had enough money available, but it is also clear that the latter were well aware of the potential of this system as a source of finance. In 1633 Oxenstierna calculated the costs of an army of 78,000 men for the Swedes and their allies in the Heilbronn League, but he did this upon two different assumptions about pay. If wages were to be paid in full twelve times a year, the annual cost of the army would have been 9.8 million Reichstaler, but this would have reduced to 5.4 million based on full payment in only one month, with advances in the other eleven, plus an issue of one pound of bread per man per day (Krüger, 1988, p. 291). Hence the princes would have saved 4.4 million Reichstaler a year in cash, although it would have accumulated as arrears of pay for eventual settlement, while the soldiers would have compulsorily financed 45 per cent of the costs of the army. This of course was a calculation, but contemporary accounts by soldiers confirm that large arrears of pay were very common in the armies of the Thirty Years War (Mortimer, 2002, pp. 29–30). In 1627 the Catholic League general Tilly complained to Duke Maximilian of Bavaria that for several years his army had been paid only once or at most twice a year, and at the time of writing had not been paid for 15 months (Ritter, 1903, p. 217). Later in the war there were several large pay mutinies in the Swedish army, and by 1647 the Swedish instructions to their negotiators at the peace conference included the demand that their common soldiers should receive a full year's pay as settlement of their dues (Lundkvist, 1988, p. 234). In the event they were only paid three months' arrears, which still amounted to some two million Reichstaler, and Imperialist and Bavarian troops received similar payments. They were luckier than some of their predecessors. Soldiers hired early in the war by the Bohemian estates accumulated wage arrears of five-and-a-half million guilders, but due to the comprehensive defeat of the rebellion none of this was ever paid (Redlich, 1964–65, pp. 492, 499, 501).

This last point demonstrates how arrears of pay could be converted from forced loans into outright donations to the cost of the war, most notably in the case of soldiers who died with large amounts due to them. The shift to maintaining armies throughout a war also led to the individual soldier signing on for the duration rather than for a fixed term, usually no more than one campaigning season at a time, as had previously been the case, and hence to greater potential accumulations of pay arrears. In practice, enlisting for the duration often meant until death. After a battle the dead were mostly buried in mass graves, and were often not even counted, let alone identified, while those who failed to return for roll-call and were not known to have been taken prisoner were simply struck off the company lists (Burschel, 1994, pp. 271–2). It is safe to assume that their arrears of pay died with them, as they did for the many deserters and the much larger numbers who died of disease. Given the short average life expectancy and the very high losses of men, the sums involved must have been substantial, although unquantifiable. It is estimated that of around 25,000 Swedes and Finns shipped to Germany in 1630–31 more than half were dead two years later (Roberts, 1992, p. 124). For a single Swedish regiment, half of the initial 1086 men died over the same period (twice as many from illness as from wounds), and a further 12 per cent deserted (Krüger, 1988, p. 296). Over the longer term, of 230 men conscripted between 1621 and 1639 from a single Swedish village, 215 were dead by 1639 (Parker, 1988, p. 304). The Imperialist general Gallas lost one-third of his cavalry and half of his infantry on a single march into Holstein and back in 1644, mainly from hunger, disease or desertion, as he had no significant encounter with the enemy (Salm, 1990, p. 43). Some hardier, luckier, or more careful men did survive to become veterans, but most of those who died left unpaid wages as a contribution to the cost of war. Where military enterprisers employed them they may well have been the initial beneficiaries, but some of the advantage will also have accrued to the princes, in the often rough and ready eventual settlement of the contractors' claims.

Reference has already been made to the role of the military contractor in supplying credit, particularly at the time of recruitment. This was crucial, as a heavy outlay was involved, not least because potential soldiers were often well aware of the uncertainties of pay once enlisted, and by this period they demanded a significant sum of cash in hand before signing on. Added to this was travelling and subsistence en route to the muster place, and while waiting for the full complement to be recruited, as well as the provision of weapons and basic equipment. This all fell at the point where a prince's resources were likely to be most stretched, and before the force being raised could begin to support itself by occupying territory and extracting contributions from the population. This was exactly the dilemma faced by the emperor in 1625, and by Gustavus Adolphus in 1630. With virtually no troops of his own, and very little cash, the emperor had to turn to Wallenstein, who had become immensely rich through the fortunate conjunction of a wealthy wife and shrewd, if none too scrupulous, financial and property dealings in the aftermath of the defeat of the Bohemian rebellion in 1620. Wallenstein in turn brought in the requisite number of colonels, and between them they recruited and financed an army which grew to 100,000 men. Wallenstein himself is thought to have lent the emperor over eight million guilders between 1621 and 1628, a sum both remarkable in itself and in relation to an estimate of his personal fortune at no more than one-and-a-half million (Redlich, 1964–65, p. 254). This indicates the working of a multiplier effect, with military contractors using not only their own funds but also their own creditworthiness, which at this time was usually greater than that of the princes, to finance the armies. Although the contractors funded the upkeep of their regiments largely from contributions, their initial loans often tended to be rolled over, and even to increase due to periodic crises in cash receipts. Hence Wallenstein estimated in 1630 that more than a million guilders of debt was outstanding to colonels whose regiments had been merged or discharged, and were thus no longer even in existence (Ritter, 1903, p. 245).

Credit from soldiers and military contractors facilitated war, but it also prolonged it. As long as contributions were coming in the armies could be supported, and arrears of pay and contractors' loans, as well as those from military suppliers and other sources of credit, could be rolled over. An end to war meant an end to contributions and discharge of the soldiers, at which point all these debts fell due for payment. In 1635–36, at the lowest point in Sweden's fortunes, Oxenstierna would gladly have ended the war if only terms could have been obtained which would have enabled these obligations to be met, but negotiations failed on the question of cash, and the war continued for a further twelve years (Roberts, 1991, pp. 43, 52). The same problem prolonged the final peace conference, which lasted for several years. In the summer of 1647 Swedish negotiators were asking for twelve million Reichstaler for the satisfaction of debts to their senior officers, military contractors and soldiers, a figure progressively reduced to ten, six and finally the agreed figure of five million (Lundkvist, 1988, p. 234).

The role of contributions

Although credit was important in recruiting armies, the contributions system supplied the core finance for the war, and indeed underpinned the availability of credit by providing the prospective means for eventual repayment. Moreover it was essentially a system created by the Thirty Years War, although it remained central to war finance long afterwards. Looting and living off the country had been the traditional methods of remunerating and feeding soldiers, but they also limited the size of armies, as there were practical constraints on how many soldiers could be supported for how long in this way by territory within range of their raids. It was also inefficient, as individual, random and uncontrolled foraging and plundering quickly exhausted an area's resources, often destroying whatever was not consumed, and hence forcing the troops to move on. Exactly this frequently happened in the Thirty Years War too, and was responsible for much of the horror, but it nevertheless increasingly arose as an abuse or a failure of the system, rather than as the basis of it. For the individual soldier, traditional concepts of war died hard, while the supply problems of large armies on the march often made resort to old methods inevitable, but organized exploitation of economic resources at a sustainable level proved able to support warfare of an entirely larger scale and duration.

The precise origin of contributions remains uncertain. The term itself derives from the name applied in the sixteenth century to a special tax levied by a prince in his own territory, usually with the consent of the estates, to finance a military campaign. The concept as developed in the Thirty Years War was quite different, however, the three essential elements of legality, consent, and taxing the prince's own subjects being replaced by systematic extortion without a legal basis, levied by or under threat of force, and frequently on the subjects of other princes in army-occupied territory. There are few, if any, definite examples before 1600, and not many before 1618. An Imperial law of 1570 did provide for soldiers to be billeted on the population and fed free of charge, but only if the soldiers themselves had not been paid, in which case they had to give receipts for later settlement, with the cost being deducted from their eventual pay. Emperor Rudolf II's generals in the Turkish wars went further in billeting their armies without paying for subsistence, to judge from complaints in the Hungarian Reichstag around 1602, and the same procedure was followed by Imperialist forces in Bohemia at the time of the rebellion, as set out in ordinances of 1621. These contain some of the earliest references to cash payments as an alternative to supplying food and drink, but a further Imperial ordinance of 1622 was more specific in providing for a general levy or cash contribution from an area, to pay for supplies to the troops over and above individual subsistence from billet hosts (Ritter, 1903, pp. 211, 219–21).

These examples still concerned a prince and his own subjects, but matters had already progressed further elsewhere. In 1620 the Spanish general Spinola invaded the Palatinate on behalf of the emperor, and he raised his troops' wages from the population there, clearly a case of levying on the subjects of another prince, although in this case one declared to be in rebellion. Even this distinction disappeared soon afterwards, when Spinola wintered his army in neutral territory over 1620–21, but extracted their wages locally in like manner (Redlich, 1959, pp. 252–3). The elector Palatine's generals Mansfeld and Christian of Brunswick followed suit, and Tilly too levied contributions in the following years, although in his case for the subsistence rather than the pay of his soldiers. In his ordinances of 1623 and 1624 for the neutral territory of Hesse, Tilly offered the alternative of payment in cash rather than in kind, but by this time there was no suggestion of eventual repayment of the costs involved. However it was left to Wallenstein to turn what was becoming custom and practice into a system. When he set out to raise his great army for the emperor he undertook to finance its recruitment and equipping, but to pay and maintain such a force thereafter was beyond his or the emperor's resources. He had, though, already had some experience of organizing contributions in Bohemia, and he immediately applied this to the new army in an ordinance of November 1625. In striking contrast to previous practice this was directed from the outset towards money rather than supplies in kind, with the objective of providing the soldiers with regular pay in cash and of raising the entire cost, not just subsistence, from contributions (Ritter, 1903, pp. 217–19, 223–6). By and large this was successful, and Wallenstein's approach was quickly adopted by others, not least Gustavus Adolphus, becoming the standard method of financing armies for the duration of the Thirty Years War, as well as spreading widely and remaining important throughout the following century (Lynn, 1993, p. 310).

As a system, contributions worked best when territory could be maintained under longer-term occupation, and collection organized on a regular basis. A study of the principality of Hohenlohe indicates how the civilian administration soon became the collection instrument for Wallenstein's contributions, while records for one of its districts show that in the years from 1628 to 1649 war levies frequently brought in twice as much as the pre-war cash taxes, and in particular years, three, four and five times as much. Nevertheless exactions were generally kept to what was economically feasible, allowing them to be sustained over a long period of years (Robisheaux, 1989, pp. 210–11). Likewise the vast majority of the costs of the Imperial army of 10,000 to 15,000 men garrisoning part of Westphalia from 1639 to 1650, estimated as at least 15 million Reichstaler over the period, was raised from systematic contributions without destroying the ability of the region to pay (Salm, 1990, pp. 165, 168, 122). Conversely the system was at its weakest in supporting large-scale active campaigning. Big armies on the move had no time to establish orderly collection systems along the way, either for cash or provisions, so that they tended to fall back on the old methods, often devastating the countryside and not infrequently imperilling their own survival – hence Gallas's disaster in Holstein referred to above.

Contributions also had two other major disadvantages. The first was that, because they were not paid voluntarily or as taxation with a legal basis, a continuous coercive military presence was required, which ultimately meant that territory had to be permanently garrisoned in order to collect the contributions needed to finance the field armies. This necessitated more troops, which in turn increased costs and required yet more contributions to be collected. Therein lies the famous paradox of Wallenstein's supposed response to the emperor's initial request that he raise a smaller force, that he could support an army of 50,000 but not one of 20,000 men (Mann, 1976, p. 272). The second drawback was that contributions could come to dictate rather than support strategy, as they arguably did for Gustavus Adolphus after the battle of Breitenfeld in 1631, when he led his army into the rich but militarily unimportant prince-bishoprics of central Germany, rather than following up his victory more directly (Krüger, 1988, p. 287).

Evaluating the importance of contributions quantitatively rather than in general terms is very difficult, for two reasons. Firstly the term is often loosely used, and at one extreme can be limited to orderly collections, akin to taxation in nature, while at the other it can encompass all resources extracted from occupied territories which went to support the armies in the broadest sense, other than individual looting – and even that cannot necessarily be excluded as it often functioned as a substitute for pay. Secondly, no comprehensive records exist. Contributions were commonly both raised and spent locally, under the control of the military, usually without being accounted for centrally and not even always in field records, while the amount which was diverted fraudulently can barely be guessed at. Thus from one of the better sets of surviving records, that for the relatively settled Imperialist garrison in Westphalia mentioned above, and here referring to orderly cash contributions according to the narrower definition, it has been noted that more than 90 per cent of the amount collected went out directly as soldiers' pay, without passing through any central treasury (Salm, 1990, p. 125). In other cases records are less informative or simply unavailable, and indeed it is easier to find details of agreements regarding contributions to be paid to the Swedish armies in the latter years of the war in the columns of contemporary published chronicles than in the state archives, although the amounts involved may have been much larger than better-recorded sources of income such as French subsidies (Böhme, 1967, p. 91). The problem is compounded by the fact that, despite Wallenstein's preference for cash, a large proportion of contributions in the wider sense were in kind, and hence even less likely to have been comprehensively valued and recorded. This difficulty is well illustrated in a contemporary note of the complex pattern of contributions required of one German village in 1647:

> In this above-mentioned year of 47 we had to give [Hohent]wiel a monthly contribution of ten florins, together with three tuns of wine, ... four wagon-loads of grain (which we exchanged with the villagers of Blumenfeld, on whose behalf we gave Mainau 16 quarters of corn, five quarters of rye and ten quarters of oats), ... and in the spring 2000 vine stakes (which Hans Schäpfl of Hausen made for us, for which we paid him 24 florins), while instead of hay and straw we regularly paid the captain of cavalry Hans Jerg Widerholt in cash, 86 florins and 6 batzen. The same year of 47 we supplied Constance with $2\frac{1}{2}$ tuns of wine, many wagons of wood for watch fires, labourers for working parties and digging fortification works every day, and 100 hundredweight of hay. Likewise to Niclaus, Baron von Gramont, commandant of Zell, two florins service money every month, and 20 kegs of wine at the beginning of the year, as well as labourers and fortification workers at that time, and we had afterwards to pay out 16 batzen a week for the labour service.
>
> (Mortimer, 2002, p. 49)

Gustavus Adolphus enunciated the maxim that war must be made to pay for itself in a letter to Oxenstierna in 1628, at that time referring to his involvement in Prussia, and almost his first action on landing in Germany in

1630 was to coerce the duke of Pomerania into agreeing to pay a large annual contribution (Roberts, 1992, pp. 119, 131). Krüger has calculated, if very approximately, the level of Swedish war expenditure in the years 1630–34, from the number of troops at various dates and Oxenstierna's own estimates of the cost per man, reaching a total of 38 million Reichstaler for the period. Against this he has identified income which he regards as certain of 16 million, and a further 10.5 million classified as probable, leaving a gap of 11.5 million, which he believes can only have come from contributions levied in occupied territories. However, of the certain and probable income 15.3 million also came from Germany, making 26.8 million in all, over 70 per cent of the total. The great majority of this will ultimately have been extracted from the population, either directly by the Swedes or on their behalf by local princes, including their allies in the Heilbronn League and unwilling contributors like the duke of Pomerania. Of the remainder, 2.4 million came from foreign subsidies, 3.2 million from tolls on port traffic in Swedish-occupied Prussia and Pomerania, and only 5.5 million (15 per cent of the total) from Sweden itself, mostly in the first two years (Krüger, 1988, pp. 288–9). Foreign subsidies played a relatively small part in these years, and also later in the war, with total French subsidies to the Swedes from 1638 to 1648 calculated at only 5.2 million Reichstaler, very much the same figure as the indemnity the Swedes finally received to pay their accumulated debts to the army at the end of the war (Lorenz, 1981, pp. 100–4).

The three factors discussed, military contracting, new sources of credit and contributions, explain how a small country, Sweden, was able to play a leading part in the Thirty Years War, but they also provide at least a partial explanation of why the war lasted so long and was never brought to a clear military conclusion. The same methods could be adopted by others, and all the principal participants in the war employed them to a greater or lesser extent, as did a number of smaller entities. Thus there were at various times not only Imperial, Spanish, Swedish and French armies fighting in Germany, but also armies belonging to Baden-Durlach, Bavaria, the Bohemian Estates, the Catholic League, Denmark, Hesse-Cassel, the Palatinate and Saxony, as well as various minor forces acting as parts of one alliance or another, while the mercenary generals Mansfeld and Christian of Brunswick early in the war, and Bernard of Weimar more successfully later, operated with what came close to being private armies. As long as credit made money available, raising troops does not seem to have presented many would-be participants with great problems, and, once in the field, shifting the cost burden on to the unfortunate population through contributions enabled armies to be maintained more or less permanently. Even defeat in battle was only rarely decisive, as armies could be rebuilt with startling speed. Tilly, for example, was heavily defeated at Breitenfeld in September 1631, but he was back in the field early the following spring. This made it very difficult to drive even minor participants out of the war by military means. Wallenstein and Tilly not only defeated Christian IV of Denmark in battle and drove him out of Germany, but also occupied a large part of his home territory, before he finally conceded and came to terms. Even the occupation and loss of all his lands did not prevent Frederick V, the elector Palatine and erstwhile king of Bohemia, from fighting on for several more years before he finally withdrew. The Swedes more than once took Prague and threatened Vienna, but it is very questionable whether even the loss of his hereditary heartland would have forced the emperor to terms. In 1648 the main parties to the Treaty of Westphalia could have fought on, as they had for years during the negotiations, and a further outbreak of war in 1649 was a distinct possibility. New mechanisms had made near-permanent war possible, but had not yet provided the means to bring about the total defeat of a major determined opponent.

Increasing army size and the 'military revolution'

This argument can be taken a step further, in order to shed some light on one of the vexed questions of the 'military revolution' debate, namely why armies grew dramatically in size during the early modern period. In the essay which started the discussion in 1955, Roberts argued that such a revolution occurred between 1560 and 1660, whereas Parker, in his response of 1976, proposed a longer timescale, noting that 'between 1530 and 1710 there was a tenfold increase both in the total numbers of armed forces paid by the major European states and in the total numbers involved in the major European battles' (Roberts, 1995, p. 19; Parker, 1995a, p. 43). Roberts saw expanding armies as 'the result of a revolution in strategy, made possible by the revolution in tactics [of Maurice of Nassau and Gustavus Adolphus], and made necessary by the circumstances of the Thirty Years War', while Parker placed the impetus earlier, noting that the development of the *trace italienne* system of fortifications in the late fifteenth to early sixteenth centuries enormously increased the number of men required both to garrison and to besiege towns and fortresses (Roberts, 1995, p. 18; Parker, 1995a, p. 45; Parker, 1995b, pp. 350–2).

There has been a considerable discussion of these and other possible reasons for the growth of troop numbers in this period, but in a sense this has largely addressed the wrong question. The key problem is not what drove army growth at this time, but what had constrained it previously, and hence what changed to bring about the observed result. Logic suggests that a warring prince in any period would seek to defeat his opponents by bringing to bear the largest possible force, whether as one army or several, while military men have always been wary of being outnumbered, 'for as you know God is usually on the side of the larger forces against the smaller'. The comment is contemporary, made by Bussy-Rabutin, a former French cavalry general, in 1677, but the thought was not new – Tacitus said something very similar – and at the time of the Thirty Years War it was the conventional wisdom underlying Wallenstein's and Gustavus Adolphus's efforts to raise their huge armies. In this and earlier periods smaller forces of high military calibre not infrequently defeated larger ones of lower quality, while brilliant generals, or new methods and tactics, or plain luck, sometimes allowed a smaller army to triumph over a larger one of equivalent standard. Nevertheless when other things were broadly equal the big battalions conquered often enough for establishing numerical superiority before a battle to be a prime objective of strategy. Why, then, were armies not larger earlier?

The question has of course been addressed before. Parker identified four pre-conditions for the emergence of bigger armies as the norm, rather than as the occasional exception which had occurred previously. These were expansion of the administrative capacity of the state, logistical improvements to supplies systems for large forces, creation of sufficient wealth in society to support higher levels of military expenditure, and development of credit and financial mechanisms such as those of the Dutch and the Bank of England (Parker, 1995a, pp. 45–8). These are valid enough in the latter part of the early modern period, but the point to note here is that much of the growth in army size preceded these advances, and the factors discussed above in the context of the Thirty Years War were in fact ways of getting round the relevant problems.

One essential precondition of army growth was the availability of sufficient suitable recruits, and this can be linked to a process of military de-skilling which occurred between the mid-fifteenth and mid-sixteenth centuries. In the later Middle Ages, typified by the battle of Agincourt in 1415, the key forces had been the knights comprising the heavy cavalry, and the archers. Both were in short supply, because of the amount of training and practice needed to achieve and maintain proficiency in the use of their respective weapons, while the cost of a knight's armour and equipment put it beyond the reach of all except noblemen and a few of their personal retainers. This began to change towards the end of the Middle Ages, with the growth in use of the pike, first as a defensive weapon, and later, particularly in the hands of the Swiss, for offensive purposes. A certain amount of skill and physical strength was still needed to manage a twelve-foot pike, but these requirements were further reduced with the advent of firearms. Despite the elaborate drill manuals of the early seventeenth century, the rudiments of musketry can be learned in a day (as the present author has done), and certainly in less than a week. While further training in battlefield disciplines was obviously desirable, the raw recruit began to be militarily employable once he could load and fire his weapon in the general direction of the enemy, which was the basic requirement at that time and for centuries afterwards. As for cavalry, the day of the knight was over once anyone who could sit on a horse and fire a pistol at the same time could bring him down. These developments, which were effectively completed with the introduction into general use of the flintlock pistol around the 1540s, made every able-bodied man between 16 and 45 into a potential pikeman, musketeer or cavalryman, so that the limited number of trained soldiers competent in the use of specialist weaponry was no longer a constraint on the rapid recruitment of large forces.

This effectively explains why military contracting did not emerge until around the end of the sixteenth century, as such activities only became possible on a significant scale once men were readily available. The status-conscious aristocratic knights and skilled men-at-arms of the late Middle Ages had tended to be individualists, conscious of their worth, and not inclined to take service with middlemen, but it was another matter when any farm-hand became potentially employable as a soldier. A second factor affecting this timing was the trend towards keeping armies, and hence regiments, together over one or more winters, which, as noted above, also emerged in the late sixteenth century. This was militarily and financially more effective for the prince, but it also created a much more attractive business and professional proposition for the would-be contractor. Raising a regiment for a single summer involved a lot of effort and risk, but smaller opportunities to make money, whereas once it became a longer-term proposition the concept of ownership by the entrepreneur could develop, bringing with it the associated recurring sources of profit, as well as an established post and salary as a colonel. Such prospects in turn enhanced the contractor's own creditworthiness, making it easier for him to raise the funds necessary to finance initial recruitment, which was itself an essential part of the growing ability to raise large forces quickly.

Military contracting solved, at least in part, the prince's or state's administrative problem, as Parker has pointed out, although there was a considerable associated cost. Meeting this, and the greater underlying financial commitment of maintaining larger armies, was taken care of by the development of the contributions system in the early seventeenth century. The real earlier constraint was not so much lack of sufficient wealth in society to support military expenditure, as lack of the absolutist power and administrative means for princes to extract that wealth through taxes, coupled with a general unwillingness to impose the necessary scale of burden on their own subjects, for fear of the disturbances or economic damage which might result. The prospect of making enemy or neutral populations pay for war was much more attractive, and again military contractors were instrumental in overcoming the administrative problem, by not only providing the troops but also arranging and enforcing the contributions necessary to pay for them. In practice the burden often also fell upon the prince's own subjects, but here too military coercion achieved what attempts at orderly taxation could not. There is thus a clear relationship between military contracting and contributions, each system being largely dependent on the other for their essentially parallel development. Both were necessary, together with the associated growth of credit from contractors and soldiers, to provide the basis upon which large armies could be recruited and maintained for extended periods much more easily in the first half of the seventeenth century than previously.

Supply logistics remained a problem which the seventeenth century could not solve, so that while the total numbers of troops in service rose sharply they had to be dispersed across a number of garrisons and field armies, the maximum size of which remained broadly unchanged. Thirty thousand men was a very large single army during the Thirty Years War, and it would have been accompanied by an even larger train of wagoners, sutlers, servants, wives, children and hangers-on of all sorts, so that the whole entity might well have numbered 100,000 people, plus a very large number of horses. This was around the size of the largest cities in Europe at the time, and larger than the biggest in Germany, noting that the population of Hamburg in 1650 was estimated at 60,000 (Franz, 1979, p. 9). Such huge additional numbers could not be supplied for long in any one place from the local countryside, and, except in the immediate vicinity of navigable rivers, bringing the necessary quantities of food and forage from any great distance was precluded by the state of the roads and the number of carts, wagoners and horses required. Hence in summer large armies had to be constantly moving on, literally to fresh pastures, while in winter they had to be dispersed into quarters over wide areas.

To sum up, it seems less likely that army growth as a Europe-wide phenomenon was driven by either the introduction of *trace italienne* fortifications, or the tactical innovations of Maurice of Nassau and Gustavus Adolphus, but more probable that it was the logical consequence of the de-skilling of soldiering, followed by the development of mechanisms which removed or greatly reduced most of the other constraints on troop numbers. Given the availability of a sufficient number of potential soldiers, a contracting system which both alleviated the administrative problems and provided credit for initial recruitment, and the ability of forces once raised to sustain themselves almost indefinitely by occupying territory and extracting contributions, it was inevitable that warring princes would set out to raise ever larger armies. Wallenstein was the pioneer with his 100,000-man Imperial army of 1625, but once he had shown how it could be done Gustavus Adolphus and others were not only able but virtually obliged to follow suit, in an early modern version of the arms races of the twentieth century.

References

Böhme, K.-R. 1967. 'Geld für die schwedischen Armeen nach 1640', *Scandia*, 33, 54–95.

Burschel, P. 1994. *Söldner im Nordwestdeutschland des 16. and 17. Jahrhunderts*, Göttingen.

Franz, G. 1979. *Der Dreißigjährige Krieg und das deutsche Volk*, 4th edn, Stuttgart.

Krüger, K. 1988. 'Dänische und schwedische Kriegsfinanzierung im Dreißigjährigen Krieg bis 1635', in Repgen, 1988, 275–98.

Lorenz, G. 1981. 'Schweden und die französischen Hilfsgelder von 1638 bis 1649', in Repgen, 1981, 98–148.

Lundkvist, S. 1988. 'Die schwedische Kriege- und Friedensziele 1632–1648', in Repgen, 1988, 219–41.

Lynn, J.A. 1993. 'How War Fed War: The Tax of Violence and Contributions during the *Grand Siècle*', *Journal of Modern History*, 65, 286–310.

Mann, G. 1976. *Wallenstein: His Life Narrated by Golo Mann*, London.

Mortimer, G. 2002. *Eyewitness Accounts of the Thirty Years War, 1618–1648*, Basingstoke.

Parker, G. 1995a. 'The "Military Revolution, 1560–1660" – A Myth?', in Rogers, 1995, 37–54.

——1995b. 'In Defense of the Military Revolution', in Rogers, 1995, 337–65.

——1988. 'The Soldiers of the Thirty Years War', in Repgen, 1988, 303–15.

Redlich, F. 1964–65. 'The German Military Enterpriser and his Workforce', *Beihefte zur Vierteljahrschrift für Sozial- und Wirtschaftsgeschichte*, 47–8, Wiesbaden.

——1959. 'Contributions in the Thirty Years War', *Economic History Review*, 12, 247–54.

Repgen, K. 1988. *Krieg und Politik 1618–1648: Europäische Probleme und Perspektiven*, Munich.

——ed. 1981. *Forschungen und Quellen zur Geschichte des Dreißigjährigen Krieges*, Münster.

Ritter, M. 1903. 'Das Kontributionssystem Wallensteins', *Historische Zeitschrift*, 90, 193–249.

Roberts, M. 1995. 'The Military Revolution, 1560–1660', in Rogers, 1995, 13–35.

——1992. *Gustavus Adolphus*, London.

——1991. *From Oxenstierna to Charles XII: Four Studies*, Cambridge.

——1958. *Gustavus Adolphus: A History of Sweden, 1611–1632*, vol. 2, London.

Robisheaux, T. 1989. *Rural Society and the Search for Order in Early Modern Germany*, Cambridge.

Rogers, C.J., ed. 1995. *The Military Revolution Debate: Readings on the Military Transformation of Early Modern Europe*, Boulder.

Salm, H. 1990. *Armeefinanzierung im Dreißigjährigen Krieg. Die Niederrheinisch-Westfälische Reichskreis 1635–1650*, Münster.

Turner, Sir J. 1683. *Pallas Armata: Military Essays of the Ancient Grecian, Roman and Modern Art of War*, London.

7

The Prussian Military State

Dennis E. Showalter

The aphorism usually attributed to the French statesman Count Mirabeau, that Prussia was not a country with an army but an army with a country, remains two centuries later a common way of introducing a discussion of eighteenth-century Prussia. Throughout absolutist Europe military expenses made up a major share of state budgets. But where 20 or 30 per cent was the norm elsewhere, the Prussian army regularly accounted for as much as three-quarters of public expenditure – and that in times of profound peace. In political, social and cultural terms as well, Prussia was generally recognized by its neighbours as centring on its army to a degree unknown elsewhere. Finally, that military focus seemed to be widely accepted at all levels and in all corners of a Prussia whose subjects were by any discernible standard no less content than those of other states.

It has been correspondingly logical for historians to present the Prussian military state, as it developed from the peace of Westphalia in 1648 to its collapse at Jena/Auerstädt in 1806, as a thing in itself, a product of objective geopolitical imperatives and the interrelated policies of successive rulers, an instrument of power, and above all an instrument of war. This chapter offers an alternative perspective. It presents the Prussian military state as, in strategic terms, a deterrent rather than an instrument of power projection, and in wider socio-political contexts essentially contingent and consensual in its nature – in short, less a predatory institution than a force for stabilization in the protean environment of early modern Europe.

I

Eighteenth-century Prussia's militarization was linked to the geopolitics of its political forebear, the electorate of Brandenburg. The Brandenburg that emerged from the peace of Westphalia was an archetypal middle-ranking German power, too large to be casually overlooked by its stronger neighbours, yet too small to pursue an independent policy vis-à-vis Bourbon France or Habsburg Austria. In that context Prussia did have the advantage of remoteness. Being further away from western Europe's centres of power and conflict than any of its German counterparts, Brandenburg possessed some diplomatic flexibility. On the other hand the electorate was also a Baltic power with two rivals, Poland and Sweden, all three being more or less equally competitive.

Not only was Brandenburg pulled in two diplomatic directions; it had neither external frontiers nor internal cohesion. With territories extending from the Rhine river in the west to deep into the Baltic lands in the east, Brandenburg was truly, to borrow a later phrase, 'a mollusc without a shell'. Sweden ignored for seven years the provisions of the Treaty of Westphalia allocating eastern Pomerania to Brandenburg. When Sweden went to war with Poland in 1655 Frederick William, the 'Great Elector' of Brandenburg, offered to transfer homage for his province of East Prussia from Sweden to Poland. The Polish king and parliament, desperate for vengeance against the heretic Swedes ravaging their heartlands, accepted the change in Prussia's status in return for Frederick William's military support. In 1660 the peace of Oliva confirmed Frederick William's full title to East Prussia – but treaties east of the Elbe tended to be short lived.

Flexibility also shaped the elector's policies in the west. In 1672 he allied with the Netherlands against France, then extricated himself from the Dutch collapse. He contributed troops to the Anglo-Austrian coalition against Louis XIV in 1675 in return for generous subsidies, but withdrew to Brandenburg after the allied defeat at the battle of Turckheim. That same year the elector's army inflicted a major defeat on Sweden at Fehrbellin, but he was forced, at French insistence, to return the resulting territorial gains four years later in the context of a general European peace. Dining with Louis XIV required a long spoon.

At the time of Frederick William's death in 1688, Brandenburg had not lost ground. It was still a middle-ranking principality depending on the goodwill of the great powers. This achievement, while no small triumph given the lack of court cards in the elector's hand, was neither consequence nor cause of Prussia's transformation to a 'military state'. Over the years its army had established a reputation in both Baltic and European contexts as a solid, reliable fighting force, but nothing special. Prussia's army, like its German and European counterparts generally, was essentially an extension of the royal household. It was a force of volunteers, with its core recruited locally while the rest came from everywhere the elector's contingents marched. There were always men footloose, desperate or adventurous enough to take the enlistment bounty.

Financing the army, as opposed to recruiting it, was Brandenburg's central problem. The electorate's tax base was too narrow and too small to support the 30,000 men Frederick William considered the minimum necessary to keep Prussia a player at the head diplomatic table. Foreign subsidies helped to make up the difference, but as the scale and cost of war increased these were more readily promised than delivered. Subsidies also invited a situation where Prussia might be constantly making war for interests not its own, in order to support the army that enabled it to survive – a vicious circle whose likely outcome was permanent client status.

Frederick William had responded by seeking both to expand his state's commercial and industrial capacity and to establish an administrative structure able to maximize utilization of private resources for public purposes. Society became increasingly subject to economic regulation at all levels, with a tax-collecting system based on that of Holland and an infrastructure increasingly shaped by government participation, ranging from canal construction to tariff legislation. As in military matters, however, none of that particularly distinguished Prussia from other middle-sized German states seeking to maintain their status in an environment where the growing scale and intensity of war-making prefigured an eventual inability to keep pace (McKay, 2001; Neumann, 1995).

The elector's heir, Frederick III, is usually described – or dismissed – as more concerned with the trappings of power than its substance. He was, however, shrewd enough to leave the army alone, and perceptive enough to maximize its value as a subsidy force. Even as the War of the Spanish Succession eroded the relative impact of the small and middle-sized forces involved, Prussian contingents nevertheless maintained consistently high levels of tactical competence and combat performance. While Vienna would in principle allow no kings within the Reich, it was worth a royal title for Habsburg Emperor Leopold to bind Prussia's ruler and his fighting men to the Habsburg colours. Allowing Frederick to call himself 'King in Prussia' (hence being known as King Frederick I thereafter) was a significant concession, and it was not mere fecklessness for the newly anointed monarch to sustain his dignity by display. Elaborate court costumes, handsome public buildings and collections of the best in modern art represented no direct challenges to Vienna's primacy in Germany (Frey and Frey, 1984).

Prussia's behaviour prefigured that of an increasing number of lesser German states which in the course of the eighteenth century eschewed military competition for a cultural/intellectual version. Often not much less expensive, the new course was easier on infrastructures and demographics (Wilson, 1995). Any possibility of Prussia playing a long-term part in this competition vanished, however, with the accession of Frederick William I to the throne in 1714.

The new monarch was determined to secure his state's position as an autonomous European power – not a rival to Austria, but its 'faithful second' in north Germany; not a rival to France, but a supporter of the European stability that best served Prussia's interests. Skilful small-scale diplomacy secured Stettin and most of Swedish Pomerania by 1721, after which Frederick assumed the role of a satiated monarch despite disappointment over Vienna's refusal to underwrite his claims to the disputed Rhenish duchies of Jülich and Berg. That commitment to the status quo was, however, accompanied by an equal determination to maintain Prussia's freedom of diplomatic action (Oestreich, 1977; Kathe, 1976). That determination transformed the achievements of his predecessors into the foundations of the Prussian military state.

II

At the apex of Prussia's administrative system in 1713 were the General War Commission, which had evolved under the king's predecessors into a focal point for tax and welfare issues, and the General Finance Administration, responsible for administering the royal properties, which were a major source of state revenue. Internal rivalries led Frederick William to combine them under a variously translated, teutonically elaborate title of General Superior Finance, War, and Domains Directory, usually shortened to General Directory. This body integrated territorial, functional and collegiate principles in a way impossible in a larger state, or under a looser hand than that of Frederick William. Each of its four departments was individually responsible for both the general administration of particular provinces and the control of particular administrative functions for the kingdom as a whole. The various provincial estates, already largely vestigial, lost their remaining powers of taxation and were forced to turn over most of their administrative functions to provincial agencies of the central government, the War and Domain Chambers. In their final versions these bodies collected revenue alike from towns and villages, from royal property, and from general levies, and passed it on to the treasury at Potsdam. There as much as possible was converted into specie and stored in kegs to finance the wars Frederick William hoped never to fight (Dorwart, 1953).

Viewed from one perspective, the reign of Frederick William I was characterized by a concentration of administrative power unprecedented in Germany, and barely matched in Louis XIV's France. On the other hand no agency was headed by a single responsible person. Instead decisions were made collectively and collegially, with corresponding opportunities for both jurisdictional disputes and principled controversies over who should exercise authority in a particular case. The rapidly expanding bureaucracy, moreover, drew most of its rank and file from existing interest groups, especially an aristocracy which was by no means the homogeneous body it later became. Loyal to the king – and literally fearing his stick – the noble bureaucrats were nevertheless able much of the time to temper the wind of state when it blew on their particular fellows. The result was a balancing of discontents, in which no group was perceived as dominant. The grievances of one were usually countered by the advantages of another, and Frederick William showed an unusual capacity to steer a course among the rocks and shoals of his still-polyglot kingdom's still-complex special interests (Rosenberg, 1958; Gothelf, 1998).

Increasingly those interests were both defined and validated by their relationship to the army. Frederick William was convinced that the army of 40,000 he inherited from his father was unsuitable to sustain the autarky he sought. It was too large for the great powers to ignore or to treat as merely another subsidy force. It was also too small to stand independently among Europe's armed forces. In Frederick William's mind, keeping Prussia out of the wars and crises that continued to characterize European diplomacy after the Peace of Utrecht depended in good part on an army large enough and effective enough to discourage attempts at compelling Prussia to choose sides in any specific situation. In modern phrasing, Frederick William sought to make the Prussian army into a deterrent force.

His projected ideal strength was 80,000 men. But how could such a force be created and maintained? Traditional sources of manpower came under unprecedented pressure even during the War of the Spanish Succession, not only in Prussia but throughout Germany, as recruiting parties came increasingly to resemble press gangs. Racketeering, corruption and kidnapping remained common even after hostilities ended, especially in a Prussian army that, unlike most others, did not cut back its establishment to correspond with the reduction of funding for bonuses and bounties. In the 1720s even honest recruiters embarked on what amounted to man-hunts to meet their quotas, generating increasing opposition from the landlords whose labourers they impressed and whose authority they challenged. As a kind of professional courtesy the recruiting parties of German states were usually allowed to operate on each other's territory. Hanover, however, nearly declared war in 1729 over the behaviour of Prussian recruiters. In other states, recruiting for Prussian service became a capital offence alongside witchcraft and parricide (Childs, 1982, pp. 52ff.).

Securing reliable regimental officers for an army even the then size of Prussia's, to say nothing of the king's projections, was a parallel problem. The free-agent system that emerged from the Thirty Years War still persisted. James Keith came from Scotland by way of Russia. Leopold von Anhalt-Dessau was sent as a boy to make his fortune under Prussian colours. But at the bottom line that approach was both random and expensive (Schrotter, 1912–14). The most obvious solution to the Prussian army's personnel problem at all levels involved tapping the state's own resources, systematically and on a scale sufficiently limited that it did not seriously diminish the labour force on which a pre-industrial economy directly depended. Frederick William I began by systematizing the dragooning of the nobility's sons into 'cadet schools', partly as a source of subalterns and partly as surety for their parents' loyalty.

That the schools were little better than holding-pens, providing neither education nor training of any consequence, made little difference in an era when an officer – like initiates of virtually every other skilled craft – was expected to learn his trade by apprenticeship and experience. The wider result of that process was the direct integration of the aristocracy into the state apparatus, by providing careers both honourable and relatively more profitable than depending on the revenues of estates that could not be alienated, and whose development required capital resources far beyond the scope of clans, let alone individual families.

For the enrolment of enlisted men a different model stood ready to hand. Beginning in the seventeenth century, Sweden's army had depended heavily on a system under which groups of farms furnished, supported and replaced a soldier. Russia under Peter the Great introduced a similar procedure. The Prussian cantonal system, introduced in 1731, was more extensive and more systematic. It divided the kingdom into districts based on the number of 'hearths', or family residences. Each regiment was assigned a specific district, and the district was divided into as many 'cantons' as the regiment had companies. All able-bodied men between the ages of 18 and 40 were registered and liable for military service. If the companies did not fill their ranks by voluntary enlistment then eligible cantonists were conscripted to fill the vacancies.

In practice Prussia's domestic recruiting policy prefigured the Selective Service system as implemented in the United States during the 1950s and 1960s. In both cases the state could not bear the cost of training seriously every theoretically eligible male. A process of random selection seemed as irrational to King Frederick William I and his advisers as it did to General Lewis Hershey and the US Congress. As a result, numerous social and economic groups were excluded from the cantonal system – nobles and businessmen, apprentices in a wide variety of crafts, textile workers, theology students – the list grew with the years, each new category having its own rationale (Harnisch, 1996).

The canton system enabled the Prussian state to maintain a force large enough in peacetime, and with a sufficient number of reserves, to sustain its great-power pretensions without emptying the treasury. It succeeded less by direct compulsion than because of the willingness of families and communities to furnish a proportion of their sons each year, and because the system allowed both institutions a significant role in deciding precisely which individuals were furnished. Public, official authority reinforced its social, unofficial counterpart in a specific area that directly impacted large numbers of people. Considered in that context the 'police states', the emerging enlightened despotisms of the eighteenth century, may have been more congruent with traditional societies than has been previously conceded, and correspondingly more positively acceptable to their subjects.

The familiar argument that the Prussian system left the burdens of military service entirely on Prussia's least favoured subjects – farm workers, smallholding peasants, unskilled urban workers – is accurate. It is also misleading. In eighteenth-century Prussia all owed service to the state. In that sense those excluded from the cantonal system proper were less exempted than occupationally deferred.

That developing consensus reflected two basic aspects of Prussian culture. The first was Pietism. This eighteenth-century religious impulse challenged the quietism of traditional Lutheranism by emphasizing service to and reform of the community. While less austere than the Calvinism to which it owed much of its theological substance, Pietism cultivated a sober, level view of the world and of mankind's place in it. It offered little room for exaltation or inspiration, and less for the kind of public posturing that confused status with hubris and performance with visibility. The Prussian state justified itself not by divine right in the manner of Louis XIV, or on prescriptive grounds of the kind later articulated by Edmund Burke, but in instrumental terms, with protection and stability being exchanged for service and obedience. It was the kind of social contract, no less firm for being unwritten, that Pietists were likely to affirm (Clark, 2000; Gawthrop, 1993).

The Pietist concept of duty provided a moral dimension to the subject of service that was by no means artificial. Self-discipline and social discipline are significant contributors to self-awareness and self-esteem – pride in tasks consciously and conscientiously performed in an environment validating those tasks. Discipline's positive aspects may also be enhanced by an environment which, like early modern Prussia, has little surplus to sustain hedonism and offers few attractive prospects for self-indulgence. Not a few officers, for example, turned to self-improvement and professional improvement from disgust or boredom with the opportunities for vice offered by a garrison town.

The second cultural prop of the Prussian military state was patriarchy. That concept has been so often defined in a model of overt dominance and submission that it merits examination in an alternative context suggested by Klaus Epstein. Conservatism, according to Epstein, is most effective when unarticulated. When it responds to 'the party of movement' by describing, let alone defending, itself, conservatism is playing on the other party's home field and by his rules (Epstein, 1966, pp. 65ff.). A similar point can be made about patriarchy. Whether in the context of family, village, or Junker estate, it was most functional when least obtrusive. For those in charge, both collective wisdom and individual experience indicated the counter-productivity of throwing one's weight around, of directly intervening in the routine course of events except when absolutely necessary. That authority which disrupted the least was also likely to be the best and most effective (Münch, 1992).

Extended upwards, while the Prussian military state was by no means invisible to its subjects, it and its representatives did not interfere at random or change their minds at whim. The aphorism 'there are still law courts in Berlin', quoted in many eighteenth-century contexts, highlights the developing image of Prussia as a *Rechtsstaat*, a state of laws – and practices with the force of law – that not even the king himself could ignore.

Pragmatic as well as philosophical issues shaped acceptance of the military state. As usually implemented, cantonal conscription was not especially oppressive. Among the registered males, only those who met the height requirement of 5 ft 7 in. (usually fewer than 20 per cent), and were non-noble, not sons of officers, did not directly own a farm, and whose families were worth less than 10,000 taler were eligible for induction. That reduced the number of eligibles in a company sector to about 18 per cent of the male population. One typical company recruiting area of 771 hearths included at any given time approximately 135 households with males who met the minimum requirements for conscription. That population had to fill a yearly requirement of about three recruits – scarcely an insupportable burden in any context.

Even when the Seven Years War is included, fewer than half of the nearly nine million men registered from first to last under Prussia's cantonal system ever donned a uniform. This degree of flexibility created ample opportunities for families and villages to assert control over their young men by deciding who went to the army and who stayed at home. On a most basic level that in turn made it possible to plan futures, as individuals and families were freed from the pressures of haphazard, uncontrolled domestic recruiting. Cantonal service had other consequences as well. A defining feature of the eighteenth-century Prussian state was its virtual resignation of rural administrative control to the *Gutsherren*. These aristocratic landlords exercised police, religious and educational authority within the boundaries of their estates. State policies affecting the countryside were usually filtered through the landlords. The resulting symbiosis was best expressed in a contemporary aphorism: 'Und der König absolut / wenn er uns den Willen tut' (the king is an absolute monarch as long as he does what we want).

There was, however, another side to the coin. As a rule Prussia's peasant conscripts initially spent from 18 months to two years with the colours, learning the basics of their new craft. They were then furloughed – returned to civilian life and the civilian economy – and recalled each year for a brief refresher course. But even on furlough men doing military service were under military law, to which they could and did appeal against both communities and landlords. The cantonist was neither soldier nor peasant in the traditional sense, but walked a fine line between the two groups. His status was perhaps best illustrated by the requirement that furloughed men always wear a piece of uniform clothing. That regulation was not, as so often stated in general accounts, intended as a safeguard against desertion. An item of clothing is easily discarded – especially since the cantonists' most common choice was the army-issue gaiters that protected their civilian breeches, and gaiters were about as common rough-labour garb as recycled fatigue jackets in the contemporary United States. Desertion for a furloughed cantonist, moreover, was a matter far more complex than sudden headlong flight across the fields. It meant permanently severing familiar ties and abandoning familiar hopes. Seldom undertaken lightly, it involved careful preparation, precise timing, secreting food, cash and clothing, and usually some help from friends and relatives.

The real purpose of the uniform clothing was to identify the cantonist as a soldier, and therefore under military authority. In a society where authority was regularly asserted through blows, army gaiters were a warning to a gang boss – and perhaps even to a Junker – to think twice before casually striking a king's man. For the assertive or the fortunate, military service could offer protection in other ways as well. Furloughed privates successfully appealed to military authorities against abuses by local officials, and they obtained permission to marry from colonels when landlords were intransigent.

The emancipating aspects of military service must not be exaggerated. The cantonist's landlord and his company commander might well be the same person, when not brothers or cousins. As the aristocracy became more closely integrated into the military and civil administrations in the course of the eighteenth century, loopholes correspondingly tended to disappear. Nevertheless a significant element in stabilizing the Prussian military state seems to have been the opportunities it offered common soldiers to challenge the oppressively deferential society in which they lived (Kloosterhuis, 1992 and Bleckwenn, 1977, are more nuanced than Busch, 1997).

Ancien régime societies as a whole were structured around the concept of privilege as opposed to the concept of rights. It is only a slight exaggeration to say that not merely the clergy and the aristocracy, but almost everyone east of Britain, west of Russia and north of Vienna belonged to a 'privileged order' in the sense of having perquisites conferred by custom and prescription, if not always by law. For most the privileges were extremely limited – but that made them correspondingly important.

Direct reciprocity between the impact of cantonal military service and increasingly respectful treatment of peasants by landlords cannot be proved definitively. It is nevertheless true that from the middle of the eighteenth century peasants were not only being summoned directly to appear before royal courts, but were addressed as *Herr*. Lease contracts were increasingly free of traditional feudal and servile formulas. Coercion was giving way to clientage, the tacit acceptance of networks of mutual obligations, as the dominant means of control in the countryside (Melton, 2000).

III

Additional light may be cast on the situation in the countryside by paying closer attention to the army. Prussia's army depended for its effectiveness on its spirit more than on its discipline. Compulsion in its varied forms might keep men in the ranks. It could not make them fight. More precisely, it could not keep them fighting. Drill and training were designed in part to inculcate automatic physical responses – loading and reloading by numbers, and moving according to orders. But neither conditioned reflex nor external force, together or separately, could keep men in the ranks at the height of an eighteenth-century battle, whose normal course resembled nothing so much as feeding two candles into a blowtorch and seeing which melted first. Instead the Prussian army integrated its conscripts and its volunteers into a cohesive and efficient fighting force by what might be called a commitment–dependence cycle.

A soldier's relationship to the state differs essentially from that of a civilian because it involves a central commitment to dying, as opposed to death as a by-product of other activities like fire fighting or law enforcement. In western societies that commitment is not absolute – a fact that can surprise even students of military history when they discover what 'fighting to the last man' means in practice (Smith, 1994). Moreover, for much of the time for most soldiers the 'death clause' is inactive. An individual can spend thirty honourable years in uniform and face only collateral risks. But all armies possess a sense of what it is legitimate to expect under given circumstances.

The soldier of Renaissance and early modern Europe originally identified himself in terms of individuality. Becoming a soldier involved being able to carry a sword, to wear outrageous clothing and to swagger at will among the women in ways denied the peasant or artisan. The introduction of uniforms and the systematic enforcement of camp and garrison discipline did much to remove the patina of liberty from a life that, while not solitary, was likely to be nasty, brutish and short. In its place emerged a pattern in which the state demonstrated concrete concern for the soldier's well-being as a means of increasing his dependence on the state. Prussian uniforms were regarded as among the best in Europe. Its medical care in peace and war was superior to anything normally available to commoners. Its veterans had good chances of public employment, or maintenance in one of the garrison companies that combined the functions of local security and soldiers' home.

The deep pool of potential recruits, especially in peacetime, made selectivity possible to a degree unknown elsewhere in Europe. Prussia's cantonists consistently impressed foreign observers as being big, well-proportioned young men, excellent raw material for an army that understood how to maximize their potential. And the relatively small number of recruits present at any one time enabled Prussian training methods to be based on levels of individual instruction impossible in the mass armies of a later generation, with their large intakes and small cadres. The usual practice was to put the recruit in the charge of a reliable soldier who, for a share of whatever food, drink or cash the youngster might possess or receive from home, provided basic instruction in dress and behaviour. The details of drill and uniform were left to the non-commissioned officers, but even they were instructed to deal patiently with recruits who showed goodwill.

That patience was relative, particularly since Prussian society generally considered cuffs and blows a natural part of any process of male instruction or socialization. It nevertheless represents no whitewash of Prussian discipline to note that many of the more vivid horror stories were reported either by officers advocating a discipline based on mutual honour and mutual respect instead of sanctions, or by men whose experiences in Prussian service had been somehow unfortunate. As in any army, a disproportionate amount of punishment fell upon a disproportionately small number – the dull-witted and the loud-mouthed, the sullen, and not least those unfortunate enough to be made scapegoats for some reason by their superiors or their fellow-soldiers. The ordinarily tractable individual with an ordinarily developed ability to blend into his surroundings in no way faced a life of unrelieved misery in an alien environment.

After his initial training the cantonist, as mentioned, spent as much as ten months of every year at home on furlough. While with the regiment, a good part of his time was spent in civilian billets, outside the immediate supervision of his officers and sergeants, and with corresponding opportunities to cultivate contacts and relationships that ranged from the romantic to the criminal. Prussian soldiers off duty were left to their own devices to a degree inconceivable in British or American armed forces until recent years. They could dress much as they pleased, seek part-time employment – a practice encouraged by the army – or practice the arts of idleness. A good many of the often-cited problems of complying with the regulations governing uniform and personal appearance on duty seem to have been consequences of earlier, avoidable sins of omission and commission regarding uniform, kit and grooming (Rush and Showalter, forthcoming).

The cantonists, however, were only one pole of the army that was the core of the Prussian military state. Even on mobilization they made up only about 60 per cent of the total force. The rest were volunteers, and without them the cantonal system could not function. The volunteers provided the institutional stability, the everyday experience that was transmitted to the cantonists through dozens of official and unofficial channels. They also bridged the gap between the number of men Prussia's civil economy could reasonably spare in peacetime and the number of men Frederick William I considered necessary to have available for immediate service. These men are frequently called mercenaries, but the latter term had a much looser definition in the eighteenth century than it does today, when 'mercenary' connotes a ruthless cosmopolitan who fights for any paymaster. In the Prussian army a mercenary was anyone who was not a conscripted cantonist. Nor were they, as general accounts often suggest, all foreigners. Many were, legally at least, Prussian subjects, among them discharged apprentices and under-employed day labourers who joined the army for financial security. Others were men who saw no prospects of improving their lot in civilian life and sought, if not liberty, at least a new form of servitude. Not a few were true volunteers. One seventeen-year-old Alsatian travelled as far as Aachen to join the Prussian army because of its high reputation. His account, while written from a perspective that often confuses positive experience with the general vigour of lost youth, nevertheless describes even his days as a recruit as full of fun and horseplay, spent in company far more interesting than that of his home village (Fann, 1990; Dreyer, 1870). The Prussian mercenary, in short, did not consider himself part of a legion of the lost. His self-image was likely to be that of a free man, following the honourable craft of arms by his own choice. And while the official contracts of enlistment might be both one-sided and absolute, a mercenary could always invoke the escape clause of desertion. The draconian penalties instituted in the Prussian army to prevent this affirm its relative ease in peacetime for someone who had no stake in the wider society. Indeed at times deserters eventually re-enlisted – though usually as far as possible from their original garrison – and officers and drill sergeants seldom asked awkward questions if a new man seemed unexpectedly familiar with the movements and exercises (Sikora, 1996).

IV

Prussia's carefully balanced social/military structure was brought to the edge of destruction by the monarch usually considered to have embodied Prussia's military state. Frederick II ('the Great') interpreted the behaviour of states as subject to rational calculation, governed by principles that could be learned and applied in the same way as one maintained a clock. As crown prince he had taken, in contrast to his father's situationally-based pragmatism, an academic approach to questions of statecraft. Beginning with the hypothesis that Prussia needed a systematic long-term foreign policy to secure its interests, he proceeded by traceable stages to the conclusion that expansion by annexation was an ultimate necessity. Frederick supported this contention by appealing to 'reason of state', a necessity outside the moral principles applying to individuals. His *Anti-Machaviel*, published in 1740, further developed the argument that law and ethics in international relations were based neither on the interests of the ruler nor on the desires of the people (Schieder, 1982; Blanning, 1990). His concept of a monarch's role rejected the representational and heroic elements that had been crucial to Europe's rulers since the Renaissance. Frederick in contrast described himself as 'Field Marshal and First Minister of the King of Prussia'. His idea of war was that it should be short, decisive, and brutal – partly to conserve scarce resources and partly to deter future challenges from the defeated party or anyone else. War's aims should be clear, positive, and susceptible of discussion. The optimal goal was to establish, by an initial victory or series of victories, the wisdom of negotiation as an alternative to continued conflict.

Between 1740 and 1763 Frederick applied these principles with single-minded determination. Prussia confronted Europe in arms and emerged victorious, but at a price that left the state shaken to its physical and moral foundations. Provinces were devastated, people were scattered, and the currency was debased. As many as 180,000 Prussians had died in uniform, to say nothing of civilian losses. The social contract of the military state – service and loyalty in return for stability and protection – was likewise shaken to its foundations.

Frederick was correspondingly determined to restore his kingdom as quickly as possible. He personally oversaw the distribution of seed grain and draft animals, the payment of officials' back salaries, and the opening of royal land to emigrant settlers. His wartime-generated reputation for controlling everything in person was sustained by the energy and detail with which he conducted inspections throughout his kingdom. The king's first tour of Prussia's ravaged provinces was remembered for years even by people who had been a hundred miles away from the royal coach when it passed through.

For a while it seemed that the king's persona might redefine the military state by personalizing it. Bureaucratization, however, worked increasingly against such a development in the postwar years. The administrative apparatus became more self-referencing and more remote as it grew more complex. A similar process took place in the legal system (Mittenzwei, 1979), and in the military one as well.

After 1763 Frederick proposed essentially to maintain Prussia's still tenuous great power status by negotiation (Scott, 1994). The army would resume its function as a deterrent, underwriting Prussia's diplomacy by emphasizing the alternative. The king had been slow to learn, but the Seven Years War finally convinced him that perceived capacity and perceived readiness to make war were far more important to Prussia's security than the waging of war itself. Standards of discipline and appearance became increasingly rigid and increasingly comprehensive, in ways inviting comparison to the British Navy in the late age of sail, and for similar reasons. A smart ship and a smart regiment were understood as possessing a certain deterrent effect by virtue of their respective grooming. Reviews and manoeuvres developed from testing grounds for war to public displays of power, designed to deter any state or any domestic dissident from thinking of trying further conclusions with 'Old Fritz' and his grenadiers.

There was another side to deterrence through display. The complex evolutions developed after 1763 were in principle designed to enable men to endure and units to manoeuvre under the worst foreseeable tactical conditions, against enemies who had long prepared to counter such battlefield tricks as the oblique order. But with clockwork regularity the order of the day, drill movements grew exacting to the point of impossibility even for experienced men.

As part of his programme to facilitate Prussia's economic recovery Frederick also increasingly skimped on his army's infrastructure. The quality of uniforms steadily declined – an important morale factor, and a significant financial burden on men required to make up loss and damage from their own pockets. Grain allowances for the cavalry were cut to the point where in spring and summer horses were expected to graze, with a corresponding adverse effect on their conditioning. These kinds of infrastructure economies made it increasingly difficult to recruit and retain the foreign professionals whose presence balanced the cantonal system by keeping draft calls low. As economic conditions improved and prices rose, moreover, foreign soldiers constrained to seek employment in the civilian economy found themselves at a significant disadvantage compared to their Prussian counterparts with better claims on garrison communities. Desertion was a logical consequence. It is not coincidental that most of the worst horror stories of preventive and punitive measures against 'French leave' in Prussia's army date from the period after the Seven Years War (Showalter, 1994).

V

Frederick's death in 1786 opened something like a window of opportunity for a rising generation of military theorists influenced by an *Aufklärung* suggestion that war, like literature, philosophy and art, was a human endeavour as well as the domain of reason. The new king, Frederick William II, supported policies calculated to restore pride as well as to emphasize duty. Amenities like family allowances and regimental schools were accompanied by bans on the more extreme forms of physical punishment, and by creation of a specialized light infantry, the fusiliers, where discipline was based heavily on appeals to professionalism and comradeship. Each line company was also allotted ten enlisted 'sharpshooters', selected for physical fitness and mental alertness, who provided a valuable source of efficient NCOs and a tangible recognition of good service (Stine, 1980).

Implemented more systematically and with more enthusiasm, such policies might have given Prussia a more professionalized army, with foreigners easier to recruit and retain and Prussian natives readier to consider making a career of military service. Even in its limited form the new order was sufficient to keep desertion rates moderate during the 1790s, despite the appeal of French propaganda stressing the advantages of coat-turning in the name of liberty, equality and fraternity. And as the passive deterrence characteristic of the final 20 years of Frederick II's reign gave way under Frederick William II into an active policy in both Poland and western Europe, the army's operational performance was generally solid. The defeat by the French revolutionary army at Valmy was generally understood as a specific problem of command rather than a general indication of institutional decline. After some seasoning, Prussian line battalions between 1792 and 1795 combined well-controlled volleys and well-regulated local counterattacks that matched, if they did not always master, French dash and courage. Prussian fusiliers proved formidable opponents against French raiders and foragers, on occasion teaching larger units sharp lessons at high tuition costs in the crafts of skirmishing and marksmanship.

Far from being hopelessly retrograde or terminally arteriosclerotic, in short, the Prussian army at the end of the eighteenth century was well able to support a Prussian state strategy of prudent territorial ambition and limited commitment to external alliances (Showalter, 1994). It was, however, increasingly clear to the state's military professionals that the standards of warfare were now being set by France. It was equally clear that French human and material resources massively exceeded anything Prussia could hope to match. For almost a century Prussia's military hole card had been a recruiting system that systematically tapped its indigenous manpower on a consensual basis. Now France too had begun mobilizing its lower classes systematically – and had many more of them. A decade of war and revolution had diminished the number of foreigners willing – or able – to don Prussian uniform. Increasing the domestic contribution to the army's cadres was theoretically possible. Official figures gave over two million cantonists available in 1799, and 2.3 million in 1805. Even if all the increasingly generous legal exemptions were continued, over 300,000 men could be conscripted in a given year without summoning the middle aged and the less physically capable. Matching France man for man in the long term was, however, impossible, quite apart from the risk that rapid increases in enrolments might gridlock an administrative system arguably already too finely tuned for the good of state and society.

Napoleon's army, moreover, was not a mass levy of armed patriots. Its regiments instead increasingly resembled those that had marched to glory with Frederick, strong cadres of professionals reinforced at intervals by conscripts not all that different in motivation from Prussia's own cantonists (Forrest,

2002). It was not a reactionary idea to assert that matching such an adversary required a quality army able to counter French mass and skill with even greater fighting power of its own. Conceptualizing the specifics of that force, however, was not easy in the context of rapid, continual changes in war-fighting, combined with a state policy which for financial and diplomatic reasons withdrew from the war in 1795, and thus kept Prussian troops and officers from updating their operational experience for ten crucial years (White, 1989).

The government's initial decision in 1805 to ally neither with Napoleon nor with the Third Coalition forming against him was a final manifestation of the Prussian military state's nature and purpose. That state, and the army that was its focal point, had developed as a deterrent in the context of a multi-polar international system. Its ultimate purpose, however, was to sustain Prussia's autonomy. Now that system faced the risk of de facto reduction to a French or Russian satellite. It was scarcely remarkable that, eventually driven into a corner, Prussia turned to its army and took the chance, in the autumn of 1806, of fighting alone, waging all-out war against a hegemonic empire.

For all the shortcomings so pitilessly exposed in the glare of hindsight, the Prussians fought well enough at Jena and Auerstädt to give their enemies more than a few bad quarters of an hour. Nor is it inappropriate to stress that in 1806 the Prussian army faced an opponent at the peak of its institutional effectiveness, commanded by one of history's great captains at the peak of his powers. The military state had not been discredited in principle. The reform movement that followed the collapse of the old order took Prussia down new roads, domestically and in the context of the European state system. But one thing it sustained – the synergistic linkage of state, society and army, with the army at the centre, that had made Prussia a great power and would make her the centre of an empire before it was finally brought low.

References

Blanning, T.C.W. 1990. 'Frederick the Great and Enlightened Absolutism', in *Enlightened Absolutism: Reform and Reformers in the Later Eighteenth Century*, ed. H.C. Scott, London, 265–88.

Bleckwenn, H. 1977. *Unter dem Preußen-Adler*, Osnabrück.

Busch, O. 1997. *Military System and Social Life in Old-Regime Prussia*, Atlantic Highlands.

Childs, J. 1982. *Armies and Warfare in Europe, 1648–1789*, New York.

Clark, C. 2000. 'Piety, Politics, and Enlightenment in Eighteenth Century Prussia', in *The Rise of Prussia, 1700–1830*, ed. P.G. Dwyer, London, 68–87.

Dorwart, R. 1953. *The Administrative Reforms of Frederick William I of Prussia*, Cambridge.

Dreyer, J.D. 1870. *Leben und Thaten eines preussischen Regiments-Tambours*, Breslau.

Epstein, K. 1966. *The Genesis of German Conservatism*, Princeton.

Fann, W. 1990. 'Foreigners in the Prussian Army, 1713–56: Some Statistical and Interpretive Problems', *Central European History*, 23, 76–84.

Forrest, A. 2002. *Napoleon's Men. The Soldiers of the Revolution and Empire*, London.

Frey, L. and Frey, M. 1984. *Frederick I, the Man and His Times*, Boulder.

Gawthrop, R.L. 1993. *Pietism and the Making of Eighteenth Century Prussia*, Cambridge.

Gothelf, R. 1998. 'Absolutism in Action: Frederick William I and the Government of East Prussia, 1709–1730', doctoral thesis, University of St Andrews.

Harnisch, H. 1996. 'Preußisches Kantonsystem und ländliche Gesellschaft: Das Beispiel des mittleren Kammerdepartements', in *Krieg und Frieden: Militär und Gesellschaft in der frühen Neuzeit*, ed. B.R. Kroener and R. Pröve, Paderborn, 137–65.

Kathe, H. 1976. *Der 'Soldatenkönig': Friedrich Wilhelm I. 1688–1740, König in Preußen; eine Biographie*, Berlin.

Kloosterhuis, J. 1992. *Bauern, Bürger und Soldaten: Quellen zur Sozialisation des Militärsystems im preußischen Westfalen 1713–1803*, Münster.

McKay, D. 2001. *The Great Elector*, New York.

Melton, J.V.H. 2000. 'The Transformation of the Economy in East Elbian Prussia, 1750–1830', in *The Rise of Prussia, 1700–1830*, ed. P.G. Dwyer, London, 111–28.

Mittenzwei, I. 1979. *Preußen nach dem Siebenjährigen Krieg: Auseinandersetzungen zwischen Bürgertum und Staat um die Wirtschaftspolitik*, Berlin.

Münch, P. 1992. *Lebensformen in der frühen Neuzeit, 1500 bis 1800*, Frankfurt.

Neumann, H.J. 1995. *Friedrich Wilhelm der Große Kurfürst: der Sieger von Fehrbellin*, Berlin.

Oestreich, G. 1977. *Friedrich Wilhelm I.: Preußischer Absolutismus, Merkantilismus, Militarismus*, Göttingen.

Rosenberg, H. 1958. *Bureaucracy, Aristocracy and Autocracy: The Prussian Experience 1660–1815*, Cambridge.

Rush, R. and Showalter, D. Forthcoming. 'Der gute Kamerad: the Life of a Prussian Soldier in the Army of Frederick William I'.

Schieder, T. 1982. 'Friedrich der Große und Machiavelli: Das Dilemma von Machtpolitik und Aufklärung', *Historische Zeitschrift*, 234, 265–94.

Schrotter, R. von. 1912–14. 'Das preußische Offizierkorps unter die ersten Könige von Preußen', *Forschungen zur brandenburgischen-preußischen Geschichte*, 26, 429 ff.; 27, 97–167.

Scott, H.M. 1994. 'Aping the Great Powers: Frederick the Great and the Defence of Prussia's International Position, 1763–1786', *German History*, 12, 286–307.

Showalter, D.E. 1994. 'Hubertusberg to Auerstädt: The Prussian Army in Decline?', *German History*, 12, 308–33.

Sikora, M. 1996. 'Verzweiflung oder "Leichtsinn"? Militärstand und Desertion im 18. Jahrhundert', in *Krieg und Frieden: Militär und Gesellschaft in der frühen Neuzeit*, ed. B.R. Kroener and R. Pröve, Paderborn, 237–64.

Smith, L.V. 1994. *Between Mutiny and Obedience: The Fifth French Infantry Division during World War I*, Princeton.

Stine, J.E. 1980. 'King Frederick William II and the Decline of the Prussian Army, 1788–1797', doctoral dissertation, University of South Carolina.

White, C. 1989. *The Enlightened Soldier: Scharnhorst and the Militärische Gesellschaft in Berlin, 1801–1805*, New York.

Wilson, P.H. 1995. *War, State, and Society in Württemberg, 1677–1793*, Cambridge.

8
New Approaches under the Old Regime

Peter H. Wilson

The 'old regime' and 'limited war'

The term 'old regime' (*ancien régime*) was invented by the French revolutionaries to distinguish their brave new world from the monarchies they hoped to displace. Thanks to the convention that their revolution was a major turning point in world history and the birth of 'modernity', it has stuck as a general label for the period from 1648 to 1789. This time is generally defined, in contrast to the preceding and subsequent eras, as a time of relative stability under 'absolute' monarchies. Just as the period after 1789 is associated with 'revolutionary warfare', so the old regime is related to its own distinct form of 'limited war'. This reflects a general assumption in historical writing and in social and political science that military and political organization are directly interrelated and that armies display the characteristics of the societies they serve (Lynn, 1996).

Limited war is likewise defined in relation to earlier and later forms of conflict. It apparently lacked the popular involvement found in either the 'religious wars' of the 'confessional age' (1517–1648) or the ideological and national struggles of the revolutionary and Napoleonic era (1789–1815). Kings and their advisers allegedly decided war and peace without reference to broader interests, giving rise to the other label of 'cabinet wars'. Later analyses of these struggles have adopted the critical language associated with the term 'old regime', depicting war as the 'sport of kings' with little impact on civilians beyond the battlefield. Many accounts imply a lack of seriousness in these 'rococo' manoeuvres by small armies of disinterested mercenaries in their powdered wigs and lace coats (Mönch, 1999).

These military problems have been related to the wider deficiencies of old-regime monarchies, because both army and state are seen as co-evolving through three stages, determined ultimately by the underlying rise of capitalism (Schnitter and Schmidt, 1987; Best, 1982). In the initial foundation phase the establishment of a permanent 'standing army' coincided with the emergence of absolutism in the mid-seventeenth century. The following period of consolidation saw the further development of both the army and absolute monarchy without either losing their essentially mercenary and feudal characteristics. The aristocracy abandoned their opposition to absolutism and accepted integration in the crown's forces as the officer corps, displacing the commoners who had previously played a major role. The army then entered a period of decline towards the end of the eighteenth century, precisely when absolutism allegedly lost its 'progressive' qualities and fossilized into a reactionary front against further social and economic change. The growing class tensions that are often held to be the cause of the French Revolution were reflected in the army by clashes between nobles and commoner NCOs and men. Desertion and other forms of anti-military activity apparently increased, while tactical and organizational innovation largely stagnated. Military development was impossible without a broader structural transformation of state and society. The French Revolution supposedly unleashed these tensions and heralded a new era for war as well as for politics. The revolutionary armies defeated their old-regime opponents because they were inherently 'superior' as military organizations associated with historically progressive forces.

War and the state

Whilst recognizing the significance of changes in the mid-seventeenth and late eighteenth century, more recent interpretations question the standard models of the old regime and limited war. The political changes in the mid-seventeenth century can be more properly labelled a 'new regime' (te Brake, 1998). Regardless of its precise character, the state emerged as the primary guarantor for internal order and external defence. It claimed far wider powers than before, including the authority to define the 'true faith', as well as justice, social behaviour and the 'common good'. Virtually all government was monarchical, since even the Venetian, Genoese and Dutch republics contained royalist elements and traditions. Many monarchies moved towards absolutism between 1620 and 1660. This term remains controversial, not least because it post-dates the period it describes. Nonetheless it serves as a convenient description, provided it is understood as a style of rule rather than a coherent system (Wilson, 2000a).

The accumulation of power was still incomplete, but a qualitative shift had taken place in most countries during the civil and international strife of the sixteenth and seventeenth centuries. Medieval politics had been characterized by a multitude of local and provincial authorities wielding practical authority, and potent but less tangible universal ideals like Christendom, represented by the emperor and the papacy. Sovereignty was fragmented, shared between kings, aristocrats and corporate institutions that often owed allegiance to more than one lord. The sovereign state emerged as an intermediary level between the universal and the particular, defined by centralized authority exercising exclusive jurisdiction over a distinct territory and its inhabitants.

This process had been decided in a series of struggles between would-be sovereigns and entrenched local interests between around 1450 and 1650. Fighting was often fiercest where differences over religion sharpened divisions, particularly after the permanent schism in western and central Europe with the Reformation of 1517. Centralized monarchy often emerged triumphant, as in the Habsburg lands with the victory over the Austrian and Bohemian rebels by 1620, in France after the defeat of aristocratic and provincial opposition by 1654, and in the British kingdoms with the failure of Scottish and Irish attempts at greater autonomy. This outcome was not preordained, however, and sovereign states also emerged from below, as in the case of Switzerland and the Dutch republic, whose existence was formally acknowledged by their respective former Habsburg masters in 1648. Other states secured independence by defeating the imperial ambitions of their neighbours, like Portugal, which shook off eight decades of Spanish rule in 1667.

These struggles were largely over by the 1660s, by which time the existence of centralized authority was generally no longer contested from within. Disputes shifted to struggles to limit, control and exploit such authority. Absolutism's success derived from its ability to direct these tensions towards more peaceful forms of conflict resolution, through court intrigue, judicial arbitration and administrative reform. The revolution of 1789 and subsequent constitutional reforms did not demolish the state, but simply institutionalized such bargaining and extended participation to broader social groups.

International conflict

The emergence of sovereign states sharpened the distinction between internal and external wars. The state monopolized legitimate violence within its own frontiers, though it took until the nineteenth century before extraterritorial forms such as piracy and mercenary service were fully suppressed (Thomson, 1994). European disputes centred on struggles to define the territorial extent of the sovereign states and their status in the evolving international order. The monarchical character of European politics, deemed so necessary for domestic stability, contributed to international instability. Intermarriage and the vagaries of human reproduction amongst European royalty created a web of dynastic rights to different territories, triggering a series of wars of succession between 1655 and 1778 as competing families settled their conflicting claims. Some of Europe's largest states were threatened with dismemberment because of their character as dynastic unions of disparate lands. Both Habsburg monarchies faced serious challenges in the wars of the Spanish (1701–14) and Austrian (1740–48) successions. The former ended with Spain losing its other European possessions but retaining its overseas empire under a new, Bourbon, dynasty. The latter saw the Austrian Habsburgs retain their possessions, but only at the price of substantial concessions to Prussia. Whilst still a composite state, Britain escaped dismemberment because its succession was regulated internally after the initial Glorious Revolution displaced the Catholic Stuart monarchy in 1688. The deposed dynasty launched repeated attempts to recover its crowns until 1746, but failed because it lacked sufficient external support.

The redistribution of provinces at the conclusion of these struggles reflected the growing concern to preserve a balance between the major European powers. Though marking a move towards the sovereign states system, the peace of Westphalia (1648) did not bury older notions of universalism. It remained unclear whether European states would interact as equals, regardless of size or the status of their rulers, or be arranged in some kind of hierarchy. The relative revival of the Austrian Habsburg monarchy, which retained the title of Holy Roman Emperor, sustained the imperial ideal of Christian Europe united behind a single secular head against external threats from unbelievers like the Ottomans. France launched a direct challenge, as Louis XIV (r. 1643–1715) sought a new pole position as 'arbiter of Europe', a title implying pre-eminence over other rulers rather than their direct subjugation (Kampmann, 2001; Lesaffer, 2001; Luard, 1992).

Material considerations remained secondary to status as the means to sustain royal *gloire* and reputation. Rights and titles were hardly trivial. Political stability rested on dynastic legitimacy and the ruler's ability to maintain peace and promote collective welfare. Monarchs had to convince their peers to respect their rights, since status only assumed validity when recognized by others. Failure to uphold rights suggested that these had lapsed, opening the way for others to claim them. Personal vanity played its part, as did the concern to bequeath a glorious legacy to posterity. Yet kings rarely embarked on war lightly. Unjustified conflict would provoke the hostility of other monarchs and endanger the domestic peace upon which their own legitimacy rested. The desire to convince others of the validity of their cause, and to resolve disputes peacefully, encouraged the growth of diplomacy and the concept of international law (Wilson, 1998b).

These concerns were reflected in the conduct of operations. Practical constraints already imposed restrictions on old-regime warfare. Though Europe's population grew from 100 to 187 million between 1660 and 1800, much of the continent remained sparsely populated. Three out of four Europeans lived in the countryside and depended heavily on agriculture for their livelihood. Productivity remained low and often little above subsistence levels. Transport relied on horses, navigable rivers and canals. Movement away from population centres or river lines was difficult, particularly when it involved large numbers of men with equipment. The agrarian cycle and the availability of food and fodder restricted large operations primarily to the spring and summer, although this varied with location as, for example, heat and water-borne diseases inhibited summer operations in Spain and Hungary. Commercialized regions with large populations and good transportation, such as the Low Countries, experienced frequent fighting, although even here logistical arrangements often failed, curtailing operations. While remaining more restricted than later conflicts, old-regime operations were far from unsophisticated. Generals had to master a wide range of practical management skills to sustain and move their armies (Lund, 1999). Concern to preserve these forces encouraged additional caution. Manpower was limited and soldiers were difficult to replace. Heavy losses in one action could endanger other operations, and most generals preferred to frustrate their enemies by simply avoiding a decisive defeat.

While falling short of modern humanitarianism, Christian morality discouraged needless sacrifice of life. Scientific advances fostered a belief in rational efficiency, whereby the enemy could be out-manoeuvred without the need for a battle. Fortresses could surrender with honour once the wall had been breached. Prisoners would be exchanged or released on parole, rather than massacred or impressed into the victorious army. There were numerous exceptions to these norms, indicating that old-regime commanders were perfectly capable of acting forcefully when they believed it necessary. The primary purpose of war, however, remained the restoration of peace by compelling the other side to accept the validity of contested rights. The general reluctance to endanger social stability by embracing extreme measures weakened the ability of old-regime monarchies to resist the ruthless French revolutionary regime.

There were signs of change long before 1789, as rational material arguments assumed greater prominence in justifications for war, reflecting the secularization of European thought and the shift away from moral and theological arguments towards a more utilitarian morality. Earlier scientific thinking already encouraged mechanistic ideas of a European balance between major and minor powers, prompting greater consideration of their economic and military potential. Such ideas persisted, but were now supplemented by a new secular spiritualism, born in the Romantic reaction to Enlightenment rationalism from the 1770s, and emphasizing the potency of the national will that revolutionaries and governments claimed to articulate after 1789.

Tactics and organization

European armies displayed a number of common characteristics from the mid-seventeenth century that reflected practical and cultural constraints on military organization. Technological change remained evolutionary rather than revolutionary. Most soldiers were armed with a handgun, particularly after the introduction of the bayonet in the 1680s eliminated the use of pikes within twenty years. This change roughly coincided with the replacement of matchlock firearms by flintlocks, which improved the concealment of troops in nocturnal operations since their position was no longer betrayed by the burning matches needed to ignite the powder. Effective range remained less than 150 metres, however, and guns were still rendered inoperable by wet weather. As muzzle-loading, long-barrelled weapons, they were also difficult to load and fire in a prone position or from horseback. Cavalry still composed between a third and a fifth of western and central European armies, but good horses were as difficult to replace as men and were also required to pull artillery and supply wagons.

Human and equine biology imposed restrictions on both strategy and tactics. Movement to and on the battlefield was limited by physical endurance. Soldiers were generally men aged 25 to 35, with only 5 per cent of French personnel aged under 18 and 15 per cent over 35 in 1789 (Scott, 1978, pp. 7–8; Corvisier, 1964, pp. 624–6). Armies relying more heavily on conscripts tended to be proportionately older, because their personnel often served for life, whereas volunteers enlisted on limited contracts. More than half of Prussian privates were over 30 in the later eighteenth century, in contrast to a century later when this was the maximum age specified even for reservists (Fann, 1977; Hanne, 1986). Physical conditions remained roughly static throughout this period. Recruitment took men who could be spared from the labour-intensive economy, generally those without land or adequate work. In turn this economy provided limited nutrition, as population growth largely outstripped the rise in productivity before the 1730s. Meat consumption declined after the Middle Ages and puberty was delayed compared to the present. Stature was taken as a sign of physical fitness, along with good teeth, which were required to bite the end off the paper cartridges used from around 1700. Even so, around a fifth of soldiers were below the official minimum height, because of the difficulty of finding enough tall recruits (Komlos, 1989; Steegmann, 1985).

Tactical formations were intended to maximize the potential of the available weapons. Close-order deployment was stressed, particularly for the infantry, who formed long lines to utilize their firepower. Whereas ten ranks was still standard around 1620, six had become the norm by 1650. This was reduced to five between 1680 and 1700, falling to four with the widespread use of bayonets, and finally to the two or three that remained standard for fire tactics for the century-and-a-half after 1750. Such formations relied on the psychological effect of both the volume of fire and the shock of bayonet attacks to break the enemy's will to resist, rather than kill him outright. Since all firearms, including artillery, used black powder, visibility quickly became restricted once firing commenced. It was difficult for officers to direct fire and movement even in the open, and while well-trained troops could operate in woods and other broken terrain, this was usually avoided. Most countries used various specialist troops to occupy such terrain and harass enemy formations. Such units evolved from the detached companies of musketeers and dragoons of the early seventeenth century into the regular light infantry and riflemen of the late eighteenth century. Cavalry and artillery played important support- ing roles, but their effectiveness was limited by the need to neutralize enemy horse and cannon before they could turn on his foot. Eastern European armies made greater use of horsemen, because they fought in relatively open, under- populated areas.

Training reflected the need to maintain formation and deliver concentrated fire or shock. It focused on instilling the discipline required to overcome the nat- ural desire to run or remain motionless in the face of enemy fire. It also addressed the structural problems created by the permanence of armies from the mid-seventeenth century onwards. While armies were still reduced in peacetime, they remained far larger than before 1618, yet soldiers' pay was eroded by infla- tion and was often insufficient to support a family. Governments were forced to extend surveillance to counter desertion, to deal with the new phenomenon of garrison towns, and to regulate relations between soldiers and the other corporate groups of old-regime society.

Discipline also reflected wider moral and theological concerns for a divinely ordained social hierarchy, and the belief that the lower orders lacked the full capacity for rational thought and responded best to external stimulus and coercion. Rulers already imposed normative behaviour through the articles of war, or written regulations, that were issued with increasing frequency from the early sixteenth century. These changed during the seventeenth century, moving from threatening punishment and other external sanctions to encour- aging self-discipline by fostering new corporate identity and self-esteem amongst ordinary soldiers. The scientific belief in a mechanistic universe re- inforced the emphasis on order, precision and harmonious movement (Eichberg, 1977; McNeill, 1995). The equation of order with social status encour- aged leaders of irregular units to accept integration within the standing army and subordination to its norms (Rink, 1999).

The imposition of discipline was related to the establishment of more hier- archical command structures. The disciplined fire and movement tactics required close supervision of soldiers, who were grouped in units of standard- ized size to facilitate greater control and direction. A new intermediary level of battalion organization was interposed between the standard sixteenth-century infantry units of the regiment and the company. While the company remained the main administrative unit for both horse and foot, new tactical subdivisions were created, either by combining two cavalry companies as a squadron, or by splitting the infantry into 'divisions', further subdivided into platoons to facilitate fire control. The ratio of officers to men increased as supplementary ranks were created, while the average size of an infantry company or cavalry squadron dropped from between 300 and 500 around 1550 to 150 a century later. The company and regiment became permanent administrative institutions for the artillery by 1700, though tactical formation into batteries remained largely on an ad hoc basis. Higher organizations also remained tactical rather than administrative, with infantry and cavalry regiments being grouped, usually in pairs, into brigades under a general on the battlefield. No permanent organization existed between the brigade and the overall structure of a field army before the Napoleonic era, though later eighteenth-century theorists already envisaged combining brigades into divisions and these into corps.

Armies and the aristocracy

Recruitment and social composition was more varied than tactics or organization, because it was determined less by the relatively universal limitations of weaponry and human physique, than by each country's social, economic and cultural conditions. The expansion in army size and the hierarchy of ranks created new opportunities for Europe's nobility, but these were not universally welcomed. Military service was not only risky but expensive, especially as kings continued to expect officers to provide their own clothing and equipment until the later eighteenth century. Officers were also required to inject cash into the 'company economy', the financial administration of their unit, which included the cost of recruiting, clothing, equipping and feeding the soldiers. Managing a company or regiment became a permanent occupation with the development of standing armies, yet nobles often had other economic or political interests that demanded their time. Despite the martial basis of aristocratic privilege, soldiering remained socially suspect and morally ambiguous, tainted by its breach of the Christian commandment not to kill and widespread hostility during the sixteenth century to the military as an alien body within society. Social relations were still feudal, binding aristocrats to protect the interests of their tenants and serfs, upon whose goodwill and continued labour their wealth and privileges ultimately rested. War represented disruption and the intrusion of royal power into the localities. Most aristocrats opposed war, using their influence in parliaments and assemblies to restrict their monarch's ability to wage it by refusing to vote the necessary taxation.

The indigenous nobility remained important to the creation of all European standing armies, but commoners and other outsiders formed a significant proportion of the officers during the seventeenth century. This began to change, usually around the 1650s to 1670s, as native nobles became more prominent. While impoverished noblemen could still be found serving in the ranks, particularly in royal bodyguards or the heavy cavalry, the traditional idea of the knight largely disappeared in western and central Europe. Most accepted the commutation of knight service into regular taxation, except in eastern Europe where the aristocratic levy remained integral to the defence of political privilege and autonomy. Eastern aristocrats were also more numerous, forming up to 10 per cent of the population, or around five times the proportion in the west, where overall numbers declined by about a third through the extinction of many families and curbs on privileges. Nobles were gradually reconciled to the new political and military conditions under absolutism, but there was no wholesale compromise between crown and aristocracy. Monarchs promoted the careers of loyal families, including commoners, by expanding patronage through the baroque court, civil administration and officer corps. The army offered the largest sphere for patronage and became more attractive as changes to military regulations and law sharpened distinctions between officers and men by 1700.

European variations

France exemplifies these general trends as well as the existence of specific local characteristics. Superficially France conforms to the standard old-regime combination of a mercenary standing army officered by the aristocracy and used in limited wars of aggression to advance purely dynastic objectives (Kiernan, 1957). However recent research has revealed the difficulties faced by French kings in monopolizing violence and fashioning a reliable army.

France was a very large, populous and relatively compact country, but the ability of its monarchs to exploit its great wealth was restricted by their own dynastic weakness, manifest through frequent royal minorities, and the presence of entrenched provincial and corporate interests. France's experience also illustrates the generally ambiguous impact of early modern warfare. War not only created states, but threatened to destroy them. It gave kings the chance to use force against domestic as well as external opponents, but the associated escalating costs threatened domestic stability and undermined royal legitimacy. The Bourbon dynasty's recovery after the internal Wars of Religion (1562–98) was interrupted by another royal minority in 1610–14. Though opposition from the Huguenot minority was crushed by 1629, royal power still rested on shaky foundations. Prolonged conflict after 1635 compelled a partial decentralization, as the crown resorted to expedients to sustain the war against Spain (Parrott, 2001). Aristocratic and provincial discontent resurfaced in another civil war in 1648–54, during Louis XIV's minority.

The crown emerged victorious because there was now little alternative to a single royal monopoly of violence. Following the suppression of each revolt after 1595, French kings destroyed the strongholds of the defeated rebels. If inflation and escalating war costs hit the crown, they affected others more severely. Nobles and municipalities could not compete with the monarchy in mobilizing the resources now required for major war. Meanwhile the crown manipulated patronage to neutralize its most dangerous domestic opponents, whilst reworking aristocratic honour into a code of loyal service to a glorious king (Rowlands, 2001, 2002). The grandees lost their status as autonomous military commanders, as French forces became dependent on a logistical infrastructure created and controlled by the crown, and supported by regular taxation. A sign of the crown's success is the rapid growth in the size of the permanent army, despite a relatively static population after 1600. Whereas no more than 20,000 men had been maintained in peacetime before 1635, Louis XIV had at least 50,000 after 1661, equivalent to the maximum war strength of the previous century. Numbers swelled to around 270,000 men during the Dutch War (1672–79) – representing the largest army in Europe since the Roman Empire – rising to 340,000 during the Nine Years War (1688–97) and probably only slightly less during the War of the Spanish Succession. Peacetime strength averaged about 150,000 until 1789, or more than the wartime peak between 1635 and 1659. Considering that these figures exclude naval personnel and militia, they represent a significant mobilization in a still agrarian country.

Nonetheless French organization remained incomplete. The king had asserted his authority over the high command, but regiments retained their autonomy, and it was not until 1763 that recruitment became a royal monopoly and soldiers swore loyalty directly to their king. Officers still enjoyed wide prerogatives, with those in the later eighteenth century entitled to seven-and-a-half months paid leave every two years. The proportion of non-noble officers had already dropped to 10 per cent by 1750, and they disappeared almost completely by 1789. Despite this there were never enough posts to go round, and many nobles had no prospect of military rank. Restrictions on commoners were a response to demands from poorer provincial aristocrats to secure appointment. Disillusionment with royal favouritism heightened tensions amongst French officers, fatally weakening the army before the revolution.

Analysis of the rank and file also challenges assumptions about old-regime armies. Foreigners comprised between 10 and 33 per cent of French soldiers during the Thirty Years War, already representing a decline on the proportion during the previous century. This figure fell to 15 per cent after 1659, and though rising briefly during the Dutch War never again moved significantly above a fifth. Most numerous among them were Swiss infantry, followed by Germans and Irish. The incorporation of Alsace (1648) and Lorraine (1766) made many of these foreigners into French subjects (Lynn, 1997, pp. 328–32; Scott, 1978, pp. 12–14). Most Frenchmen joined as volunteers, serving for a bounty and regular pay (Corvisier, 1964, pp. 167–89, 281–341). Nevertheless

France made growing use of coercion as its rising demands for manpower after 1672 coincided with an economic downturn, worsening agrarian conditions, and a static population. A militia was established in 1688, drawing on earlier systems and the king's powers to summon his subjects in wartime. Every parish had to provide recruits, initially by election, but from 1691 this was replaced by a lottery, which was extended to married men in 1703. The militia was intended to defend France while the regular forces campaigned elsewhere, but shortage of troops compelled the deployment of 100,000 militiamen in offensive operations during the War of the Spanish Succession. Another 145,520 were mobilized during the War of the Austrian Succession, though the number serving at any one time was rarely above 30,000. The system was reorganized in 1778, effectively recognizing its role as a recruitment pool for the field army by attaching the former militia units as depot battalions to the line infantry. The relatively static size of the regular establishment after 1714 reduced the burden on the French population, which rose by at least six million across the century, creating a new potential that was ruthlessly tapped by new forms of more universal conscription after 1793.

Though involving a considerable degree of coercion, the French experience illustrates the capital-intensive route to a monopoly of violence, whereby a country mobilized men and materials by paying for them (Tilly, 1992). In addition to its own forces, maintained by royal taxation, France subsidized the war efforts of its allies, and also hired large numbers of foreign auxiliaries in all its wars between 1635 and 1783.

Despite France's status as Europe's pre-eminent military power in this period, Britain represents a more successful variant on capital-intensive war-making. Britain deployed an average of 76,400 men during the Nine Years War, increasing this to 92,700 in the following conflict over the Spanish succession. The peacetime establishment of 35,000 rose to 45,000 in mid-century, and well over 100,000 were deployed worldwide during the American War of Independence (1775–83). However no more than two-thirds of the wartime totals were British, since the rest were hired auxiliaries, usually Germans. Subsidies to allies and auxiliaries totalled £24.5 million between 1702 and 1762, or around a quarter of Britain's total military spending. Though the Militia Act of 1757 created a reserve force of about 30,000, there was little need for direct coercion to fill the ranks except in years of crisis. Britain's population roughly doubled between 1688 and 1801, while its economy expanded even more rapidly. New forms of production permitted the release of large numbers of men when required. Around half a million Britons served during the American War of Independence, or about one in eight males of military age (Conway, 1995, pp. 37–8).

Domestic political stability contributed to British power. John Brewer has argued that consensual government and fiscal accountability through

parliament created a potent fiscal–military state after 1688, enabling governments to finance war through long-term low-interest loans secured on rising
tax revenues tapping goods in flow (Brewer, 1989). Nevertheless Britain's
undoubted successes should not obscure serious problems. Given the absence of
firm party organization, parliament often proved unreliable as administrations
lost the support of MPs, while taxation continued to stir popular opposition
(Black, 1999). The transition from a relatively small peacetime establishment
often proved difficult, delaying Britain's effective entry into continental struggles like the Seven Years War (1756–63). Britain's land forces were scattered in
small provincial and colonial garrisons, spending much of their time on anti-
smuggling duties and other police activities to the detriment of training
(Houlding, 1981).

More fundamentally, the basis of British military power disproves the traditional Whig association of representative government and low taxation
(Hoffman and Norberg, 1994). The failures of both the royalist and parliamentar-
ian forces during the civil wars after 1637 exposed the deficiencies of the
country's neo-medieval military organization, forcing its remodelling on centralized professional lines (Gentiles, 1992; Wheeler, 1999). These reforms were
continued by the restored monarchy after 1660, creating a relatively efficient
fiscal and military administration, and channelling more of the country's
resources into war. Whereas the army and navy consumed only a quarter of
total government spending before 1640, they accounted for around twice that
after 1660 in times of peace and nearly three times during war.

The Dutch republic also followed the capital-intensive route,, having created
a powerful fiscal–military infrastructure during the independence struggle
against Spain (1568–1648). It managed to field around 100,000 men each year
in the wars against Louis XIV, but around a third of these were hired auxiliaries. The republic continued to rely heavily on foreign troops in wartime
until its collapse in 1795, but the heavy cost of maintaining its fortified southern
frontier encouraged a defensive strategy, and the army became primarily a
garrison force (Ten Raa, 1911–59; t'Hart, 1993).

Spain also adopted a defensive strategy from the 1630s, even if it did not
decline to the extent perceived by earlier historians. It relied heavily on its other
European possessions for recruits, notably the southern Netherlands, Milan and
Naples. Loss of these lands during the War of the Spanish Succession represented a serious blow, particularly as it coincided with civil war in Spain itself.
The new Bourbon dynasty reorganized its forces along the lines of its French
ally. Regiments and battalions replaced *tercios* as the principal administrative and tactical units after 1706. The country's existing militia was used as
the basis of a new form of conscription after 1704. Though the militia
remained a distinct organization alongside the regular regiments, it now
provided around half the army's recruits. Retrenchment and the burden of

colonial defence kept the army underfunded and under strength throughout the rest of the eighteenth century, and it had to rely on impressment to mobilize in wartime.

The Italian states generally followed this mixture of coercion and capital, particularly Naples, which formed its army with direct Spanish help after 1735. Savoy exploited its strategic position to draw in foreign subsidies, which provided around a fifth of its revenue under Victor Amadeus II (r. 1675–1730), rising to 40 per cent in the crisis year of 1706, when Britain and the Dutch republic paid it to resist France. The standing army grew from a few thousand to over 26,000 by 1704. This level was sustained throughout the eighteenth century, in contrast to the other independent Italian states, which generally reduced their forces. However around a third were recruited in Switzerland and southern Germany, while after 1690 many of the rest came from a limited form of conscription that was based, like that in Spain, on an existing militia organization.

Such systems featured prominently in the more coercion-intensive resource mobilization favoured by the less commercialized, under-populated Scandinavian countries, as well as central and eastern European states. Sweden had followed the capital-intensive route prior to 1680, financing war by extensive borrowing. This produced a vicious circle as the country embarked on new wars to capture the resources needed to repay its existing loans, and Gustavus Adolphus (r. 1611–32) only maintained the offensive momentum by introducing limited conscription. Charles XI (r. 1660–97) changed tack, tying military expenditure to fixed sources of revenue, such as the crown lands expanded by confiscating estates from his nobles. Conscription was replaced by the *Indelningsverket* system after 1681, allocating land to around half the army. Soldiers were given individual farms to support themselves until called up. The remaining 30,000 men were recruited from volunteers, mainly in Sweden's Baltic provinces, and maintained from central taxation. This system proved inadequate when Charles's successor plunged the country into the protracted struggle of the Great Northern War (1700–21). Defeats deprived Sweden of its outlying provinces at a time when harvest failure and plague reduced its manpower, compelling renewed conscription from 1709. Total losses of around half a million men between 1620 and 1719 fell heavily on a country with fewer than two million inhabitants, and represented the death of about a third of all adult males, or about three times the casualty rate suffered by Spain over the same period (Lindegren, 2000, pp. 138–41).

Protests from the aristocracy forced the reintroduction of the *Indelningsverket* in 1719 and it lasted until 1901. The army liked the system because it gave units a provincial *esprit de corps* and paid salaries in kind at a time of high inflation and coinage devaluation. It was extended to include the cavalry, leaving the guards and the artillery as the only fully professional soldiers.

Training was reduced to three weeks a year, while the army aged, as younger men could only be recruited when farms became vacant. The desire to balance the budget reinforced Sweden's defensive orientation. The Swedish parliament, the *riksdag*, objected to wars of aggression, refusing credit during the Seven Years War and forcing the government to finance its already limited involvement by a series of expedients that fuelled inflation lasting into the nineteenth century.

Denmark followed a similar path. Christian IV (r. 1588–1648) intervened in the Thirty Years War with an army of 25,000 mercenaries, paid from his personal treasury accumulated from tolls imposed on Baltic shipping. Even these riches rapidly proved insufficient, contributing to Denmark's series of crushing defeats by 1645. Denmark remained heavily reliant on mercenaries, mainly recruited in northern Germany, but introduced a new system of 'cavalry lands', whereby peasant taxes were replaced by the obligation to support soldiers quartered on their farms. Like Sweden, the Danish monarchy also sought to reverse the alienation of crown lands and to tie military expenditure to specific revenues. Further defeat in 1699–1700 accelerated the trend to greater coercion. A new militia (*vaern*) of 15,500 men was created in February 1701, ostensibly because the regular army of 20,000 was now serving outside the country as auxiliaries during the War of the Spanish Succession. Militiamen were drafted to sustain the regular army following renewed defeats after 1710. The system was widely resented because, unlike that in Prussia, it directly reinforced the imposition of serfdom on free Danish peasants (Holmgaard, 1999), but attempts to reform it were defeated by aristocratic landowners in 1771–72.

The larger German principalities in the Holy Roman Empire established their own regular armies during the 1650s, but continued to rely on traditional militias as cheaper supplementary forces, despite often poor performance during the Thirty Years War. All experienced difficulties during the Dutch War, despite the significant injection of subsidies from foreign powers keen to hire German auxiliaries. Operations became a scramble for billets, as these *Armierten* (armed princes) seized food and money from their unarmed neighbours. Emperor Leopold (r. 1658–1705) accepted this continuation of the earlier contributions system to ensure that the princes still contributed to Imperial defence against French incursions (Wilson, 1998a). Constitutional reforms stabilized collective defence in 1681–82, obliging even the unarmed territories to contribute small contingents in return for preservation of their political autonomy. Mobilization was coordinated by the *Kreise* (Imperial circles), the Empire's regional subdivisions, where the smaller territories had greater influence, reinforcing the primarily defensive character of the arrangements. The more powerful armed princes accepted integration within this system, since it helped to break opposition from their own territorial estates, or assemblies, to the military taxation which became an unavoidable duty of all inhabitants of the Empire. They were also permitted to field their troops separately, and to hire out additional forces to foreign powers prepared to back their involvement in European politics.

Even with the additional subsidies, few rulers could maintain the numbers of men their dynastic ambitions required. While the larger territories all expanded their armies after 1679, they also introduced limited forms of conscription by adapting their militia structures, whilst granting a third or more of the regular soldiers extended leave in peacetime. Prussian militarization after 1713 essentially adapted this mixed system to local requirements, to sustain a disproportionately large army without destabilizing the country's agrarian base. Prussia exploited its growing political weight within the Empire to extend its search for additional volunteers into other German lands. These provided the majority of the so-called 'foreigners' who constituted around a third of Prussian soldiers alongside the native conscripts (Wilson, 2000b, 2002).

The different experience of the Austrian Habsburg monarchy reflected its established position as the leading central European military power. The monarchy already maintained a small permanent army by the 1590s, supplemented by garrison troops and a frontier militia to resist Ottoman attacks. Larger field forces were raised by calling on the German princes as the emperor's vassals when necessary. Political opposition during the Thirty Years War forced the emperor to rely on expedients, notably Wallenstein's army, funded by confiscating land from his German opponents. Despite the reverses in Germany, the Habsburgs retained their immense hereditary lands, together with the Imperial title, in 1648. These lands sustained an army that remained larger than that of any other German entity, including Prussia, for the next 150 years. Imperial prerogatives enabled the Habsburgs to call on additional assistance during major wars, such as those against Louis XIV or the Ottomans. A string of victories doubled the size of the monarchy by 1718, making it a European power in its own right, but growing disillusionment with Habsburg Imperial rule, compounded by international defeats during 1733–39, lessened German support for the dynasty just as rivalry with Prussia erupted into open warfare after 1740. As the monarchy was thrown back on its own resources, existing forms of mobilization proved inadequate, prompting major internal reforms after 1744, including the introduction of Prussian-style conscription after 1771 (Wilson, 2004).

At first sight Russia appears the most extreme example of the coercive route. Yet its export-oriented agrarian system brought a substantial influx of bullion into the country during the seventeenth century, while administrative growth enabled central government to tap the resources of a population that more than doubled between 1600 and 1719. Discussions of Russian military development are dominated by the controversy surrounding the relative influence of western technology and ideas (Ralston, 1990, pp. 13–42; Duffy, 1981). However, like that of the Ottoman Empire, Russia's experience indicates that foreign methods were rarely superior unless tailored to local conditions, and that change was generally a process of gradual adaptation rather than sudden reform.

Russia developed a characteristically eastern European army between 1460 and 1600, combining a predominantly cavalry force with units of musketeers (*strel'tsy*). Like the Ottomans and Habsburgs, it protected its long frontiers with fortified lines, notably those of Belgorod, built in 1636–53, that stretched for 800 miles. It also introduced regular 'new formation regiments' (*polki novogo stroia*) in 1632–34. Though the initial units were disbanded, they were replaced after 1645 by new formations of Russians trained by 200 foreign instructors to use the disciplined tactics of fire and movement. From around a third of Russia's field army in 1632–34, the proportion of new-formation troops doubled during the next war of 1654–67. Peacetime retrenchment reduced their overall numbers only temporarily, and another 78,000 were fielded in the campaigns against the Tatars between 1687 and 1696, while traditional gentry cavalry and *strel'sty* accounted for only 17 per cent of field strength (Kagan and Higham, 2002, pp. 34–5).

Peter the Great (r. 1689–1725) thus inherited an army that already contained substantial western elements. The significance of his reforms is five-fold. First, he adopted a new, more offensive strategy, seeking not merely to neutralize previous external threats from the Tatars and Ottomans, but to conquer new land. Second, these conquests secured ports on the Black Sea and, later, on the Baltic, enabling Russia to develop naval power. Third, he created two guards regiments as an elite force of around 7000 men, which his successors supplemented with another infantry regiment and cavalry units. Intended as the solid core of the regular army, the guards had already played an important political role in 1689 when they helped Peter overthrow Regent Sophia. Like the Janissaries, the guards remained a key element in Russian domestic politics, including assisting in the overthrow and murder of Peter III in 1762. Fourth, regular drill and standardized training were extended to other units, effectively converting the entire army into new-formation troops. Finally, while foreigners remained important, Russians were compelled to accept discipline and subordination. Here Russia followed a similar pattern to most other European monarchies, albeit at an accelerated pace. The gentry were compelled to serve as officers or officials after 1714, but once state institutions were firmly established these obligations were relaxed after 1762.

Coercion proved more lasting for ordinary Russians. Conscription was introduced in December 1699, taking serfs for life service with the assistance of their landlords. The draft was used extensively as Peter sought to establish Russia as a European power. There were 59 call-ups during his reign, compared to 94 over the next hundred years. No less than 337,196 men were conscripted in the crisis years of 1705–13, followed by another 700,000 in 1724–59 (Hellie, 1990, p. 94; Kagan and Higham, 2002, p. 55). This sustained the regular army, which remained supplemented by various militias and auxiliaries that were only slowly integrated within a uniform military system.

The Petrine system proved victorious on the battlefield, but strategically inflexible. Having fought his way to European status, Peter bequeathed an empire that could barely sustain its new role. Field Marshal Count Münnich (1683–1767) addressed the problem of underfunding by trying to Germanize the army after 1730, reducing the peacetime establishment to 123,500 and placing a greater emphasis on drill and firepower. While many of these reforms were necessary, they became mired in political opposition to externally-inspired change. Empress Elizabeth Petrovna (r. 1741–62) reintroduced Petrine organization and regulations, but it became obvious that the old system was defective. Reforms continued, provided advocates of change distanced themselves sufficiently from foreign associations. A rough balance was achieved between Petrine ideas and western methods under Catherine the Great (r. 1762–96), contributing to spectacular Russian victories in 1768–74 and 1787–91.

Poland failed to make a comparable transition to the new model armies of the later seventeenth century. Like Russia and the Habsburg monarchy, it faced both western and eastern opponents, compelling it to develop methods capable of defeating both. This task was achieved during the sixteenth and early seventeenth century with a combination of an eastern cavalry army and western-style disciplined infantry. Indeed it was the need to combat the Poles which prompted the introduction of new-formation troops in Russia. However Poland failed to match Russia or the Habsburgs in infrastructural development, because centralization conflicted with the entrenched liberties of its aristocracy. The Hungarians held similar views but were defeated by the Habsburgs by 1711, and whilst they retained considerable political autonomy they accepted integration within the Habsburg regular army. The Poles refused, defending their right to provide their own forces to assist the weak royal army in times of invasion. While their retention of body armour and edged weapons gave their forces a neo-medieval appearance, the real failing was the lack of cohesion and experience of regular troops. Reluctance to sacrifice traditional liberties or to relax serfdom frustrated all reform, particularly as foreign interference in Polish politics grew during the eighteenth century.

War and military innovation

The varied experience across Europe indicates the uneven nature of military development and the ambiguous relationship between war and wider change. The Thirty Years War interrupted earlier trends towards the accumulation of military power in many monarchies, but by indicating the limitations of existing arrangements it also forced the pace of change, particularly as the scale and duration of the conflict forced rulers to abandon traditional forms of negotiation with their subjects and to resort to more authoritarian expedients. These new forms of rule coalesced as absolutism around the mid-seventeenth century, as monarchs refused to accept customary constitutional constraints on their authority. In the larger, better-established French, Spanish and Austrian monarchies this was accompanied by the consolidation and expansion of existing permanent forces. Elsewhere it created 'armies that were left standing' by the peace (Burkhardt, 1992, pp. 213–24). Other states, particularly the smaller German and Italian principalities, founded their own new model armies in response to renewed warfare after the 1650s.

All these forces were characterized by hierarchical control exercised by a central government, though the extent to which this power penetrated to the lower echelons of military organization varied widely. Personnel were subject to greater discipline, as their behaviour was governed by written regulations intended to harmonize relations with civilians and to improve combat effectiveness. While overall numbers fluctuated, these forces remained permanent and were funded, in part at least, by equally permanent taxation.

Variations were dictated by the natural environment, as well as by social, economic and political structures. The circumstances of the formative years exercised a lasting impact, conditioning characteristics that became institutionalized and difficult to change, particularly if proven successful in battle. All armies experienced minor modifications in line with experience and external influences, but fundamental change only followed major reverses, such as those experienced by Austria in 1740 or France in 1757. Emulation of other successful powers was often superficial, as evidenced by the widespread adoption of Prussian-style uniforms in the later eighteenth century, while the fashion for Janissary dress for army bandsmen between 1690 and 1750 indicates that even defeated foes could provide inspiration for change. New ideas were never employed successfully without substantial modification, and what worked against one enemy did not guarantee success against another.

Continued development in the later eighteenth century is obscured by the absence of major wars between 1763 and 1792. Discussion of reforms had little practical effect in some countries, Prussia as well as Poland. Nonetheless the experience of both the Seven Years War and colonial conflicts stimulated new thinking on tactics and organization, which contributed to developments during the French Revolutionary and Napoleonic Wars. Military institutions also changed. In one sense they became more uniform, as most adopted similar characteristics by 1750. While tactical manuals continued to be revised, fewer administrative regulations were issued after the 1720s, as the basic systems were now in place. Time also fostered a new outlook, as officers assumed a corporate identity less associated with their social status as noblemen. The more professional outlook was reflected in the growing dissemination of military theory and practice through publications and academies. Such changes reflected wider cultural shifts, as the reaction against enlightened rationalism encouraged new ways of thinking (Kleinschmidt, 1999). The armies that faced revolutionary France were far from being institutions in decline. While unable to defeat France, they nonetheless proved a resilient basis on which to build the forces that overcame Napoleon.

References

Best, G. 1982. *War and Society in Revolutionary Europe, 1770–1870*, Leicester.

Black, J.M. 1999. *Britain as a Military Power 1688–1815*, London.

Brewer, J. 1989. *The Sinews of Power. War, Money and the English State 1688–1783*, New York.

Burkhardt, J. 1992. *Der Dreißigjährige Krieg*, Frankfurt am Main.

Conway, S. 1995. *The War of American Independence, 1775–1783*, London.

Corvisier, A. 1964. *L'armee française de la fin du xviie siècle au ministère de Choiseul: le soldat*, Paris.

Duffy, C. 1981. *Russia's Military Way to the West. Origins and Nature of Russian Military Power 1700–1800*, London.

Eichberg, E. 1977. 'Geometrie als barocke Verhaltensnorm. Fortifikation und Exerzitien', *Zeitschrift für historische Forschung*, 4, 17–50.

Fann, W. 1977. 'On the Infantryman's Age in Eighteenth-Century Prussia', *Military Affairs*, 41, 165–70.

Gentiles, I. 1992. *The New Model Army in England, Ireland and Scotland, 1645–1653*, Oxford.

Hanne, W., ed. 1986. *Rangirrolle, Listen und Extracte ... von Saldern Infanterie Regiment Anno 1771*, Osnabrück.

Hellie, R. 1990. 'Warfare, Changing Military Technology and the Evolution of Muscovite Society', in *The Tools of War*, ed. J.A. Lynn, Urbana, 74–99.

Hoffman, P.T. and Norberg, K., eds. 1994. *Fiscal Crises, Liberty and Representative Government*, Stanford.

Holmgaard, J. 1999. . . . *uden at landet besvaeres. Studier over Fredrik 4.s Landmilits med saerligt henblik på sorgsmålet om stavnsbånd og bonderkarlenes vilkår I ourigt*, Norrejylland.

Houlding, J.A. 1981. *Fit for Service: The Training of the British Army, 1715–1795*, Oxford.

Kagan, F.W. and Higham, R., eds. 2002. *The Military History of Tsarist Russia*, Basingstoke.

Kampmann, C. 2001. *Arbiter und Friedensstiftung. Die Ausseinandersetzung um den politischen Schiedsrichter im Europa der frühen Neuzeit*, Paderborn.

Kiernan, V.G. 1957. 'Foreign Mercenaries and Absolute Monarchy', *Past and Present*, 11, 66–86.

Kleinschmidt, H. 1999. 'Mechanismus und Biologismus im Militärwesen des 17. und 18. Jahrhunderts', *Aufklärung*, 11, 51–73.

Komlos, J. 1989. *Nutrition and Economic Development in the Eighteenth-Century Habsburg Monarchy*, Princeton.

Lesaffer, R. 2001. 'War, Peace and Interstate Friendship and the Emergence of the Ius Publicum Europaeum', in *Frieden und Krieg in der frühen Neuzeit*, ed. R.G. Asch and others, Munich, 87–113.

Lindegren, J. 2000. 'Men, Money and Means', in *War and Competition between States*, ed. P. Contamine, Oxford, 129–62.

Luard, E. 1992. *The Balance of Power. The System of International Relations, 1648–1815,* Basingstoke.

Lund, E.A. 1999. *War for the Every Day. Generals, Knowledge and Warfare in Early Modern Europe, 1680–1740,* Westport.

Lynn, J.A. 1997. *Giant of the Grand Siècle. The French Army 1610–1715,* Cambridge.

—— **1996.** 'The Evolution of Army Style in the Modern West, 800–2000', *International History Review,* 18, 505–45.

McNeill, W.H. 1995. *Keeping Together in Time. Dance and Drill in Human History,* Cambridge.

Mönch, W. 1999. ' "Rokokostrategen". Ihr negativer Nachruhm in der Militärgeschichtsschreibung des 20. Jahrhunderts', *Aufklärung,* 11, 75–97.

Parrott, D. 2001. *Richelieu's Army. War, Government and Society in France, 1624–1642,* Cambridge.

Ralston, D.B. 1990. *Importing the European Army. The Introduction of European Military Techniques and Institutions in the Extra-European World, 1600–1914,* Chicago.

Rink, M. 1999. *Vom 'Partheygänger' zum Partisan. Die Konzeption des kleinen Krieges in Preußen 1740–1813,* Fankfurt am Main.

Rowlands, G. 2002. *The Dynastic State and the Army under Louis XIV. Royal Service and Private Interest, 1661–1701,* Cambridge.

—— **2001.** 'The Monopolisation of Military Power in France, 1515 to 1715', in *Frieden und Krieg in der frühen Neuzeit,* ed. R.G. Asch and others, Munich, 139–60.

Schnitter, H. and Schmidt, T. 1987. *Absolutismus und Heer. Zur Entwicklung des Militärwesens im Spätfeudalismus,* Berlin.

Scott, S.F. 1978. *The Response of the Royal Army to the French Revolution. The Role and Development of the Line Army 1787–93,* Oxford.

Steegmann, A.T. Jr. 1985. '18th Century British Military Stature', *Human Biology,* 57, 77–95.

te Brake, W. 1998. *Shaping History. Ordinary People in European Politics 1500–1700,* Berkeley.

Ten Raa, F.G.J. and others. 1911–59. *Het staatsche Leger 1568–1795,* The Hague.

t'Hart, M.C. 1993. *The Making of a Bourgeois State. War, Politics and Finance during the Dutch Revolt,* Manchester.

Thomson, J.E. 1994. *Mercenaries, Pirates and Sovereigns. State-Building and Extra-Territorial Violence in Early Modern Europe,* Princeton.

Tilly, C. 1992. *Coercion, Capital and European States AD 990–1992,* Oxford.

Wheeler, J.S. 1999. *The Making of a World Power. War and the Military Revolution in Seventeenth-Century England,* Stroud.

Wilson, P.H. 2004. *From Reich to Revolution. German History 1558–1806,* Basingstoke.

—— **2002.** 'The Politics of Military Recruitment in Eighteenth-Century Germany', *English Historical Review,* 117, 536–68.

—— **2000a.** *Absolutism in Central Europe,* London.

—— **2000b.** 'Social Militarisation in Eighteenth-Century Germany', *German History,* 18, 1–39.

—— **1998a.** *German Armies: War and German Politics, 1648–1806,* London.

—— **1998b.** 'War in German Thought from the Peace of Westphalia to Napoleon', *European History Quarterly,* 28, 5–50.

9

The Sixty Years War in North America, 1754–1815

Francis D. Cogliano

Introduction

Early in the morning of 28 May 1754 a contingent of more than 40 Virginia militiamen, guided by Iroquois warriors, surprised a party of 35 French soldiers camped in a wooded glen in south-western Pennsylvania. A skirmish ensued in which the French were overpowered and asked for quarter. The French commander, a 35-year-old ensign named Joseph Coulon de Villiers de Jumonville, was wounded in the fighting. Jumonville explained through an interpreter that he had come as an emissary of Louis XV with a message enjoining the British to withdraw from the Ohio River valley. Jumonville claimed that he had a letter explaining his mission and he asked his translator to read it. During the translation Tanaghrisson, the chief of the Iroquois party, suddenly attacked the French officer, splitting Jumonville's skull with a hatchet. The Iroquois then washed his hands with Jumonville's brains. Tanaghrisson's warriors set upon the other wounded French soldiers, killing and scalping them. Within minutes all but one of the wounded prisoners were killed. The Virginians, under the direction of George Washington, a 22-year-old militia lieutenant-colonel who had experienced combat for the first time minutes earlier, struggled to protect the remaining French prisoners – around 21 in number – from the Iroquois. The Virginians returned to their camp at Great Meadows, Pennsylvania, to await a French response to the killing of Jumonville and his men. They hastily built a palisade which they dubbed Fort Necessity. A large party of French and Canadians attacked the fort on 3 July. On 4 July Washington surrendered and signed a capitulation, written in French, under the terms of which he admitted responsibility for the murder of Jumonville. The Virginians returned home in humiliation (Anderson, 2000, pp. 5–7, 42–65).

The small, bloody incident which led to the death of Jumonville and his men had wide repercussions. The skirmish initiated a war in North America between the British, the French, their colonists and the Native Americans. That war, known in British North America as the French and Indian War, became the North American theatre of the Seven Years War. How did the paths of an aristocratic French army officer, a Seneca chief and young Virginia militia officer come together to ignite a conflict which would engulf much of Europe and North America, as well as the West Indies and parts of Asia and Africa?

During the seventeenth and eighteenth centuries several different types of warfare prevailed within the extra-European colonies and possessions claimed by the European imperial powers. These included conflicts between indigenous peoples and the invading European colonizers. Examples of such conflicts are King Philip's War in New England in 1675–76, the Pueblo uprising of 1680 which drove the Spanish from New Mexico, and the Yamasee War in 1715 which pitted colonists in North and South Carolina against the Cherokees. A second type of warfare which was common was conflict between the European powers. Sometimes, as in the case of the Seven Years War, conflict actually began in the colonies. More commonly colonial warfare involving colonists, indigenous peoples and Europeans stemmed from European conflicts such as the War of the Spanish Succession (1701–14) and the War of the Austrian Succession (1740–48). The final type of colonial war was armed struggle for independence by colonists against their European rulers. The best example of this type of warfare is the American War of Independence (1775–83).

Although these three types of warfare – between native peoples and colonists, among imperial powers, and between colonists and their rulers – can be identified throughout the early modern period and throughout the parts of the world colonized by Europeans during the age of sail, these categories should not be viewed as rigid and distinctive. On the contrary they often overlapped. The death of Jumonville reveals the complexity of colonial warfare. Jumonville's mission had been to warn British colonists against settling the Ohio River valley and to assert the French claim to the region. George Washington and his men had been despatched to the region to protect the interests of Virginians who had invested in Ohio lands. Tanaghrisson and his Seneca warriors from the Iroquois confederacy entered the fray not so much as allies of the Virginians but to extend and consolidate Iroquois control over the Native Americans of the Ohio Valley, which was threatened by the French. The confluence of these different and competing interests brought Jumonville, Washington and Tanaghrisson together in a Pennsylvania glen and ignited the largest war of the eighteenth century.

The purpose of this chapter is to examine early modern colonial warfare through a detailed consideration of the military history of mainland

North America between 1754 and 1815. Between Jumonville's death in 1754 and the battle of New Orleans in 1815 eastern North America witnessed almost continuous warfare among the various groups – European, colonial and Native American – who sought control over the continent. Historians have normally viewed these conflicts – especially the Seven Years War, the American War of Independence, the War of 1812 and the numerous conflicts between Europeans (and Euro-American colonists) and Native Americans – as distinctive and successive events. This chapter argues that they should be seen as aspects of a broader conflict, a six-decade struggle for domination over eastern North America. The incessant fighting which characterized eastern North America from 1754 until 1815 is best understood as a single prolonged struggle among Native Americans, Europeans and colonists for control of the vast territory bounded by the Atlantic Ocean in the east, the Mississippi River in the west, Hudson Bay in the north and the Gulf of Mexico to the south. Victory in the Sixty Years War would be shared between the British and the Americans. The losers were the Spanish, the French and especially the Native Americans.

The Seven Years War

From the mid-sixteenth to the mid-eighteenth centuries Spanish, French and English (later British), as well as Dutch and Swedish imperialists and colonists, vied with each other and Native Americans for control over eastern North America (Taylor, 2001, chs 3–9; Steele, 1994, chs 1–6). Prior to 1700 the predominant type of colonial warfare consisted of armed conflicts between incoming European colonists and indigenous Native Americans. Often Native Americans were initially receptive and accommodating to the incoming Europeans, particularly as they valued European manufactured goods. However when it became apparent that the Europeans intended to settle and ultimately to displace the indigenous peoples, armed conflict often then occurred. During the first generation of settlement the Native Americans had a military advantage in terms of numbers whilst the Europeans benefited from superior technology, particularly access to firearms. Perhaps of greater significance than guns was the Europeans' biological advantage, as they carried common diseases such as influenza and smallpox against which Native Americans had little or no immunity. These decimated Native American populations, making armed resistance more difficult while diminishing the numerical advantage enjoyed by Native Americans (Crosby, 1976; Fenn, 2001).

A clear pattern of European–Native American relations emerged by the late seventeenth century. Initial cooperation gave way to violent conflict as the incomers increased and encroached on ever-increasing amounts of native land. The Europeans, benefiting from superior technology and assisted by the effects of imported diseases on native populations, usually prevailed in these conflicts and used native resistance to justify the violent displacement of native peoples. To be sure, differences among the numerous native peoples and European colonists, as well as particular circumstances such as geography and demography, meant that many local variations to this pattern occurred. Nonetheless by 1700 there was a substantial European colonial presence in eastern North America. The most populous colonies were those of the English, which ranged down the Atlantic coast from New England to South Carolina. The French presence was smaller in terms of population but more ambitious geographically, stretching from the Saint Lawrence valley to New Orleans in a vast arc which followed the internal waterways of North America – the Great Lakes and the Ohio and Mississippi river valleys. The Spanish laid claim to Florida in order to protect their more substantial colonial holdings in the Caribbean and Mexico (Taylor, 2001; Steele, 1994).

Colonial warfare between European colonists and Native Americans had a number of distinguishing characteristics. In the first place the number of combatants was relatively small. From the sixteenth to eighteenth centuries the Native American population steadily declined owing to disease and warfare. This decline made it difficult for Native Americans, sub-divided into linguistic and tribal groups, to commit large numbers of warriors to resisting European encroachment. The Europeans for their part did not establish large and self-sustaining populations until the late seventeenth century. The British colonies were far more populous than those of France or Spain. Nonetheless in 1700 the population of the British colonies was just 250,000, whilst New France had fewer than 20,000 settlers and the Spanish presence in Florida consisted of fewer than 100 Franciscan missionaries and a handful of soldiers.

Despite the small numbers involved, colonial warfare between Native Americans and Europeans was often very bloody. The emphasis was not on large battles but on raids and ambushes on population centres. Both sides routinely attacked the settlements of their adversaries, with the result that women, children and the elderly were often combat victims. Starvation, deprivation and torture were accepted as legitimate tactics. Europeans, viewing Native Americans as racially inferior and non-Christian, felt that the use of such tactics was legitimate. For Native Americans the adoption of European technology made warfare, even among Native Americans, much more deadly. Much of the fighting on the European side was done not by professional soldiers but by militias composed of colonists who adapted to their environment in order to fight 'Indian style'. There were more soldiers among the Spanish and French settlers in real and proportional terms, but even these adapted their tactics to suit the demands of colonial warfare (Steele, 1994, chs 2–6; Taylor, 2001, ch. 9; Richter, 1983).

Wars between Native Americans and Europeans were not the only type of colonial warfare. Also prevalent were wars between the various European powers, which often involved their colonists as well as native peoples. Between 1689 and 1754 the European powers with imperial aspirations in North America fought three major although largely inconclusive wars. The empires fought for dominance in Europe, colonial pre-eminence, and control over trade and natural resources. They carried out their struggle in Europe, North America, the Caribbean, Asia, Africa and most of the world's oceans. In North America these wars shaped and often destroyed the lives of colonists and Native Americans as well (Steele, 1994, chs 7–9).

By the mid-eighteenth century, colonial pressures and disputes had increased. The population of the British colonies continued to grow, which threatened the Native Americans of the interior. Settlers and land speculators from the British colonies, especially Virginia, Pennsylvania and New York, cast covetous eyes on the region to the west of the Appalachian mountains. Relations between and among Native Americans were disrupted by the westward pressure exerted by British North Americans. The French, sensing a threat to their claims to the transmontane region, sought to assert their sovereignty in the Ohio River valley. It was these circumstances which brought Ensign Jumonville, Colonel Washington and Tanaghrisson together in their deadly encounter in May 1754.

The death of Jumonville marked the beginning of a deadly and ultimately decisive phase of the contest for imperial control over eastern North America. The British and their colonists were ill-prepared for the war which Washington had helped to ignite. In June 1754 representatives from the New England colonies, as well as New York, Pennsylvania, Maryland and Virginia, together with the Six Nations of the Iroquois, met at Albany, New York, to discuss the threat posed to their colonies by the French. Although Benjamin Franklin, representing Pennsylvania, proposed the creation of a union of the American colonies which would provide for a common defence, the Albany Congress was a failure as the colonists could not overcome their local differences. Nor could they convince the Iroquois to give up their neutrality to attack the French. The failure of the Albany Congress revealed the problems which had beset Britain's colonies throughout the seventeenth and eighteenth centuries when it came to waging war. The colonies, which in peacetime had enjoyed a large degree of local autonomy, were ill-prepared to make common cause in time of war. This meant that British Americans, despite outnumbering their French, Spanish and Native American adversaries, often failed to take advantage of their superior numbers and resources. Indeed, American reluctance to cooperate across colonial boundaries extended to a frequent unwillingness to accept the authority of British army and navy officers. As a consequence of this colonial tradition of independent action the early years of the Seven Years War went very badly for the British (Anderson, 2000; Greene, 1994). (The following account of the war is based mainly on Anderson, 2000; Steele, 1994, chs 10–12, and Taylor, 2001, ch. 18.)

In 1755 the British sent an unprecedented number of troops to North America to fortify their frontier against the French. The major expedition of 1755 was intended to avenge Washington's humiliation of 1754. General Edward Braddock led 2200 regular and colonial troops against Fort Duquesne, which lay in the contested Pennsylvania-Ohio borderlands (present-day Pittsburgh). Braddock was contemptuous of the fighting abilities of colonists and Native Americans. He refused to employ Native American warriors as scouts and guerrillas, which had been a common practice in the forest warfare of the previous decades. Although the French and their Native American allies had only half as many men as Braddock, they did not wait at Fort Duquesne for Braddock to subject them to a siege. They set an ambush ten miles from the fort, taking advantage of the cover provided by the forest to fire into the exposed ranks of British and colonial soldiers. The result was the slaughter of Braddock's command. The British sustained nearly a thousand casualties, including Braddock, who was killed in the battle, compared to forty casualties sustained by the French and their Indian allies. The Virginian, George Washington, now experienced at forest warfare, redeemed his reputation by skilfully organizing and leading a retreat of the battered remnants of Braddock's command.

Braddock's defeat emboldened the Native Americans of the Ohio River, such as the Shawnee and the Lenni Lenape, to attack British settlements in western Pennsylvania, Maryland and Virginia. These attacks rolled back the frontier of British American settlement and distracted colonial American forces, allowing the French to take the initiative in the north. In 1756 and 1757 forces which combined French regulars, Canadian militia and Indian warriors captured British forts on Lake Ontario and Lake George. The French forces were commanded by the Canadian-born Governor-General of New France, Pierre de Rigaud de Vaudreil, and General Louis-Joseph de Montcalm. Montcalm was an aristocrat with little appreciation for warfare which featured irregular forces engaging in frontier raiding. Vaudreil, by contrast, argued that such warfare was the best means of defending sparsely populated New France.

The conflict over tactics came to a head in August 1757 when Montcalm's forces captured Fort William Henry. Among Montcalm's forces were approximately 1700 native warriors, including Abenakis, Algonquins, Caughnawagas and Nippissings from New France itself, and Ottawas, Ojibwas, Menominees, Potawatomis and Winnebagoes from the Great Lakes region. These had been recruited and supplied by Vaudreil and encouraged by the promise that they could win trophies, plunder and prisoners, as their counterparts had at Braddock's defeat. Despite serving well as scouts and raiders during the William Henry campaign, Montcalm was unwilling to use the natives during the siege of the fort, which was conducted according to the dictates of eighteenth-century European warfare. When the British commander, Lieutenant-Colonel George Monro, surrendered on 9 August Montcalm gave him generous terms. The British would be allowed to march back to nearby Fort Edward and to keep their muskets, colours and personal property, in exchange for returning all French, Canadian and Native American prisoners. Montcalm's native allies were disgusted with terms which denied them an opportunity to win the spoils of war – prisoners and booty – which were crucial to winning prestige and power for warriors in native societies. When the prisoners, guarded by French soldiers, began their march to Fort Edward, angry warriors entered the British camp to plunder what had been left behind. In so doing they killed and scalped seventeen wounded prisoners who were too ill to travel. They also seized Native Americans and African Americans serving with the British. Warriors then streamed out of the French camps and attacked the main body of prisoners. After a few minutes of fighting at least 69 were killed and a further 115 were unaccounted for, while several hundred prisoners were taken from the French by the natives.

The attack on the prisoners at Fort William Henry was immortalized in the minds of the British and Americans as a treacherous massacre. In his study of the incident Ian Steele has reconstructed the event from the perspective of the native warriors involved, to demonstrate that Montcalm's failure to under-stand and appreciate native warfare contributed to the frustration which resulted in the killings. The 'massacre' at Fort William Henry had several significant consequences. In the first place it strengthened British and American resolve to prosecute the war. After 1757 the British and Americans cooperated more closely and waged war much more ably. This is partly attrib-utable to the widespread anger over events at Fort William Henry. The inci-dent undermined the French war effort. Montcalm's open disdain for native warriors, expressed before and after the siege at Fort William Henry, alienated many of the warriors, most of whom refused to fight for the French for the remainder of the war. Historically the French had enjoyed better relations with native peoples than the British, and native warriors had allowed the French to offset their numerical inferiority when fighting the British in North America. After 1757 this was no longer the case. Finally, the incident at Fort William Henry caused a rift within the French command between Montcalm and Vaudreil. Vaudreil had appreciated the value of native warriors and understood the native way of waging war to a degree that Montcalm never did. In the wake of the William Henry campaign Vaudreil denounced Montcalm, producing lingering bitterness which divided and weakened the diminishing French forces just as the British renewed and strengthened their own forces (Steele, 1990).

Following the poor showing of British forces in America, William Pitt emerged as Prime Minister in 1757. Despite the spread of the war to Europe in 1756, Pitt focused British efforts on North America, giving priority for men, materiel and money to the American theatre of operations. Pitt sought to promote colonial cooperation by paying for men and supplies rather than requisitioning them. By 1758 the British had 45,000 troops, split evenly between regulars and colonial forces, whilst the French could only put 6800 regulars and 2700 Canadian militiamen in the field (Taylor, 2001, p. 430). Although the British sent increasing numbers of regular soldiers to North America, and most of these fought according to traditional European methods with an emphasis on manoeuvre and siege, they also recruited colonial ranger units, which adopted the techniques of native warfare to counter the irregular tactics of the Canadian militia and the dwindling numbers of native warriors who still fought for the French. These units allowed the British to use their regular forces with deadly effect against their weaker French opponents.

The tide of the war turned against the French in 1758, when separate British expeditions captured the French forts at Louisbourg, Frontenac and Duquesne. In 1759 they captured forts Ticonderoga and Crown Point. In September General James Wolfe led a daring British attack on Quebec, which was defended by Montcalm. Wolfe, frustrated by the defences around Quebec, sent his men up a cliff in the middle of the night to gather his forces before the city on the Plains of Abraham. Montcalm abandoned the relative security of the city walls to engage Wolfe in a conventional European-style battle. Both Montcalm and Wolfe were mortally wounded in the battle, in which the British triumphed. Quebec surrendered on 18 September 1759. The war in North America had turned decisively in favour of the British. In the spring and summer of 1760 the British mopped up the last French resistance and Montreal fell on 8 September. Although war continued in Europe and the West Indies for two more years, the fall of Montreal marked the end of New France.

The Seven Years War ended with the Treaty of Paris, which was concluded in February 1763. Under the terms of the treaty France ceded to Britain its claim to Acadia, Canada, Cape Breton and all of Louisiana east of the Mississippi except New Orleans. Britain agreed to restore islands it had captured from the French in the West Indies. Britain also agreed to return Havana, which it had captured during the war, to Spain. In exchange for Havana, the British received Florida. The Spanish also received France's territory west of the Mississippi River, and New Orleans. After 150 years France ceased to possess territory on the North American mainland.

Traditionally historians have portrayed the Seven Years War as the end of a prolonged historical struggle between France and Britain. It has also been interpreted as a prologue to the American Revolution. Both interpretations have merit. The war was the fourth conflict between France and Britain in North America in 75 years. It was also decisive in the sense that the British expelled the French from mainland North America. The war also set in motion the chain of events which would lead to American independence.

While these interpretations have much to commend them, the Seven Years War should best be viewed not as the end of a historical period or as the prelude to another more important event. Rather the war is best seen as the first part of a prolonged armed struggle for control of eastern North American. The Seven Years War did not end this struggle. On the contrary it marked the beginning of a particularly violent and intense phase of the conflict which had been waged intermittently since the seventeenth century. In the six decades between 1754 and 1815 eastern North America was the scene of incessant armed conflict. This conflict involved all of the major players who had participated in the Seven Years War – the British, the French, the Spanish, the Native Americans and the provincials, both Canadian and American. At issue was control over the continent and its resources. The apparent defeat of France in 1763 did not mark a definitive peace but rather a brief truce.

The American War of Independence

The third type of armed colonial conflict during the early modern period was the war of independence. Probably the most famous such conflict was the American War of Independence (1775–83). Historians have suggested that the war represents a departure from past practice. According to this view the American War of Independence was one of the first of what came to be known in the twentieth century as colonial wars of liberation. It was a conflict in which the combatants (at least in its North American aspects) were motivated by ideology and a desire for national self-determination. In this respect the American Revolutionary War anticipated the experiences of the wars of the French Revolution. The conflict over American independence, according to Stephen Conway, one of its leading historians 'was the first appearance, on a significant scale, of a people's war; the participation of a large proportion of the free male population and the political commitment of many of those who fought for the United States certainly suggest that the Americans became a people at arms nearly two decades before the French' (Conway, 1995, p. 247). This view has much to commend it. However by stressing the modernity and distinctiveness of the American War of Independence historians somewhat neglect the degree to which the conflict was consistent with previous patterns of colonial warfare. Indeed, as this chapter suggests, the war must be seen in the context of previous and subsequent colonial wars. At issue was control over eastern North America.

The American War of Independence was a consequence of the British victory in the Seven Years War. In the first place the apparent removal of the threat posed by France to Britain's North American colonies rendered those colonies less dependent on Britain for protection. The cost of the war left Britain with a massive budget deficit, which made it imperative that imperial administrators reassess the question of colonial governance and taxation. In response to the budgetary crisis successive governments sought to impose taxes on the American colonies. Between 1763 and 1775 disputes over taxation escalated to the point where some Americans questioned the value of the imperial connection. Relations deteriorated to the point where armed conflict broke out between rebellious Americans and British soldiers at Lexington and Concord, Massachusetts, in April of 1775 (Cogliano, 2000, chs 1–2).

Initially the War of Independence was an ad hoc affair. Thousands of rebellious militiamen from around New England besieged the British in Boston in the wake of the fighting at Lexington and Concord. In June the British attempted to break through the rebel lines by launching a bloody frontal assault on rebel positions in Charlestown, Massachusetts, at the battle of Bunker Hill (17 June 1775). Also in June the Continental Congress named George Washington to command the rebel forces. When Washington arrived in Cambridge, Massachusetts, in July of 1775 to take command of the rebels' 'Continental Army' he was confronted by 17,000 poorly trained, poorly equipped and poorly disciplined soldiers. His soldiers were not yet prepared by training or inclination for a prolonged conflict with British regular soldiers. Washington recognized at the outset that a more disciplined, stable force – an American standing army – would have to be created if the rebels were to succeed. It is one of the paradoxes of the American Revolution that the rebel struggle for liberty could only be achieved through the creation of an institution, the Continental Army, by curbing the democratic excesses of its members (Royster, 1979; Wright, 1984).

Throughout the war the rebels drew on four sources for soldiers. The first was the Continental Army, which evolved under Washington's leadership into a competent force which could meet British regular soldiers in combat. Although it fluctuated in size the Continental Army usually numbered a few thousand men. The second and major source of men was rebel militiamen like those who originally besieged the British in Boston. These were men who turned out to fight when the British or their allies threatened their region or state. Although they were sometimes unreliable in combat the militias were a vital source of manpower for the rebels, and the majority of men who fought on the rebel side during the war did so on a part-time basis as militiamen. The third source of manpower was French soldiers. The French, eager to revive their empire in North America, entered an alliance with the rebels in 1778. In 1780 the French sent an expeditionary force to North America, which greatly enhanced the rebel war effort. Finally the rebels cultivated allies among various Native American tribes, who supplied a small number of irregular soldiers and scouts to assist the rebels (Royster, 1979; Kwasny, 1996; Neimeyer, 1996; Carp, 1984; Higginbotham, 1971).

The British also drew on a myriad of sources to suppress the rebellion. They waged war with tens of thousands of regular soldiers from the British army.

These were supplemented by soldiers from other sources, including American militiamen who remained loyal to the crown, runaway slaves and Native Americans. The most important source of additional manpower, however, was German mercenaries. In late 1775 and early 1776 Britain entered into agreements to pay the rulers of the German principalities of Hesse-Cassel, Hesse-Hanau, Waldeck and Brunswick for 18,000 soldiers. In 1777 subsequent agreements with additional princes yielded 3000 more German troops for the British war effort. All told approximately 30,000 German mercenaries served with the British in America. These German soldiers, generically referred to as Hessians by the Americans, provided vital manpower for the British effort to suppress the rebellion in America. Not only did they provide the British with trained and disciplined troops who could immediately be sent to America, but when the war spread beyond America in 1778 the presence of the Hessians in America freed British troops for service in the West Indies, the Mediterranean and India. After 1776 the British army derived approximately one-third of its strength from German auxiliaries. Although the Hessians provided essential support to the British war effort, their presence came at a cost beyond the £4.7 million paid by the British government to the various German princes. The hired German soldiers who went to America brought with them a fearsome reputation for rapacity. Their presence frightened and angered many Americans, convincing many neutral and even loyalist-inclined colonists to support the rebels. The Hessians exemplified the fundamental difficulty the British faced in prosecuting the American war; in order to defeat the rebels the British had to resort to methods which were sure to alienate the Americans, thus making the ultimate objective, the restoration of British authority, more difficult (Atwood, 1980; Mackesy, 1964; Conway, 1997).

The American War of Independence was similar to the Seven Years War in that it combined aspects of regular and irregular warfare as understood in the early modern period. The conventional war, whereby the standing armies of the British, the American rebels, and the French sought to out-manoeuvre each other and force the surrender of their opponents, was fought mainly in the northern colonies between 1775 and 1778 and in the southern colonies from 1779 to 1781. The irregular war, which often pitted small bands of loyalist and rebel militiamen against each other, took place throughout the colonies, though it was especially intense in New York and New Jersey in 1776 and across the southern colonies after 1779 (Kwasny, 1996; Ferguson, 1979). The conventional war was something of a draw. The British won most of the war's set-piece battles but they were unsuccessful in destroying Washington's Continental Army and thus suppressing the rebellion. After 1778, when France entered the conflict on the side of the Americans, the balance in the regular war shifted. Aided by the French, the rebels performed better in conventional warfare to the point that a Franco-American force compelled the surrender of Cornwallis's army at Yorktown in 1781, ending the major fighting in the War of Independence. In the irregular war the British and their supporters fared less well. In the partisan fighting which occurred the British were frequently blamed for the attendant disorder which beset the colonies. The anarchic civil war which occurred in the southern back-country, for example, did much to alienate potential supporters of British rule. In short, the irregular war did much to undermine the effort to restore British rule in America. The campaigns of 1777 are especially revealing with regard to the nature and outcome of the war.

The British undertook two separate and uncoordinated campaigns in North America in 1777. During the winter of 1776–77 General John Burgoyne had won approval in London for a plan to lead a combined force of British regulars, Hessians, Indians, Canadians and loyalists south from Montreal through the Champlain and Hudson valleys to join with the main British forces in New York. The objective of such a campaign would be to isolate the New England colonies, already subject to a British naval blockade, and thus suppress the rebellion. General William Howe, meanwhile, planned to use the main body of British forces in North America, based in New York City, to attack the rebel capital at Philadelphia and thus force Washington and the Continental Army into a decisive struggle. Both plans were intended to bring about a timely end to the American rebellion, yet both ultimately failed (Cogliano, 2000, pp. 77–80).

William Howe decided not to undertake an overland march from New York to Philadelphia. He elected to take advantage of British naval superiority and to make a seaborne movement towards the rebel capital in Pennsylvania. After delaying several months, during which provisions ran low and his men endured the summer heat of New York, Howe loaded 13,000 men, their horses and supplies, and put to sea on 23 July. After six weeks he landed his sickly army at the head of Chesapeake Bay, barely 40 miles closer to Philadelphia than they had been when they left New York. As Congress and civilians fled, and loyalists prepared to greet their liberators in Philadelphia, Washington's Continentals unsuccessfully tried to stop Howe's advance at Brandywine Creek on 11 September. On 26 September the British captured Philadelphia. Washington counter-attacked, and was defeated by Howe at the battle of Germantown on 4 October.

The impact of the loss of Philadelphia was lessened because the city fell at almost the same moment as the rebels received good tidings from the north; Burgoyne and his entire army had surrendered to General Horatio Gates at Saratoga, New York. Burgoyne and his force of 8000 regular and irregular soldiers departed from Montreal in mid-June. Initially the campaign went as planned, as Burgoyne's army floated down Lake Champlain in flat-bottomed boats and easily captured Fort Ticonderoga. Once the troops left

Lake Champlain and sought to traverse the wilderness towards the Hudson River valley they ran into difficulty. Burgoyne's men were heavily laden with materiel and supplies which were better suited to the plains of north-western Europe than the American forest. Moreover the troops were subject to harassment by rebel militiamen, who attacked stragglers and placed obstacles in the way of the advancing army. Several fierce skirmishes took place which delayed Burgoyne's advance. His army had covered more than 100 miles during the first three weeks of the expedition. During the subsequent three weeks it made progress of barely more than a mile a day.

Like so many British commanders during the American war Burgoyne had hoped that loyalists would flock to his standard, augmenting his troops and undermining rebel authority. The presence of British forces did much to create rebels out of neutral-inclined Americans. Burgoyne's Native American allies were particularly problematic in this regard. In several instances during the expedition's advance Burgoyne's Iroquois warriors attacked outlying farms, killing several families. In a much-publicized incident a young woman, Jane McCrea, who was engaged to a loyalist officer, was killed by two of Burgoyne's Indians. Once Native Americans and whites came into conflict along the frontier, political considerations took second place to racial enmity. In the wake of the killings hundreds of militiamen from northern New England and New York turned out to oppose the British advance.

In August things began to go wrong for the northern campaign. As Burgoyne descended from Lake Champlain a second, smaller British force was to approach Albany from Fort Oswego on Lake Ontario to support Burgoyne. This force was turned back in a hard-fought battle with rebel militiamen at Oriskany, New York, on 6 August. Meanwhile Burgoyne's troops, bogged down in the wilderness, were running out of supplies. The general dispatched a force of nearly 900 Hessians, Canadians and Indians to search for supplies for his hungry army. On 16 August the foraging party was destroyed in a battle with New England militia at Bennington, Vermont. Burgoyne did not cross the Hudson and head for Albany until mid-September. His forces clashed with the Continental forces in successive battles at Freeman's Farm on 19 September and 7 October. Having failed to defeat the rebels and having sustained significant casualties (1200 to less than 500 for the rebels) Burgoyne was surrounded. He realized that he could not expect assistance from the small garrison remaining at New York. On 17 October 1777 he surrendered the remnants of his army, approximately 6000 men, to General Horatio Gates. For the first time the rebels had defeated the British in a sustained campaign (Ketchum, 1997; Martin, 1997, chs 15–16).

The 1777 campaigns epitomized the difficulties which faced the British in waging the American War of Independence. Burgoyne commanded a large well-equipped army when he departed from Montreal. Its mix of regular soldiers, militia and Native Americans was similar to the forces which had acquitted themselves so well on behalf of the British during the latter stages of the Seven Years War. Burgoyne, however, had little experience of American warfare. He was not prepared to cope with the American environment and nor did he manage his irregular forces well. Like Montcalm before him Burgoyne alienated many of his Native American troops, who deserted his army immediately prior to the battles around Saratoga. Burgoyne's own rhetoric as expressed in his various proclamations during the campaign further alienated the Americans.

By contrast William Howe's campaign was a more conventional affair in which his forces achieved their objectives. They won several large complex battles with Washington's army and captured the rebel capital at Philadelphia, but the British did not manage to destroy the Continental Army, which had fought well despite its battlefield defeats. The loss of Philadelphia did not lead to a collapse of the rebellion, as Howe had hoped. Neither Howe nor Burgoyne realized that this was a different type of war from the previous conflicts fought in North America. Whereas previous wars had concerned subjugation of native peoples or imperial rivalries, the War of Independence was a political struggle. The experience of the first years of the war had given the rebels new symbols and institutions, especially the army and its commander George Washington. As long as Washington could keep his forces in the field and he could rely on local militias to turn out in times of crisis to augment his forces and resist the British, the rebellion could continue (Royster, 1979).

Saratoga immediately changed the nature and scope of the American War of Independence. When news of Burgoyne's defeat reached Paris in December the balance was tipped within the French government in favour of a formal alliance between France and the United States. Treaties between the United States and France were signed in February 1778. With the conclusion of the Franco-American alliance the American War of Independence became a European conflict in which the colonial war in America was but one theatre. Eventually Britain found itself at war simultaneously with the American rebels, France, Spain and the Netherlands. While Britain sought to retain its North American colonies, after 1778 suppressing the American rebellion was only one of several objectives, including protecting and enlarging their holdings in the West Indies, Africa and India, and protecting the British Isles from a Franco-Spanish invasion. In consequence the government could not devote the military resources to the North American theatre of the war that it had during the period from 1775 to 1777. Some 65 per cent of the British army was in North America in 1778, but by 1780 only 29 per cent of British troops were in North America, with 55 per cent guarding Britain against invasion. After 1778 London had far fewer resources to devote to the American rebellion, while at the same time the rebels benefited from additional assistance in the form of arms, materiel and men from the French, distraction of the British by the Spanish, and money from the Dutch. Crucially, the presence of the French navy challenged British naval superiority in American waters (Conway, 1995, pp. 157–8).

The French alliance decisively tipped the balance of the war in favour of the American rebels. After three more years of fighting and two years of negotiations the war was concluded by a peace treaty agreed at Paris in 1783. Under its terms the British recognized American independence. The borders of the new United States stretched from the Mississippi River in the west to the Atlantic Ocean in the east. Florida was returned to Spain while Britain retained Quebec and Nova Scotia. A new potent power had forced its way into the military and political equation in North America. The new United States would be an aggressive rival to the traditional European powers and to Native Americans. Indeed it had demonstrated its acquisitive and expansionist tendencies even as it had fought for its independence.

War in the west

At the same time as Americans were fighting to free themselves from British rule along the Atlantic littoral, to the west of the Appalachian mountains a bloody racial conflict between settlers and Native Americans took place. If the war in the east was concerned with protecting and extending American liberty, in the west the struggle concerned survival and the subjugation of the Native American population. The war in the west was a war of conquest. (The following analysis is based on Cogliano, 2000, pp. 88–92; Faragher, 1992; and Calloway, 1995.) ·

When the War of Independence commenced Native Americans had to choose between supporting the British, supporting the rebels or attempting to maintain their neutrality. Depending on local circumstances some Indian groups sided with the rebels. Ultimately, however, circumstances compelled most Indians to pursue policies of neutrality or to fight alongside the British. Native Americans recognized the threat to their livelihood posed by a rebel victory. Should the Americans win their independence then the likelihood of unfettered white expansionism and subsequent Indian displacement would increase dramatically. In consequence many Native Americans, armed and encouraged by the British, fought against the settlers. The British cultivated and encouraged the Indians because they had so few troops of their own at their western posts when the war began. There were several thousand native warriors to both the north and the south of the Ohio River who could be encouraged to attack the white settlements. The British hoped, as a minimum, to prevent the western settlements from lending support to the military efforts of the rebels in the east, and at best to require the rebels to divert precious troops and supplies to the west.

From western New York to Georgia the same pattern was played out along the frontier during the war. In the early stages of the conflict Indians attacked white settlements. The settlers, although they suffered grievously, usually withstood the onslaughts and retaliated. Sometimes the counter-attacks were conducted under the auspices of the Continental Army. Other campaigns were organized by the states, as when Virginia and the Carolinas banded together to attack the Cherokees in 1776. Most commonly settlers took matters into their own hands in conjunction with state or national authorities. The complexity and brutality of the war in the west is revealed by events in the Ohio River valley (Faragher, 1992; Hinderaker, 1997; White, 1991; Dowd, 1992).

Between 1776 and 1778 the Indians of the Ohio River region, mainly Shawnees and Delawares, attacked the American settlements in Kentucky, which in recent years had seen an influx of white settlers from Virginia. This campaign was a success. In 1778 and 1779 the settlers began to launch frequent attacks on native villages in Ohio. The struggle was marked by brutality and atrocity by both sides and quarter was rarely given. East of the Appalachians, where the main campaigns of the war were fought, there was one war-related death for every 1000 people. In Kentucky there was one death for every 70 inhabitants (Faragher, 1992, p. 144). A notorious incident which epitomized the frontier conflict was the massacre of 96 defenceless Christian Delaware Indians at the Moravian mission at Gnadenhütten, Ohio, by rebel militia from Pennsylvania.

After they had no further use for them the British withdrew support from their Indian allies, which left them at the mercy of the American rebels. This occurred throughout the south in 1781 and 1782. Under such circumstances the tribes had little choice but to sue for peace or attempt to carry on resistance without outside support. In most cases Indians opted for the former. As a result the United States concluded treaties of dubious legal and moral value at Fort Stanwix, New York and Hopewell, South Carolina, in 1784, in which it obtained concessions of land from the Iroquois, Choctaws, Chickasaws and Cherokees respectively. Only in the region north of the Ohio River and south of the Great Lakes – then known as the North-West – were the Indians able to continue their resistance.

The situation in the region was complicated. According to the 1783 Peace of Paris the North-West was American territory. Accordingly Congress adopted a series of laws, the North-West Ordinances of 1784, 1785 and 1787, which created a system for the subdivision and sale of the territory. Despite the fact that Great Britain was a signatory to the 1783 treaty British troops still occupied posts in the region. According to the treaty the British should have turned these posts over the United States. They failed to do so because they claimed that the United States had not honoured its pledge to compensate loyalists for their losses. The natives of the region – the Delawares, Shawnees, Miamis,

Chippewas, Ottawas and Potawatomis – formed an alliance, the Western Confederacy, to resist American encroachments. Violent conflict between settlers and Indians continued unabated despite the peace of 1783. Covertly armed by the British, the Western Confederacy proved a serious obstacle to American settlement of the region and an embarrassing challenge to the sovereignty of the new nation.

The struggle to conquer the North-West went very badly for the United States. Twice, in 1790 and 1791, warriors from the Western Confederacy destroyed American armies along the present-day border between Ohio and Indiana. The first occasion was in October 1790, when a combined force of United States regulars and militiamen under General Joseph Harmar was routed. A year later General Arthur St Clair led another American army, nearly a thousand militiamen and regulars, into the Ohio country in the autumn of 1791. St Clair, who had had an undistinguished record during the War of Independence, was an incompetent officer, and on 4 November he camped without taking the precaution of posting sentries. Warriors under the Miami war chief, Little Turtle, attacked the encampment. The militiamen broke and fled while the regulars sought to fight. The result was an overwhelming defeat for the Americans, who sustained 632 dead and 264 wounded out of a force of 920 officers and men. By contrast 66 of Little Turtle's warriors were killed and 9 wounded. In 1794 Washington sent a third army under General Anthony Wayne to take on the Western Confederacy, and on 20 August 1791 he defeated them at the battle of Fallen Timbers. In 1794 the British finally agreed to withdraw from the western forts and further resistance was impossible. In 1795 the western tribes agreed to the Treaty of Greenville, by the terms of which they ceded their claim to most of the land in the present state of Ohio. The United States, while committed to republican government for its own citizens, had demonstrated that it could be as rapacious as its European imperial rivals (Sword, 1993).

The War of 1812

In January 1815 British and American forces fought the largest battle ever waged between the two countries. Approximately 5300 British regulars commanded by Major General Edward Pakenham, assisted by Admiral Sir Alexander Cochrane, attacked New Orleans. New Orleans, with its port at the mouth of the Mississippi River, was the key to American settlement in the west. American settlers in the west depended on access to the Mississippi River and New Orleans to market their produce. Without access to the port at New Orleans American farmers would have had to transport their crops overland, which was both expensive and extremely difficult. Indeed New Orleans was of such great strategic importance that the United States purchased the city, as well as whole of the Louisiana Territory, from France in 1803 for $16 million. If the British could have captured New Orleans they would have been able to stifle the westward expansion of the United States. New Orleans was defended by a mixed force of 4700 men – US Army soldiers, free blacks and militiamen from Kentucky, Louisiana and Tennessee, as well as pirates from the Gulf of Mexico – commanded by General Andrew Jackson. After a series of minor engagements Pakenham assaulted Jackson's lines on 8 January. The attack failed and the British suffered 2400 casualties and prisoners (Remini, 1999).

The battle was the culmination of the War of 1812, often referred to in the United States as the second war of independence. The war began after a prolonged dispute between Britain and the United States over the right of Americans to trade with both Britain and France during the Napoleonic Wars. The United States championed the doctrine of free trade and claimed its right as a neutral carrier to trade with both France and Britain. The British, who had subjected Napoleonic Europe to a blockade, contended that American trade with France was a belligerent act and their shipping would be subject to seizure. In consequence the British seized hundreds of American vessels between 1803 and 1812 (Perkins, 1968).

As in the War of Independence, the War of 1812 was actually two concurrent conflicts, a war between the United States and the British, and a war between the United States and Native Americans. Beginning in 1805 two Shawnee brothers, Tecumseh and Tenskwatawa (known to whites as the Prophet) sought to promote a pan-Indian confederacy in order to resist American encroachments. Tenskwatawa was one of several Native American prophets who preached a message of cultural renewal, resistance and revival. Simultaneously Tecumseh sought to forge a military alliance among the remaining eastern tribes. The resistance movement was centred on a Shawnee settlement, Prophet's Town, at the confluence of the Wabash and Tippecanoe rivers in Indiana Territory. Violent clashes between American settlers and Indians prompted the governor of the Indiana Territory, William Henry Harrison, to launch an attack on Prophet's Town in November 1811. Harrison's forces destroyed Prophet's Town at the battle of Tippecanoe. Since the Native Americans of the North-West had been traditional allies of the British, westerners incorrectly suspected that the British were behind the growing movement for Indian unity. When war broke out in 1812 American forces waged unrestrained war against Native Americans in the territory to the north and south of the Ohio River. In so doing they completed the forced displacement of Native Americans in eastern North America begun by European colonists two centuries earlier (Dowd, 1992; Remini, 2001).

The war with the British was mainly fought in the borderland between the United States and British Canada. The conquest of Canada, many Americans believed, would not only be a blow to the British but would constitute a welcome addition to the expansive American republic. American strategy called for the invasion of Canada on three fronts: along the Champlain corridor to Montreal, across the Niagara frontier and from Detroit. The American campaigns undertaken in the summer and fall of 1812 all ended in disaster. Despite winning the naval battle of Lake Erie and the battle of the Thames in Canada, the Americans were unable to make serious inroads in Canada in 1813. Surprisingly, the greatest American successes in the early years of the war occurred at sea, where the vessels of the fledgling United States Navy won a series of dramatic victories in single-ship actions against the British (Stagg, 1983; Hickey, 1989; Horsman, 1969; Quimby, 1997).

In 1814, as the European war began to wind down, the British were able to undertake offensive actions against the United States. In July the British attempted to invade the United States along the Niagara frontier and encountered stiff resistance from the Americans. In August, however, British forces captured and burned Washington. The latter part of the year saw a revival of American fortunes. The force that occupied Washington was unable to capture Baltimore. In September the Americans won another naval battle on inland waters at the battle of Plattsburg Bay on Lake Champlain, stopping another British invasion force. Meanwhile American and British negotiators had held talks in Belgium since August 1814. With the European war ending and the defeat at Plattsburg Bay the British did not have a strong interest in pursuing the conflict further. The two sides reached final agreement in the Treaty of Ghent on 24 December 1814. The treaty provided for the return of captured territory and a return to the *status quo ante bellum*. Since peace had been restored in Europe the issue of neutral rights and commerce ceased to be significant and the reason for the war evaporated, although news of the peace of Ghent did not reach America in time to forestall an unsuccessful British attempt to capture New Orleans.

Conclusion

The battle of New Orleans was the final action in the six-decade struggle to control eastern North America. The conflict had begun with a bloody skirmish between British American colonists and the French, during a nominal time of peace, near the headwaters of the Ohio River. It ended with the biggest battle ever fought between the British and the Americans at the mouth of the Mississippi River, hundreds of miles to the south-west, where the waters of the Ohio eventually empty into the Gulf of Mexico. In the intervening period the French, Spanish, British, Americans and Native Americans fought for control over eastern North America. Warfare, declared and undeclared, was incessant in North America between 1754 and 1815. The victors in the war were the British and the Americans. They jointly defeated the French, Spanish and

Native Americans in the Seven Years War. This gave Britain nominal control over the whole of eastern North America for a brief period of time. Almost immediately relations between the British state and its American colonists began to deteriorate. The result was a lengthy period of violent confrontation between the colonists and their governors, which resulted in the American War of Independence. The American rebels, with the assistance of the French, won their independence. Despite expectations that the rebellion would spread to Canada, Britain retained Quebec and Nova Scotia and would soon expand into upper Canada (modern Ontario). Despite their victory in the American War of Independence the French were unable to revive their North American empire. The Spanish remained on the periphery of the power struggle in eastern North America and ultimately sold Florida to the United States in 1818. By 1815 there were two dominant powers in North America – Great Britain and the United States of America.

The ultimate losers in the power struggle which engulfed North America in the eighteenth century were the continent's indigenous peoples. Parallel to the conflict between the Europeans for dominion over North America was a struggle between Europeans and Native Americans. The rules of war as understood by Europeans in the eighteenth century did not apply when fighting Native Americans. Atrocities were commonplace. This conflict, which was a war of conquest conducted along racial lines, revealed the nature of imperialism during the early modern period. This aspect of the Sixty Years War was brutal, acquisitive, racist, violent and immoral. When it came to the war of racial conquest between Europeans and Native Americans the citizens of the new American republic proved themselves to be more adept at prosecuting racial war than their European rivals. Where Native Americans were concerned the republican United States was a more dangerous imperial threat than were the monarchies of France, Spain and Britain.

The apotheosis of the Sixty Years War was the hero of the battle of New Orleans, Andrew Jackson. Jackson's life had been shaped by the North American colonial wars. He was born in South Carolina in 1767. As a 13-year-old boy he had fought in the War of Independence. During the war Jackson's entire family perished as a result of the chaos the conflict brought to the southern back-country. Jackson himself was captured by the British and beaten by a British officer, who left the boy with a permanent scar on his face. As a young man Jackson moved west with the frontier, settling in Tennessee, where he made his fortune as a plantation owner, lawyer and politician, and secured a commission in the Tennessee militia. In 1813 Jackson came to prominence when he led the Tennessee militia in a ruthless campaign against the Creek people in present-day Alabama. In 1814 Jackson was given a major-generalship in the United States Army and command of the Gulf Coast region. He seized Pensacola in Spanish Florida and moved to counter the British invasion of Louisiana in December 1814. After the war of 1812 he retained his army commission and continued to wage war against the southern Indians, as well as against the Spanish in Florida. Jackson's aggression ultimately compelled the Spanish to sell Florida to the United States. Jackson was immensely popular in the United States and was elected president in 1828. As president his most notable achievement was forcing tens of thousands of Native Americans to give up their lands east of the Mississippi River and move to Oklahoma during the 1830s. Jackson's formative experiences had been war, and as leader of a republic similarly forged by war he completed the conquest of eastern North America begun in 1754 (Remini, 2001).

References

Anderson, F. 2000. *Crucible of War: The Seven Years' War and the Fate of Empire in British North America, 1754–1763*, New York.

Atwood, R. 1980. *The Hessians: Mercenaries from Hesse-Kassel in the American Revolution*, Cambridge.

Calloway, C. 1995. *The American Revolution in Indian Country: Crisis and Diversity in Native American Communities*, Cambridge.

Carp, E.W. 1984. *To Starve the Army at Pleasure: Continental Army Administration and American Political Culture, 1775–1783*, Chapel Hill.

Cogliano, F.D. 2000. *Revolutionary America: A Political History*, London.

Conway, S. 1997. 'The Politics of British Military and Naval Mobilization, 1775–1783', *English Historical Review*, 112, 1179–1201.

—— 1995. *The War of American Independence, 1775–1783*, London.

Crosby, A.W. 1976. 'Virgin Soil Epidemics as a Factor in the Aboriginal Depopulation in America', *William and Mary Quarterly*, 33, 289–99.

Dowd, G.E. 1992. *A Spirited Resistance: The North American Indian Struggle for Unity, 1745–1815*, Baltimore.

Faragher, J.M. 1992. *Daniel Boone: The Life and Legend of an American Pioneer*, New York.

Fenn, E. 2001. *Pox Americana: The Great Smallpox Epidemic, 1775–1782*, New York.

Ferguson, C.R. 1979. 'Functions of the Partisan-Militia in the South during the American Revolution: An Interpretation', in *The Revolutionary War in the South: Power, Conflict, and Leadership*, ed. W.R. Higgins, Durham, 239–58.

Greene, J.P. 1994. 'Negotiated Authorities: The Problem of Governance in the Extended Polities of the Early Modern Atlantic World', in *Negotiated Authorities: Essays in Colonial Political and Constitutional History*, ed. J.P. Greene, Charlottesville, 1–24.

Hickey, D. 1989. *The War of 1812: a Forgotten Conflict*, Urbana.

Higginbotham, D. 1971. *The War of American Independence: Military Attitudes, Policies, and Practice*, New York.

Hinderaker, E. 1997. *Elusive Empires: Constructing Colonialism in the Ohio River Valley, 1673–1800*, New York.

Horsman, R. 1969. *The War of 1812*, London.

Ketchum, R. 1997. *Saratoga: Turning Point of America's Revolutionary War*, New York.

Kwasny, M.V. 1996. *Washington's Partisan War, 1775–1783*, Kent.

Mackesy, P. 1964. *The War for America, 1775–1783*, Cambridge.

Martin, J.K. 1997. *Benedict Arnold: Revolutionary Hero*, New York.

Neimeyer, C.P. 1996. *America Goes to War: A Social History of the Continental Army*, New York.

Perkins, B. 1968. *Prologue to War: England and the United States, 1805–1812*, Berkeley.

Quimby, R.S. 1997. *The United States Army in the War of 1812: An Operational and Command Study*, East Lansing.

Remini, R.V. 2001. *Andrew Jackson and his Indian Wars*, New York.

—— 1999. *The Battle of New Orleans*, New York.

Richter, D.K. 1983. 'War and Culture: The Iroquois Experience', *William and Mary Quarterly*, 40, 528–49.

Royster, C.A. 1979. *Revolutionary People at War: The Continental Army and American Character, 1775–1783*, Chapel Hill.

Stagg, J.C.A. 1983. *Mr. Madison's War: Politics, Diplomacy, and Warfare in the Early American Republic, 1783–1830*, Princeton.

Steele, I. 1994. *Warpaths: Invasions of North America*, New York.

—— 1990. *Betrayals: Fort William Henry and the 'Massacre'*, New York.

Sword, W. 1993. *President Washington's Indian War: The Struggle for the Old Northwest, 1790–1795*, Norman.

Taylor, A. 2001. *American Colonies*, New York.

White, R. 1991. *The Middle Ground: Indians, Empires and Republics in the Great Lakes Region, 1650–1815*, Cambridge.

Wright, R.K. 1984. ' "Nor is Their Standing Army to be Despised": The Emergence of the Continental Army as a Military Institution', in *Arms and Independence: The Military Character of the American Revolution*, ed. R. Hoffman and P.J. Albert, Charlottesville, 50–74.

10
Sea Power: The Struggle for Dominance, 1650–1815

Richard Harding

Sea power in early modern history

By 1650 war at sea had many of the characteristics that were to be familiar for the next 160 years. Warships had assumed the basic form and design that developed into the classic line-of-battle ship and frigate (Lavery, 1983; Gardiner, 1992). The purpose of navies was generally agreed. States put fleets to sea with the intention of fighting their enemies, destroying their trade and invading their territory, as well as defending their own lands and trade. The warship was also a symbol of state power for domestic and diplomatic purposes. The size and decoration of ships such as the English *Sovereign of the Seas* (1637) and the French *Soleil Royal* (1669) were self-conscious expressions of royal power. These warships were extremely expensive and complex, and the need for basic administrative systems to support large-scale state navies was recognized and, in some states, in place.

With so much progress already made, it is tempting to see the developments of the next 150 years as simply a working out or perfecting of well-established principles of naval warfare under sail. Warships got bigger, became better armed, and sail plans improved. It was possible to keep warships at sea longer and send them further. With greater control, reach and duration the benefits of sea power became more attainable and desirable. From this perspective Great Britain was the prime example of the sea power. From Cromwell to George III there was a conscious incremental development of the state's navy that steadily outpaced its rivals. By the mid-eighteenth century Britain achieved an ascendancy over its rivals that was never fully eclipsed. With the exception of the years 1778–81 and 1796–98 British ships dominated the world's oceans. The French Revolutionary War (1793–1802) and the Napoleonic War (1803–15) confirmed Britain's dominance of the seas and ushered in a period of imperial domination that was effectively unchallenged until the 1890s. The simple reason appears to be that British naval policy was more focused, and consequently she simply out-built and outfought her enemies, thus assuring her domestic integrity and imperial predominance.

This 'navalist' reading of history presents the early modern period as a series of stepping stones towards mature state naval policy, guided by the fundamental principle of modern sea power – the professional state battle fleet focused upon clearing the enemy from the seas. This notion, popular at the beginning of the twentieth century, contains some truth, but it does not reflect the ambiguities and problems of sea power in this period. The purpose of sea power and the manner in which it could be exercised were far more varied, and the apparent path to domination of the world's oceans far more contested, than this simple idea of evolution allows.

Sea power in the early modern world, 1650–88

In the mid-seventeenth century the processes and benefits of sea power were far from clear. Sea communication for trade and military purposes was vital. Highly valuable cargoes such as spices and bullion, and bulky cargoes ranging from coal, salt and fish to troops, ordnance and military stores, travelled by sea. While merchant vessels plied the world's oceans individually they were vulnerable to pirates and privateers. From the Middle Ages ship-owners often gathered their vessels into convoys for protection. Large concentrations of shipping, such as coastal convoys, annual fishing fleets and trade fleets to the Americas or the East Indies, offered protection against small predators, but they were slow moving and vulnerable to the concentrated firepower of state warships. Likewise military forces, particularly invasion forces, were gathered in convoys. Thus the battle fleet had a defensive and an offensive purpose – to protect or destroy concentrations of shipping poised for invasion or engaged in valuable trades.

Nevertheless different states had different perceptions of the threat and the opportunities offered by huge investment in the large line-of-battle ship. Britain, Denmark and the United Provinces were probably the most vulnerable to seaborne invasion. With limited hinterlands the landing of a relatively small seaborne army could have disastrous effects. In 1639 large Dutch naval forces disrupted a Spanish fleet transporting money and troops to the Army of Flanders (Alcalá-Zamora, 1975). The Dutch invasion of England in 1688 demonstrated the catastrophic impact a seaborne invasion could have. These countries were also vulnerable to economic dislocation by enemy action at sea. The threat of a blockade of the Thames by royalist sympathizers in 1648 and 1660, and by the Dutch in 1667, caused consternation in London. Sir Richard Holmes's 'bonfire' of Dutch merchantmen sheltering behind the island of Vlie in August 1666 had significant repercussions in the United Provinces (Capp, 1989, pp. 5–41; Ollard, 1969, pp. 148–61). Denmark was under constant threat from Swedish invasion or blockade, and Sweden needed to move troops to and from her German empire, so strategic or trade disruption could be a danger to their interests (Anderson, 1969). Most other states were less vulnerable to invasion or strategic or trade disruption. France had little to fear from small seaborne armies or the temporary disruption of trade. Spain was believed to rely on her treasure fleets, but these were not easily captured or interrupted. Treasure ships were lost to storm and capture, but the wholesale loss of convoys was extremely rare. Outside the Baltic and obvious choke-points like the Channel or the Straits of Gibraltar, sailing fleets at sea could not apply enough pressure, maintain themselves for long enough, nor cover enough coastline to have a decisive impact on trade or military events. The most immediate naval concerns of France and Spain were in the Mediterranean, where they were rivals and were faced by Barbary corsairs. Here the galley fleet played a significant role in short-range coastal operations. While Louis XIV built up his sailing navy on the Atlantic coast and in the Mediterranean to be the largest in the world by 1675, he continued to invest large sums in his Mediterranean galley fleet (Bamford, 1973, pp. 23–9). By 1660 Spain was crippled by war and had to focus her limited sailing naval forces upon covering her treasure fleets (Torres Ramirez, 1981; Serrano Mangas, 1985). During the Franco-Spanish War of 1674–78 the French and Dutch (allied to Spain) sailing battle fleets fought each other in the Mediterranean but could not effectively influence the land war in Sicily, nor destroy the inshore galley squadrons. The strain of maintaining these fleets made consistent operations very difficult (Anderson, 1971). Thus it was by no means clear that naval power had to be, or could be, built around the large sailing battleships.

An alternative lay in the maritime community as a whole. Private ships of war, or privateers, had always been a feature of war at sea. They could not threaten the integrity of a state, but most of the damage done to trade in this period was by privateers. Effective blockade of most ports was out of the question for naval powers until the mid-eighteenth century, when the size and composition of the Royal Navy made a blockade of the French Atlantic coast practicable. For long-term attacks on trade small raiders were vital. They could cover more of the trade routes than battle fleets and they could go inshore more easily. They were unlikely to have the dramatic political or economic effect of the battle fleet by destroying or capturing valuable convoys, but in the mid-seventeenth century they did far more damage than state warships, at no cost to the state, whilst enriching the maritime community (Bruijn, 1977, pp. 89–90).

Sea power and war, 1688–1713

The Nine Years War (1689–97) was fought primarily to limit Louis XIV's ambitions in Europe, but from England's perspective it was also to preserve the

Protestant succession. William of Orange's invasion of England in November 1688 was a great shock. James II's navy completely failed to prevent William landing, and the realm fell quickly into William's hands. While it was a tremendously difficult and hazardous enterprise, its apparent ease may have done much to develop British fears of invasion and the desire for a strong navy. The Anglo-Dutch fleets exceeded the French by over 60 line-of-battle ships, but the role that sea power played in the eventual Peace of Nijmegan was limited. Exhaustion, and stalemate on the European battlefields, drove the two sides to make peace. The allied fleets did eventually choke off supplies to the Jacobites in Ireland (1690–92), but not before the French successfully reinforced them at Bantry Bay in May 1689. In June 1690 the Comte de Tourville defeated the Anglo-Dutch fleet off Beachy Head and gained control of the Channel, but was unable to capitalize on the victory (Vergé-Franceschi, 1996, p. 64; Taillemite and Guillaume, 1991, pp. 25–6).

In 1692 the allies regained control of the Channel by defeating the French at the twin battles of Barfleur and La Hogue. It gave the allies control of the Channel and the western approaches, ending the French invasion threat, but it did not decisively shift the balance of the war in their favour (Aubrey, 1979). A large French fleet could still operate and cause serious problems. In 1693 Tourville successfully raided the outward bound Smyrna convoy off the Spanish coast, causing near panic in London. Privateers continued to damage allied trade and commercial confidence. Throughout the war French squadrons continued to get out to the West Indies to support their colonies and threaten those of the allies. The greatest colonial raid of the war, de Pointis's capture of Cartagena de las Indias in 1697, illustrated the continued capability of a nominally inferior naval power (Buchet, 1991, p. 179; Nerzic and Buchet, 2002).

Nevertheless changes were taking place. For England, defence of the home islands demanded a strong battle fleet. While both France and England continued to build, the numerical margin of superiority shifted markedly. England entered the war with six fewer battleships than France and ended it with 19 more (Glete, 1993, pp. 551, 576). With the Dutch as allies this margin of safety increased. The English established a squadron in the Mediterranean over the winter of 1694–95, marking an intention to maintain a continuous presence in that sea in protection of trade. Four significant expeditions were organized to the West Indies and North America, demonstrating both a willingness and a capability to undertake offensive trans-Atlantic operations. Assisted by deficit financing by the Bank of England from 1694, the English state steadily increased its investment in naval infrastructure. The royal yards at Portsmouth and Plymouth were developed to meet the French threat, shifting the balance of naval resources from the Channel yards which had been essential for fighting the Dutch. English reliance on private vessels of war continued to decline, but effective means of working with private yards for building royal warships were developed (Ehrman, 1953).

In France different lessons were being drawn. France emerged from the war in 1697 with a satisfactory record at sea. The royal battle fleet was not rejected; building continued, but funds were scarce and its role was less fundamental to the nation's security. The advantages or objectives of war at sea could be achieved with less direct investment. Squadrons continued to be sent out, but private initiatives remained much more important. The *guerre de course* became more significant from 1695. Royal ships were hired out to join privateering operations (Symcox, 1974, pp. 157–62; Dessert, 1996). The court was an investor in expeditions such as de Pointis's attack on Cartagena, rather than the principal instigator.

The peace was short lived. The allies were determined not to allow the huge and rich Spanish empire to fall into the hands of Louis XIV's grandson, Philip, Duc d'Anjou. While Flanders remained the primary battleground, the Spanish inheritance in Europe and America presented much more obvious targets for operations. Once again for England naval defence against invasion was a primary objective. Naval operations were conducted in the North Sea, the Atlantic, the West Indies and the Mediterranean. The general naval superiority enjoyed by the Anglo-Dutch navies throughout the war enabled them to conduct significant operations in all these theatres. It gave the allies, and Britain in particular, a degree of strategic flexibility to switch the emphasis of operations as the need arose. Stagnation might occur in Flanders, but Britain had the power to try to shift the balance of advantage in Spain (1707–13), Italy, the West Indies and North America (1708–11). Nonetheless in the last resort these operations did not have a decisive impact on the eventual outcome. The peace in 1713 left Spain and her American empire in Philip's hands. The Italian possessions passed to Austria and Sardinia. Sea power had not shifted the fundamental advantage to the allies, nor had England (Britain from 1707, after the union with Scotland) been able to exercise it entirely to her advantage. She had to fend off an invasion attempt in 1708, and she could not stop French expeditionary forces going to the West Indies, causing great damage and, like de Pointis in 1697, achieving a spectacular capture – this time Dugauy Trouin's capture of Rio in 1711. French privateers continued to prey heavily upon her trade (Bromley, 1987, pp. 213–41). Despite this there were significant changes in the relative naval balance between Britain and France.

Britain left the war in 1713 with a navy that was double the size of her nearest rival. The trade dislocation caused by privateers which had occurred in the 1690s was not repeated (Jones, 1988, pp. 130–5). While Marlborough had won some splendid victories on the Continent from 1704 to 1711, Britain emerged from the war with tangible gains that were unquestionably the result of her naval power. St Kitts (1702), Gibraltar (1704), Minorca (1708) and

Newfoundland (1711) extended British possessions in key regions of the world. The rhetoric of liberty and defence by a large navy, as opposed to slavery and a large army, which had informed the political debate since the fall of Cromwell, gained ground after 1710, when the new Tory government sought to justify negotiating a separate peace with France. Jonathan Swift's famous pamphlet, *The Conduct of the Dutch* (1711), summed up the arguments for the British maritime war against a continental war which primarily benefited Britain's ungrateful allies. The Royal Navy had reached another high point in its political popularity. Parliament, convinced of its vital role in protecting the British Isles and expanding trade, voted funds for expansion and development of the infrastructure. The navy debt was allowed to rise as the national debt rose from £16.7m in 1697 to £36.2m in 1713, and taxes were raised to service it. The need to man the navy at least partly by compulsion, through the press and quotas, did not sit easily with the rhetoric of liberty, but was recognized as a necessary evil which Parliament endorsed. The Royal Navy also emerged from the war with a valuable accumulated experience of operations. The administration had been able to mobilize ships for large and distant operations consistently for 12 years. The parliamentary distrust of the administration that had been common in the debates of the 1690s largely disappeared after 1708. The long years of combat had created an experienced officer corps, who knew how to conduct battles and long-distance campaigns (Harding, 1999, pp. 183–7).

Against this, the Dutch were gradually falling behind, exhausted by the land war and natural disasters. France still had the second-largest battle fleet in the world, but it was weaker than it had been in 1688, and the navy emerged from the war with no clear role for its battle fleet. Her squadrons had continued to cruise in distant waters and to have a clear diplomatic role, but they had not played a decisive part in the war. Once again privateers and private entrepreneurs had carried on the most spectacular aspects of the war at sea in a satisfactory manner. It was clear that in terms of operational flexibility and sustainability Britain was gradually outpacing its rivals.

While Europe was convulsed by the War of the Spanish Succession, another war was disturbing northern Europe. The Great Northern War (1700–21), principally between Russia and Sweden, straddled the Baltic from east to west. The Swedes and Danes had long maintained large battle fleets, but were challenged by an emerging Russian fleet being built by Tsar Peter I. Here battle fleets to protect troop convoys were vitally important, but so were the smaller vessels, especially oared galleys, able to operate on the shallow shores of the southern Baltic and the convoluted coastline of Finland and the Gulf of Riga. A Swedish battle fleet, allied to an English squadron, successfully covered a landing near Copenhagen in 1700 which compelled Denmark to renew the peace, but it was a clash between Russian and Swedish galley forces off Hango Head in July 1714 that proved to be the most decisive single naval action of the war. The Russian victory enabled her vessels to dominate the Finnish archipelago and forced Charles XII of Sweden to turn to privateers to continue operations at sea. After 1714, with the Elector of Hanover now George I of Great Britain, British naval forces were sent on a number of occasions between 1716 and 1727 to support Hanoverian interests in the Baltic, but her battle fleets were not ideal to influence predominantly coastal operations (Glete, 1993, pp. 233–9).

The war ended in 1721, although tensions continued. Across the Baltic lay the vital transport network for a war that spread along its shores. Here sea power could only be exercised by a mix of battle fleet, privateers and small vessels of war. States still had to make a judgement about the investment they were willing and able to put in to maintain sea power. Sweden and Denmark were exhausted by the war, and the Russian fleet went into decline with the death of Peter I in 1725.

An armed peace, 1714–39

By 1715 the idea that sea power was founded on the great state battle fleet was firmly entrenched in one state – Britain. In Britain the link between national security, political liberty, economic growth, fiscal strength, diplomatic strength and state naval power had assumed the status of an ideology. To other countries the value of the battle fleet was more questionable. The value of the state's battleships in projecting military power across the seas and protecting the homelands was not doubted in Denmark, Sweden and the United Provinces, but this had to be offset against the cost of building and maintaining the ships. The seaborne threat was still real, but the political and economic imperatives that the British perceived were not so clear to others. The French navy continued to decay for the first five years after the peace, and in 1720 it consisted of 33 line-of-battle ships and frigates against the British 154. The link between sea power and national security for most states was not as direct as in Britain. Economic growth did not depend on sea power. French trade in the West Indies grew faster than Britain's in the decades after 1714, giving rise to great concern in Britain. Likewise the supposed diplomatic strength conveyed by sea power was more limited than British ministers presumed. Intervention in the Baltic achieved far less than British or Hanoverian ministers had hoped. The disputes with Spain, which rumbled on throughout the 1720s and 1730s, erupting into war in 1718–20 and 1726–27, were not resolved through the decisive application of sea power. Spain's vulnerability to blockade of the American treasure fleets was less than expected, although the failure of the treasure to arrive in 1727 did have a direct impact on Spanish diplomacy, while naval power undermined Spanish ambitions at Gibraltar and in the Mediterranean. Nevertheless it did not resolve the fundamental points of dispute between Britain and Spain during this period. An important element of Britain's diplomatic power lay in her alliance with France from 1716 to 1731, which gave her a powerful army in Europe. The ending of this alliance forced Britain to rely almost exclusively on her navy for diplomatic weight, which in the great question of the Polish Succession (1733–38) was very little. To many of the political nation, convinced of the reciprocal advantages of sea power and domestic liberty, the refusal of Sir Robert Walpole's ministry to throw its weight against French ambitions in Europe seemed to threaten both liberty and power. To Walpole, sea power could not make a decisive contribution and neutrality seemed to be the most practical option.

This is not to suggest that Walpole ignored Britain's navy, rather that its diplomatic influence was more limited than a great deal of the political rhetoric of the period expected. The Royal Navy remained the principal force for both defence and projection of power overseas. Britain maintained a fleet of over 100 vessels 'in ordinary' – stripped down and watertight. Over this period Britain continued to invest in infrastructure that gave her the capability to send large squadrons over greater distances and maintain them there for longer periods. Plymouth dockyard was reorganized between 1717 and 1722. Portsmouth was expanded during the same years. The facilities at Port Mahon, Minorca, were adequate for a squadron in the Mediterranean, and after the siege of 1727 facilities at Gibraltar began to be developed. Port Antonio, on the north coast of Jamaica, was developed from 1729 in the hope of providing local protection to trade going through the Windward Passage. Port Royal was developed from 1735. English Harbour on Antigua was developed from 1728 to provide a secure, if limited, anchorage for warships. The administrative bodies, the Admiralty, the Navy Board and the Victualling Board, had a continuity of personnel which militated against innovation but ensured a degree of consistent expertise. This investment gave Britain a distinct advantage. Large numbers of ships could be despatched across the Atlantic and maintained there for longer than her rivals. At home Britain could expect to maintain a clear superiority over any enemy. Most important, the infrastructure that Britain had built up would enable her to weather the effects of attrition over a series of campaigns. There were still major problems of mobilization and maintenance, but when war came it was soon clear that British capabilities were far in excess of her rivals (Baugh, 1965).

To most powers the wars of 1689–1713 had not fundamentally altered their perception of sea power. The royal fleet was a powerful symbol of prestige. Battle squadrons could play important parts in projecting power and defending colonies and convoys, while wreaking havoc upon an enemy. On the other hand navies were hugely expensive and it took a long time to develop the necessary technical expertise, systems and practices. Nevertheless during the 1720s both France and Spain took a renewed interest in their fleets. The new Bourbon monarchy in Spain was determined to protect the empire in America and further its ambitions in Italy. Both depended on sea communications. In 1717 a naval and amphibious force overwhelmed the Savoyard garrison on Sardinia. In 1718 another force was landed on Sicily to drive out the Austrians. The British ability to operate substantial forces at a distance was soon demonstrated by the destruction of the Spanish fleet off Cape Passero in July 1718. The struggle for Sicily dragged on until October 1719, when the Austrians finally captured Messina, and the war was only concluded after a French army invaded Spain early in 1720.

Sea power was essential to Spanish plans, and José Patiño, the Intendant General of the Navy from 1717, continued the process of building up the fleet (Béthencourt Massieu, 1954). Between 1725 and 1740 the Spanish battle fleet grew from 16 to 43 warships. Naval yards were developed, including the large facility for building and repair at Havana, Cuba (Harbron, 1988, pp. 29–35). The navy was never powerful enough by itself to achieve significant diplomatic results. Gibraltar was not recaptured in 1727. The treasure was blockaded by the British in the Caribbean in the same year, and the British naval presence in the Tagus in 1735 could not be challenged effectively. Nonetheless the Spaniards had decided to invest in a substantial new navy of high quality ships.

France also began building again after 1725, when the young Comte de Maurepas became Secretary of State for the Navy. The plan was to expand the line of battle to 54 ships, and although this was not achieved there was a surge in building after 1720, and by 1740 France had about 47 line-of-battle ships. These ships were large seaworthy two-deckers, with good cruising capability and solid artillery platforms (Lavery, 1983, p. 80; Glete, 1993, pp. 259–61). There were, however, still many weaknesses. Crucially, funding did not grow at the same pace as the fleet. Under such circumstances, although Maurepas did a great deal, he could not develop the infrastructure significantly at home or overseas. The French navy remained superficially powerful but in practice extremely fragile. It could not stand long campaigns of attrition. During the 1730s French squadrons went on missions to Barbary, Genoa and Danzig, with limited success, but Maurepas's view of the role of the royal navy was not as an oceanic cruising battle fleet to challenge the British Royal Navy. Rather it was as squadrons supporting specific actions, such as merchant convoys or expeditionary forces, working in conjunction with privateering squadrons (Vergé-Franceschi, 1996, pp. 84–101; Villiers, 2002, pp. 104–10).

War, 1739–48

Anglo-Spanish disputes had never been properly settled since 1713. Spain was resentful at the British occupation of Gibraltar and Minorca, and highly suspicious of British traders interloping on the prohibited Spanish-American markets. British merchants were equally incensed at Spanish *guada costas* stopping and seizing vessels on spurious grounds. By mid-1739 the political room for manoeuvre had all but disappeared. Built upon a conviction that British sea power would rapidly reduce Spain to peace by seizure of Spanish territories in the Americas, seizure of the annual treasure fleets and disruption of her local commerce, the political pressure on the Walpole government to attack Spain became unstoppable (Woodfine, 1988). Expectations of British sea power ran high from the autumn of 1739, but by early 1744 disillusion had set in. It had not been possible to blockade the Spanish squadrons in their home ports. In the summer of 1740 the Ferrol and Cadiz squadrons got out to pre-empt a British expedition to the Caribbean. Another squadron got out of Barcelona in December 1741 to escort Spanish troops across to Italy. In April 1740 the belief that British ships and seamen were superior to the Spaniards was rudely shattered by the spirited if ultimately unsuccessful defence of the *Princessa* against three British seventy-gun ships. The large expedition sent out in September 1740 to take and hold significant Spanish territories in the Caribbean had achieved almost nothing by the autumn of 1742.

Worse was to come. From December 1740 Europe had been at war over the Austrian Succession. France had maintained a sort of neutrality in the Anglo-Spanish war, but the movements of her squadrons defended Spanish shipping and deflected British offensive action against Spain. In February 1744 the neutrality ended. A French squadron escorted a Spanish squadron out of Toulon. The Franco-Spanish force was attacked by Admiral Mathews's Mediterranean squadron on 22 February 1744, but the result was inconclusive. In the Channel a French invasion squadron moved from Brest to Dunkirk without being brought to battle by the home fleet under Sir John Norris. It was fortunately dispersed by gales. As the war with France broadened, British naval power did not achieve the results expected of it. During 1745 and 1746 French squadrons got out to the West Indies, Canada and the East Indies. Expeditions to the coast of France in 1746 and operations on the Indian sub-continent achieved little. With these disappointments, there was concern that British naval officers were not doing their duty to bring the French to battle. There were also some successes. In June 1744 Commodore George Anson returned from a circumnavigation of the world with a great quantity of plunder. A small squadron assisted New Englanders to capture the French town of Louisbourg, Cape Breton, in July 1745. The navy effectively deterred French intervention in the Jacobite rising throughout the summer and autumn of 1745, and later assisted the army's advance north to crush the Jacobites at Culloden in April 1746. In 1747 events at sea gave cause for cheer. In May Anson ran into a convoy off Cape Finisterre heading for Canada with a small escort. In a chase action he overwhelmed the escort and captured a few merchantmen. In June Captain Fox made a rich haul from a returning West Indian convoy. In October Admiral Hawke intercepted a convoy off Cape Finisterre and chased and captured most of the escort.

It seemed at last that sea power was having some clear results, but it had little impact on the peace negotiations. French victories in Flanders cancelled out the capture of Louisbourg. Superficially, little seemed to have altered in relation to the impact of sea power on diplomatic events. French and Spanish squadrons had largely achieved their missions (Vergé-Franceschi, 1996, pp. 91–101). Privateers had again done much of the damage to trade on all sides. France had lost about half her merchant shipping, 23 line-of-battle ships and 18 smaller ships, but her trade had not been destroyed nor had she been compelled by naval pressure to seek peace (Bosher, 1995). Spain had lost about half her pre-war naval tonnage (Glete, 1993, p. 264). Yet sea power had brought neither France nor Spain to their knees. Nevertheless a great deal had changed which was not entirely obvious at the time.

The infrastructure investment was clearly making a difference. Britain could maintain large forces in West Indian waters for years, while the French could hardly maintain a fleet there for a few months. The expedition sent out in 1740 under the Marquis d'Antin stayed hardly any time, and returned to France devastated by sickness. The expedition to Canada in 1746 took a long while to organize and was in poor condition when it reached Chibouctou Bay (later Halifax) in Nova Scotia. It too could not stay long before it was forced to withdraw, ravaged by sickness. In future any challenge to British local superiority in the Americas was going to be difficult. In European waters, the investment in Plymouth had made it a suitable base for a large squadron deployed in the western approaches – the Western Squadron. Supplied from Plymouth and Torbay, this force could maintain a watch off Ushant for convoys or battle fleets. The chances of either getting through unnoticed were shrinking. The Royal Navy had also been able to maintain larger numbers of cruising and small warships. These vessels had sounded the coasts of France from 1745, making themselves familiar with these waters. In future French coastal shipping would be far less secure. The impact of the privateers was less than in the previous wars. Trade had been disrupted, but economic dislocation, which had been a threat in the earlier wars, particularly the 1690s, did not reoccur. All nations, Britain included, seemed less vulnerable to privateering action.

All this added up to a further strengthening of British sea power relative to her rivals. British sea power, in the form of the battle fleet and the supporting maritime industries, was an increasingly robust, flexible long-range instrument. Neither France nor Spain had developed in the same way and for much of the Seven Years War (1756–63) France faced Britain alone at sea. The consequences rapidly became clear.

The Seven Years War, 1756–63

After the War of the Austrian Succession ended, France and Spain rebuilt their fleets. The achievement looked impressive. By 1756 France had 54 line-of-battle ships and Spain 39. The French officer corps were developing an increasing understanding of the maritime world with the establishment of the *Académie de la Marine* at Brest in 1752. The galley fleet which had been traditionally used to combat Spanish and Barbary maritime forces was increasingly irrelevant and was suppressed in 1748. The Bourbon navies looked as though they were developing the materials for truly oceanic sea power (Pritchard, 1987). Major weaknesses remained. The ships were high quality vessels, but the effort to produce them was exhausting. All navies suffered from a shortage of manpower and naval stores, but the order of magnitude of these problems was far greater in France and Spain than in Britain. While the British maritime population was expanding, the French and Spanish populations were relatively stagnant. By 1746–48 perhaps half the maritime labour force in France was needed for the navy in time of war (Le Goff, 1990). Despite an administrative system that looked far more rational than the 'press' operating in Britain, the French navy needed to dig much deeper into the labour pool. The French navy's ability to survive long-term attrition was extremely limited. Despite the expansion of the battle fleet it was still nowhere near the size of the Royal Navy. In 1755 the Royal Navy outnumbered the French navy by 66 line-of-battle ships and 43 frigates. Meeting the Royal Navy in battle at sea was an unattractive proposition. Squadron warfare in defence of convoys and expeditions, supported by privateering operations, remained the best option but exposed the navy, privateers and merchant marine to defeat in detail. In 1755, when war broke out again, Spain did not join France. British forces were less stretched than between 1739–48.

While with hindsight it is possible to see the great advantage Britain possessed in 1755, contemporaries were not so fortunate. Britain was vulnerable to pressure upon Hanover and to the threat of invasion. British naval forces had not destroyed French overseas commerce or colonies. Privateers of all nations had continued to cause more damage to trade than the royal navies. It was not entirely obvious that Britain would be able to mobilize or maintain its theoretical numerical advantage. Britain too could suffer from attrition. Neither the effectiveness nor the impact of sea power could have been foreseen in 1755.

For both Britain and France the conflict which broke out in 1755 had a much stronger colonial and maritime focus than any previous conflict. For both countries, results in the colonies were seen as both practicable and important. A clash at sea opened the war, and attrition quickly began to take its toll on France. Britain seized French merchantmen at sea, denying France the opportunity to mobilize a significant proportion of its limited labour pool. Perhaps 6000 seamen were captured in 1755 alone, enough to man one-fifth of the entire French navy. By 1763 about 60,000 French sailors languished in British gaols, of whom 70 per cent were skilled seamen (Villiers, 2002, p. 111; Harding, 1999, p. 210).

During the early years of the conflict French squadrons still got in and out, successfully escorting convoys. They threatened Britain with invasion, captured Minorca and even gained temporary superiority in North American waters. But the strain was apparent. Desertion, disease and capture were wearing down the pool of French sailors. The Minorca campaign dramatically reduced the manpower of the Toulon fleet. One more campaign in 1757 and the pool was exhausted. The Commissaire of Classes estimated that there were only 6800 seamen available on the Atlantic coast by the end of 1757. Meanwhile Britain's maritime resources matched the expansion of her naval forces. Despite a crisis in 1759, the press, bounties, and encouragement to foreign seamen enabled her to man 277 ships in that year. During the war Britain and her American colonies put over 1700 privateering expeditions to sea, compared to 710 French operations (Harding, 1999, pp. 209–10). The French maritime strategy was collapsing in an unexpectedly dramatic manner.

This domination at sea by the end of 1758 was to have consequences that had not been experienced before. By this date British confidence, experience and numbers overwhelmed the French. There were very few large battles, and these were largely chase actions. In October 1759, when the Marquis de Conflans prepared to put to sea with the Brest fleet to cover an invasion attempt on Britain, he was aware that his chances of either evading or beating the powerful Western Squadron under Admiral Hawke were slim (Le Moing, 2003). The Battle of Quiberon Bay on the afternoon of 20 November, when Hawke chased Conflans's fleet into the dangerous waters of Quiberon in the teeth of a gale and in gathering darkness, provided the practical and symbolic seal to British dominance.

Far more than in the previous war, French trade suffered. The Royal Navy's dominance enabled warships to cruise for trade in oceanic and coastal waters. Warships captured more French vessels than privateers. A more rigorous policy of seizing French trade in neutral ships applied further pressure. By the end of 1759 the royal yards in France were largely exhausted of naval stores, commerce was stopped, and the Treasurer of the Navy was bankrupt. The other consequence of the collapse of French naval power was the operational opportunities it gave to British forces across the globe. Sea power supported the conquest of Canada, the French West Indies and Bengal, all between 1759 and 1761. When Spain entered the war in 1761 her navy was completely unable to tip the balance in favour of the Bourbon monarchies. Havana and Manila fell in 1762 (Corbett, 1907).

The security which this domination gave to British trade was a major fillip to parliamentary confidence, which was the foundation of access to credit. Funds not only supported the continuing expansion of the Royal Navy, but also the expansion of the army and the provision of subsidies to colonies and to European allies. The expansion of the army in the Americas and the exploitation of provincial forces made the conquests of the West Indies and Canada possible. The despatch of a small army to Europe to assist Prussia, and the provision of subsidies, contributed to containing French gains in Europe. This time there would be no countervailing conquests by France in Europe with which to regain her colonial empire. The link between naval power and British military success was an essential part of the rhetoric that underpinned William Pitt's political position from 1757 to 1761. Although he was out of office when the Peace of Paris was signed in 1763, this relationship seemed to have been conclusively demonstrated. Martinique and Guadeloupe were returned, but Canada and Bengal were now in the British orbit. Prussia had been preserved. In British, French and Spanish eyes, sea power, in the form of the royal fleet, had had a decisive impact on European diplomatic events.

To some extent this overstated the case. Prussian resistance had prevented French gains in Europe, and it was not British credit or soldiers alone that were responsible. Frederick II's military skill and a great deal of luck had preserved his kingdom by the end of 1762. Nonetheless sea power was now seen as having a direct and powerful effect on diplomacy.

The rebuilding of sea power, 1763–75

Even before the Peace of Paris the French Minster of Marine, Choiseul, began to rebuild the French fleet. The treasury was empty but patriotic subscription provided funds to build some powerful new three-deck line-of-battle ships. From 1760 to 1766 Choiseul could not significantly improve funding, but he provided a critical determination to challenge Britain at sea by 1767. Under Choiseul and his successors, reforms of the officer corps were undertaken, tactical doctrine was developed, and bodies of marine infantry and artillery were established. The dockyard administration was reformed, Toulon and Brest were developed and strengthened, and new arsenals and hospitals were established. The ambitious building plan could not catch up with Britain, but between 1766 and 1770 France built twice the tonnage of Britain. By 1770 France had 68 line and 35 cruising warships against Britain's 126 line and 76 cruisers (Villiers, 1991).

While Britain maintained a healthy superiority over France, the development of the Spanish fleet, if joined to France, could pose problems. The re-organization of the central administration of the Spanish navy, new schools for engineers and shipwrights, and an expansion of the officer corps all suggested a strengthening of the basic infrastructure of the Spanish navy. The growth of the navy, when added to that of France, provided the Bourbon powers with a greater naval tonnage than Britain. The superiority Britain had enjoyed in the Seven Years War could not be relied on in the future (Merino Navarro, 1981).

Other powers were also investing in naval forces. The balance of power had not changed much in the Baltic since the death of Peter I of Russia in 1725.

The mixed fleets of galleys and sailing warships remained the foundations of amphibious and coastal operations during the Swedish–Russian War of 1741–42 and the Seven Years War. In the 1770s the Swedish navy underwent a number of administrative, organizational and operational reforms, but the fundamental structure, operational capabilities and roles of the fleets remained unchanged during the Swedish–Russian War of 1788–90.

Russian interest in naval power extended to the Black Sea and the Mediterranean. War with Turkey broke out in 1768, and in 1769 the Baltic fleet was sent to the Mediterranean. The annihilation of the Turkish fleet at Chesme in July 1770 gave the Russians complete domination of the Levant (Anderson, 1952, pp. 286–91). It was a spectacular expression of sea power, but it was unable to apply decisive pressure on Constantinople and it was to be another four years before the Turks accepted a peace.

Sea power in balance, 1775–83

The American War of Independence showed Britain both the limits and intrinsic strength of her sea power (Stout, 1973). Attempts to use sea power to bring the colonists to submission between 1768 and 1775 completely failed. Once the war had broken out, the great resources that had supported British sea power disappeared. About half of all British mercantile tonnage was built in American yards by 1775. The facilities in American ports were gone and the provisions and naval stores that maintained the facilities in the West Indies and Halifax were now cut off. Worse, to maintain a large army in North America required a huge and continuous transport operation to ferry troops, stores and provisions from Britain. The focus of effort had to be on the army, and to keep finances under control the fleet was not fully mobilized. In 1776 New York was captured to provide a base of operations. The Royal Navy ravaged the coastline of rebel-held territory, but it could not stop American privateers attacking transports and merchantmen, nor could it prevent Americans trading with or receiving assistance from neutral powers.

When France entered the war in 1778 Britain was unprepared to fight a battle-fleet war, and the revived French navy could initially meet the British on nearly equal numerical terms. This got worse in 1779 when Spain joined the war, and a Franco-Spanish fleet entered the Channel in the summer to cover an invasion force. The crisis was weathered, but the Royal Navy was pulled in many directions, having interests to protect ranging from Canada to India. North America was by then slipping down the list of priorities. By 1780 the British were outnumbered in battleships, and in December of that year the Dutch joined the coalition. Sea power successfully defended the home island, the West Indies, Gibraltar and India, but it could not suppress the rebels nor prevent the French from assisting them. At the critical point in the autumn of

1781 it could not provide the succour needed by Cornwallis's besieged army at Yorktown.

   On the other hand the basic strength of British maritime resources was beginning to tell. Britain began to out-build the allies. Two hundred and seventy thousand tons of naval shipping was launched between 1776 and 1785 (Glete, 1993, p. 274). In the West Indies Rodney outfought the French during 1782. In India even the most powerful French intervention in the region during the eighteenth century failed to shake British control. By 1785 Britain again outnumbered the Bourbon navies in ships of the line. It was too late, however. America was lost, as was Minorca. To all the powers involved, sea power, as expressed in the royal battle fleets, seemed to have been decisive. French squadrons had played an important role in keeping the American rebellion going in the critical period of 1780–81, while Britain had been brought to crisis in 1779 by the threat of invasion. However the Royal Navy had preserved vital British interests at this time, and had emerged from the war with a strengthened reputation. Privateers had not had a major impact on the course of events, except for the Dutch, who suffered greatly from the depredations of British privateers. While financial retrenchment was necessary for all nations following the demands of this war, it did not fall on the navies. Sea power had become a central strand of European military ambition.

The European naval race and the dominance of Great Britain, 1783–1815

The period between 1783 and 1789 saw the high point of naval building. The Royal Navy continued to expand after 1785, albeit more slowly than in the preceding five years. In 1790 Britain had 145 line and 131 cruising warships. The Dutch virtually rebuilt their fleet after the disasters of 1781–84. The French added 27 ships of the line and 25 frigates to their navy by 1785, replacing losses and bringing it to its most powerful point during the entire eighteenth century by 1793. The ships were well designed and built. Spain added 60,000 tons of naval shipping between 1783 and 1789 (Glete, 1993, pp. 553, 589, 635). The Turks rebuilt their fleet after Chesme and carried out reform of the administration. The advances in shipboard hygiene, medicine, organization and diet at sea were also becoming more general (Lloyd and Coulter, 1961; Buchet, 1997).

   The fleets of the great powers had never been larger or individual ships more powerful and seaworthy. The integration of line-of-battle ships, cruising warships and smaller vessels to project effective sea power, from oceanic encounter battles to local blockades, coastal raiding or invasion, had never been so complete. The maritime resources of the countries were now integrated with the state navies to support such operations. Privateering remained an important feature of most maritime economies in time of war, when normal trade was disrupted, but it could not answer the needs of states employing sea power. By 1789 power at sea depended on the state's navy, which in turn depended on an expanding maritime economy, an effective bureaucracy in all aspects of naval life, and growing professionalization of the officer corps. All these things were happening in Europe in the last twenty years of the eighteenth century. The maritime economy continued to grow, and reforms of naval administration continued across Europe. The officer corps of France, Spain and Turkey continued to reform. Only in the United States, where bureaucracy and professionalism within the navy smacked dangerously of royal patronage and absolutism, did the debate about the battle-fleet navy continue (Symonds, 1980).

The state fleet had become a powerful, flexible and influential weapon with a long reach, but it was still extremely fragile due to its expense and complexity. The revolution in France in 1789 dealt a crippling blow to the French navy. Already largely immobilized due to lack of funds throughout the 1780s, the revolution drove the majority of the officer corps from their posts by 1791. The dockyards were crippled by a crisis of authority. The war in Europe had a major impact on navies. French sea power collapsed with the revolution. Mutinies, losses to the Toulon fleet during the Anglo-Spanish occupation in 1793, the battle of the First of June 1794 and smaller actions took their toll on the French fleet (Acerra and Meyer, 1988). It revived owing to victories on land during 1795–97, as Spain and the United Provinces joined the French Republic against Britain. Britain was again outnumbered at sea by 1796, but the attrition of naval warfare between 1797 and 1801 gave the advantage back to Britain. Spanish naval forces damaged at the battle of St Vincent in February 1797 decayed in port. The Dutch fleet was largely immobilized after the defeat at Camperdown in October 1797. The French Mediterranean fleet was destroyed at Aboukir Bay in August 1798. French ports were blockaded and their yards were gradually starved of vital stores. Seamen were captured and the vital pool of maritime resources was drained. Napoleon's hold over Europe from 1801 to 1814 gave the French empire the naval resources of Holland, Denmark and Venice, but his attempts to unite them at one point to provide overwhelming force were never realized. The Trafalgar campaign of 1803–05 was the last serious challenge to British naval supremacy.

Britain's use of sea power was by this time highly sophisticated. The battle fleet and the inshore cruising squadrons ranged around most of Europe's coasts, disrupting trade and starving the dockyards of stores and seamen. Naval forces covered colonial expeditions to the West Indies (1793–98) aimed at increasing wealth in Britain in the face of the financial strains of war. Other expeditions secured the Dutch colonies at the Cape of Good Hope and in the East Indies. Naval power, by bombardment or expeditionary forces, countered

French attempts to gather naval strength from other countries, such as Denmark in 1801 and 1807, or Holland in 1809. French possessions in the West Indies were again captured in 1809–10. Naval forces covered the operations of merchants as they broke the attempts by Napoleon to exclude British trade from continental Europe. Forces at Malta supported trade to southern Europe. Forces in the North Sea provided protection for access to the Baltic, where initially false papers and from 1809 a small naval force supporting Sweden gave protection to trade. Sea power lay at the heart of Britain's contribution to the defeat of Napoleon. It made possible the long campaign in Portugal and Spain. While it did not cause the resistance of Russia, Austria and Prussia which eventually destroyed Napoleon's empire in 1813–14, the subsidies and supplies that followed the resistance helped the campaign.

Oceanic sea power did not cause the collapse of the Napoleonic empire, but Britain clearly possessed a dominance unseen before. Sea power had saved Britain from invasion, protected its vital economic interests and provided the basis to support those allies whose armies destroyed the *Grand Armée*. By 1815 sea power was a complex and expensive weapon. At its core lay the state battle fleet, but sea power was exercised as much by cruising and smaller warships, without which it would not have had much effect. It required the integration of large and small naval forces, a highly professional officer corps, the resources of the maritime economy, including manpower, building and maintenance skills, credit facilities, merchant vessels for transport and to a lesser extent privateers, together with the legal system, the state fiscal system and colonial governments. Even with superiority in all these factors by 1800 sea power was not easily or consistently applied. Britain faced a crisis between 1796 and 1798. She suffered defeats in most parts of the world, but on the whole the effects of attrition on her enemies destroyed the fabric of their fragile naval forces.

References

Acerra, M. and Meyer, J. 1988. *Marines et Révolution*, Rennes.

Alcalá-Zamora y Queipo de Llano, J. 1975. *España, Flandes y el Mar del Norte (1618–1639)*, Barcelona.

Anderson, R.C. 1971. 'The Sicilian War of 1674–1678', *Mariner's Mirror*, 57, 239–65.

—— 1969. *Naval Wars in the Baltic, 1522–1850*, London.

—— 1952. *Naval Wars in the Levant, 1559–1853*, Liverpool.

Aubrey, P. 1979. *The Defeat of James Stuart's Armada*, Leicester.

Bamford, P.W. 1973. *Fighting Ships and Prisons: The Mediterranean Galleys of France in the Age of Louis XIV*, Minneapolis.

Baugh, D. 1965. *British Naval Administration in the Age of Walpole*, Princeton.

Béthencourt Massieu, A. 1954. *Patino en la Politica Internaçional de Felipe V*, Valladolid.

Bosher, J.F. 1995. 'Guerre et activities de la Marine Marchande au Canada 1743–1763', in *Etat, Marine et Société*, ed. M. Acerra and others, Paris, 49–71.

Bromley, J. 1987. *Corsairs and Navies 1660–1760*, London.

Bruijn, J.R. 1977. 'Dutch Privateering during the Second and Third Anglo-Dutch Wars', *Acta Historica Nederlandicae*, 9, 79–93.

Buchet, C., ed. 1997. *L'Homme, la Sante et la Mer*, Paris.

—— 1991. *La Lutte pour l'Espace Caraibe et la Façade Atlantique de l'Amerique Centrale du Sud (1672–1768)*, Paris.

Capp, B. 1989. *Cromwell's Navy: The Fleet and the English Republic, 1648–1660*, Oxford.

Corbett, J.S. 1907. *England and the Seven Years War*, London.

Dessert, D. 1996. *La Royale: Vaisseaux et Marine du Roi Soleil*, Paris.

Ehrman, J. 1953. *The Navy in the War of William III*, Cambridge.

Gardiner, R., ed. 1992. *The Line of Battle: The Sailing Warship 1650–1840*, London.

Glete, J. 1993. *Navies and Nations: Warships, Navies and State Building in Europe and America, 1500–1860*, Stockholm.

Harbron, J.D. 1988. *Trafalgar and the Spanish Navy*, London.

Harding, R. 1999. *Sea Power and Naval Warfare, 1650–1830*, London.

Jones, D.W. 1988. *War and Economy in the Age of William III and Marlborough*, Oxford.

Lavery, B. 1983. *The Ship of the Line: The Development of the Battlefleet 1650–1850*, London.

Le Goff, T.J.A. 1990. 'Problèmes de recrutement de la marine française pendant la Guerre de Sept Ans', *Revue Historique*, 283, 205–33.

Le Moing, G. 2003. *La Bataille Navale des Cardinaux (20 novembre 1759)*, Paris.

Lloyd, C. and Coulter, J.L.S. 1961. *Medicine and the Navy*, vol. 3, Edinburgh.

Merino Navarro, J.P. 1981. *La Armada Española en el siglo XVIII*, Madrid.

Nerzic, J.-Y. and Buchet, C. 2002. *Marins et Flibustiers du Roi Soleil – Carthagène 1697*, Paris.

Ollard, R. 1969. *Man of War: Sir Robert Holmes and the Restoration Navy*, London.

Pritchard, J. 1987. *Louis XV's Navy, 1748–1762: A Study of Organisation and Administration*, Kingston.

Serrano Mangas, F. 1985. *Los Galeones de la Carrera de Indias, 1650–1700*, Seville.

Stout, N.R. 1973. *The Royal Navy in America, 1760–1775: A Study of Enforcement of British Colonial Policy in the Era of the American Revolution*, Annapolis.

Symcox, G. 1974. *The Crisis of French Sea Power 1688–1697; From Guerre d'Escadre to Guerre de Course*, The Hague.

Symonds, C.L. 1980. *Navalists and Antinavalists: The Naval Policy Debate in the United States, 1785–1827*, Newark.

Taillemite, E. and Guillaume, P. 1991. *Tourville et Beveziers*, Paris.

Torres Ramirez, B. 1981. *La Armada de Barlovento*, Seville.

Vergé-Franceschi, M. 1996. *La Marine Française au XVIIIᵉ, Siecle: Guerres– Administration– Exploration*, Paris.

Villiers, P. 2002. 'Les Convois Coloniaux en Atlantique de Louis XIV à Louis XVI', in *Bordeaux et la Marine de Guerre (xviie–xxe siècles)*, ed. S. Marzagalli, Bordeaux, 104–10.

—— 1991. *Marine Royale, Corsaires et Trafic dans l'Atlantique de Louis XIV a Louis XVI*, Dunkirk.

Woodfine, P. 1988. 'Ideas of Naval Power and the Conflict with Spain, 1737–1742', in *The British Navy and Uses of Naval Power in the Eighteenth Century*, ed. J.M. Black and P. Woodfine, Leicester, 71–90.

11

The French Revolutionary and Napoleonic Wars

Alan Forrest

If the years from 1740 had seen repeated trials of strength between the armies of the European powers, these were dwarfed by the Wars of the French Revolution and Empire. Between 1792 and 1815 France was almost constantly in a state of war with coalitions of European states, and from 1803 – after the collapse of the truce signed at Amiens – there was no peace across the greater part of the continent until Napoleon's final defeat at Waterloo. Napoleon himself moved restlessly from one campaign to another, fighting some sixty battles in all and winning the great majority of them (Gates, 1997, p. 5). Indeed, the sheer scale of warfare made it difficult for contemporaries to regard the Revolutionary and Napoleonic Wars as simply the continuation of the traditional struggles between states that had characterized the eighteenth century. They distorted trade patterns and consumed an unprecedented proportion of the country's economic wealth. And French objectives were not limited to the customary aims of traditional European wars, be they the acquisition of granaries, of neighbouring territories or of overseas colonies, dynastic successions, or (as with Louis XIV) dreams of attaining natural frontiers. France, it appeared, now thought on an altogether more ambitious scale, attempting to impose its new polity on much of continental Europe during the revolutionary years, before aspiring to create a new Carolingian empire under Napoleon. French troops fanned out across Europe as far as the Peninsula and Russia, they crossed the Mediterranean to Egypt and North Africa, and in a moment of misguided over-ambition they attempted to overturn the new black government in Haiti. They did not hesitate to open up several fronts at once or to take on powerful coalitions of states. Indeed, by the early years of the nineteenth century there seemed no limit either to French territorial ambitions or to her military capability. France, it appeared, had created a new kind of warfare, and many contemporary observers were convinced that 1789 had ushered in a military as well as a political revolution across Europe.

But did it? French revolutionary leaders consistently spoke as though this war was different in kind, where the revolution had to conquer or risk obliteration.

196

This had a number of consequences. It changed the purpose of military engagement, it made the drawing up of peace treaties more difficult, and most importantly it changed the character of armies as the nature of personal allegiance was undermined. It also, as Vergniaud and others recognized, made it virtually impossible for the French to rely on any allies in what was an essentially ideological conflict. For the revolution provided Frenchmen with a constitution that guaranteed their liberty, in contrast to the despotism that reigned elsewhere. Vergniaud, warming to his theme and supporting Brissot's call for war against the emperor – and it was specifically the emperor, not the Austrian people – argued that no compromise was possible with kings and tyrants, since the very existence of the French constitution posed an intractable threat to their authority: 'It makes men free, whereas they want to rule over populations of slaves.' The crowned heads of Europe, moreover, had not responded neutrally to the French Revolution; they were already at work undermining France's achievement, resorting to three different 'armies of reptiles' to destroy the revolution from within – an army of intriguers and slanderers who exploited their links with *émigré* nobles and with the court faction grouped around the queen, Marie-Antoinette; an army of priests who sought to subvert Catholic opinion in the provinces; and an army of speculators, fired by greed to destroy the country's economy. For the war party, of whom Vergniaud was a highly eloquent spokesman, this was a war quite different from those that had gone before, a war of principle between a sovereign people and ambitious tyrants, between citizens and slaves, opposing two systems of government that were mutually antagonistic and unable to coexist in peace.

It is, however, significant that in this same speech to the Convention Vergniaud spoke in two quite different registers. On the one hand he talked of moral absolutes, the essential rightness of a war to secure the liberty of the peoples of Europe: 'I see the spirits of past generations crowding into this temple to beg us, in the name of the evils which slavery made them suffer, to preserve from these evils those future generations whose destinies we hold in our hands.' He asked his fellow deputies to listen to these prayers, since 'by meriting the title of benefactors of your country you will also merit that of benefactors of the human race'. This was heady stuff, and it secured the orator a standing ovation from the Convention. It also provided proof of his revolutionary credentials. But he took care also to base his case for war on much narrower diplomatic claims that would help sway those deputies who were well versed in eighteenth-century diplomatic convention. For technically the *casus belli* was less grandiosely universal – the claim that Leopold had broken the 1756 treaty between France and Austria when he signed the Treaty of Pilnitz. This resulted in an untenable situation, Vergniaud claimed, whereby the emperor was now free to break all his treaty obligations, while being able to insist that France abided by hers. This was all the more difficult to support in that the 1756 treaty had been highly disadvantageous to France, reducing her role to that of an impotent spectator while Austria dismembered Poland and Bavaria, and forcing France to betray her historic obligations to the Ottoman empire, 'the most ancient and loyal of her allies'. To applause he neatly combined the diplomatic case with the case for human liberty: 'It is easy to see that breaking this treaty is as necessary a revolution for Europe as the demolition of the Bastille was for France' (Stephens, 1892, I, pp. 276–8, 284–5, 280).

If I have lingered somewhat long over this one speech, it is because it illustrates the essential ambivalence which lay even at the heart of the war party in the Convention – a recognition that France needed credible justification for going to war, credible, that is, to contemporaries inside and beyond France, and was reluctant to break entirely with the conventions of international diplomacy. France could not afford to be regarded as an irresponsible warmonger, and if there was to be a war, then it had to be one that the rest of Europe could accept and understand. Once war started, of course, the political leaders threw caution to the winds, declaring the *patrie en danger*, summoning up a national effort against the enemy, and equating the other European powers – Austria and Prussia in 1792, soon to be expanded to Britain and Spain – with reaction and counter-revolution. They warned that the price of defeat would be the destruction of liberty and the reimposition of monarchy, and that if Paris fell the civilian population would be slaughtered to avenge the killing of Louis XVI. Fears and conspiracy theories helped to fan the flames of the war effort, while responsibility for national defence was placed on the population at large, as France turned to mass levies and armed the people against the enemy. The idea of the 'nation in arms', of an entire population mobilized to defend the country against attack, became one of the watchwords of the First Republic, and once in uniform the soldiers were subjected to regular doses of political propaganda. During the 1790s the Convention sent out deputies-on-mission and *commissaires* to the armies to remind the men of the cause for which they were fighting, and to underline their patriotic duty as citizens. The revolutionary content of this message reached its peak under the Jacobins, when the deputies did not hesitate to equate the defence of the *patrie* with that of the revolution, or to portray the armies as an instrument of politics (Biard, 2002, pp. 286–96). Radical newspapers were distributed to the troops, political clubs flourished in the battalions, and ordinary soldiers were encouraged to denounce any officer suspected of treason or of harbouring counter-revolutionary ambitions. The Jacobins did not want an army that discussed and disagreed about political issues, but they did want an army of citizens, of men who were valued by others for their sacrifice to the nation and who, while accepting the inevitable restrictions on their personal liberty imposed by military discipline, enjoyed the status and dignity of *hommes libres*. Robespierre never tired of telling the soldiers of his confidence in them – as opposed to their officers, whom he regarded with an almost pathological distrust – and of his belief that they were, as men of the people, good and moral beings on whom the future of the republic was dependent. 'Carefully avoid', he told the Convention, 'everything that could unite in the souls of the *citoyens-soldats* such military spirit as cuts off soldiers from citizens and which yokes glory and self-interest to things that make for the ruin of citizens' (Déprez, 1910–67, VII, p. 263).

This was, of course, revolutionary rhetoric, and how far it actually improved the morale of the soldiers or caused them to fight with greater commitment must remain a moot point. Certainly there are few historians writing today who would echo Albert Soboul when he wrote that ideology could 'arouse the mass of the common people and inspire them to make even the supreme sacrifice' (Soboul, 1959, p. 4). What evidence we have – largely that of soldiers' personal correspondence and journals – is predictably inconclusive. There were, of course, among the soldiers some committed Jacobins and militants from the Paris sections, who relished the ideological language of the period and dreamed of preaching revolution across Europe. Such men wrote home gleefully recounting the execution of an *émigré* officer or the forcible closure of local churches during the dechristianization campaign. They dutifully kept in touch with their local clubs and municipal councils, offering their opinions on political developments and distributing praise and blame where these seemed appropriate. They evidently saw the army as an instrument of political progress, repeating the accounts of victories that they had been given and showing their approval for the work of the deputies who accompanied their battalions. But they were not numerous. Indeed, it is striking how the vast majority of soldiers' accounts of their time in the armies deliberately eschew political discussion, confining themselves to the things that really mattered to them – food and clothing, the shortage of firewood, training, forced marches, fatigue and fear of battle (Forrest, 2002). Besides, with the passage of time the political content of military rhetoric faded significantly, giving way to the more traditional demand that the troops take a professional pride in soldiering, and to the encouragement of corps loyalty. If there was still an ideological tone to the discourse of the Directory and the Consulate it was less revolutionary than it was patriotic, the identification of the military effort with the nation and the interests of France.

All rhetoric is of course propagandist, a means both of motivating and enthusing those in uniform and of persuading the civilian population to accept the hardships that accompanied the war effort. How far should we allow ourselves to be swayed by the revolutionary message which the French were preaching, especially in the ideologically charged period of the Jacobin republic? Among contemporary observers, Karl von Clausewitz was one who was deeply impressed by the work of the revolution and by the reforms it generated, and this vision, which lies at the heart of his famous treatise, *On War*, would have a profound influence on succeeding generations. In Clausewitz's view, the real novelty of the revolution lay in its linking of service with citizenship, the identification of the military with the nation and the French people, which, he believed, gave the French a level of energy which no other state could rival. 'It is true', he wrote, 'that war itself has undergone significant changes in character and methods, changes that have brought it closer to its absolute form. But these changes did not come about because the French government freed itself, so to speak, from the harness of policy; they were caused by the new political conditions which the French Revolution created, both in France and in Europe as a whole, conditions that set in motion new means and new forces and have thus made possible a degree of energy in war that otherwise would have been inconceivable' (Paret, 1985, p. 33). This energy had its basis in the key concept of citizenship. Thirty million Frenchmen were now prepared to make a sacrifice for the nation, since all thirty million regarded themselves as citizens of the French state. It was to this energy, he believed, rather than to tactical innovation, that Napoleon owed his great victories over the Austrians and Prussians in 1805 and 1806, and their leaders were at fault in not reforming their own political and military systems to take account of it. For, Clausewitz insisted, it brought about an upheaval in the conduct of war which deserved to be called a 'revolution', a moment which would change forever the scale and character of European armies (Paret, 1992, p. 77). Prussia, for instance, which had prided itself on using tactics inherited from its foremost military leader of modern times, Frederick the Great, was forced to rethink its recruitment and deployment strategies in the light of Napoleon's obvious superiority in the field.

Clausewitz's interpretation not only dominated military thinking throughout much of the following century; it has also had a profound effect on the way in which historians have discussed the Revolutionary Wars in particular. Historians sympathetic to the revolution and to the French republican tradition, from Jules Michelet through to Albert Soboul, have emphasized what was new about the revolutionary armies and about the nature of the war, and they have suggested that an army consisting of citizens, and thus representative of the people, must have had greater motivation to fight than the hirelings and mercenaries who filled the ranks of their enemies. It was, they implied, a new kind of army, one made necessary by the new kind of society which France had become. Others have preferred to see the period in more traditional terms, dismissing the revolutionaries' talk of innovation as part of a wider attack on a now-discredited *ancien régime*. On the ground there was little that was truly new. The French, insists one historian, fought in formations and deployed tactics that would have been instantly recognizable to most eighteenth-century generals (Black, 1999, pp. 192–4), while more conservative nineteenth-century historians of the French army, many of them serving officers, saw a necessary conflict between a revolutionary state which sought to deny its past, and an army that was the principal defender of the nation's heritage (Bertaud, 1979, pp. 13–14). That is not to imply that the revolution had no effect on the French military; it clearly had, both on the army's size and its composition. But it is important to distinguish between political and social changes instituted by the revolution – like citizenship and the destruction of the corporate social order of the *ancien régime*, which changed utterly both the character of the officer corps and the approach to recruitment – and tactical innovation on the battlefield. The revolutionaries were not noted for their mastery of military tactics. Even Carnot, the greatest strategist of the period, was more gifted as an organizer than as a tactical innovator. And if Napoleon was the most creative tactician of his times, he also insisted on the importance of study and reflection in winning battles, annotating the great French strategists of the past and applying their lessons to his own campaigns. He learned from them all – from Folard and Bourcet, de Saxe and Guibert – taking key concepts from each which he then incorporated into his own strategy, notably the importance of destroying the heart of the enemy, the immense value of surprise attacks, the advantages of swift manoeuvres, and the use of quick-marching columns. He also learned from studying the victories of the revolution in the early 1790s, particularly the value of surprise attacks from the wings to cut off the enemy from the rear. His genius lay in adapting existing ideas as much as in innovating, applying the battlefield tactics he had learned from others to the situations he faced at Ulm or Jena or Eylau (Serman and Bertaud, 1998, pp. 165–6).

There is certainly strong evidence to suggest that in purely military terms the Revolutionary and Napoleonic Wars were more evolutionary than revolutionary, relying on traditional manoeuvres and well-tested tactics. Military drill and training were laid down in the infantry manual of 1791, itself a reworked version of the provisional drill-book of 1788 and a publication deeply rooted in eighteenth-century practice (Règlement, 1792). It called for battles to be fought by a mixture of line and column, with the three-deep line to maximize fire power in battle and to structure assaults on the enemy, and the column for the approach and for bayonet charges against fortified defences (Rothenberg, 1978, p. 114). This would change little over the twenty-three years of war; indeed, at Waterloo Jeremy Black can talk of much that was utterly traditional in the armies' formations, adding, only half-facetiously, that 'the squares that resisted Ney's cavalry looked back on nearly half a millennium to Crécy, where English longbowmen had defeated attacking French cavalry: firepower bringing low physical force' (Black, 1994, p. 194). In practice, of course, the French did not always have either the discipline or the training necessary to carry out these manoeuvres. The old line army could perform them, as could the first volunteers of 1791, but the increasing resort to conscription and mass levies meant that most units were composed of young soldiers poorly trained in the art of warfare. For this reason much was made of the natural swagger and *élan* of the French troops, and their appetite for battle, and many of the engagements of the 1790s disintegrated into mass assaults on the enemy, with loose and largely unplanned skirmishing. Skirmishing, indeed, would remain an essential tactic throughout the Napoleonic Wars, complementing the more formal manoeuvres of the line. It was, above all, the role of the light infantry, on which Napoleon relied so heavily on the battlefield, especially as a response to artillery attack. To be fully effective, skirmishers needed both skill and experience; the skirmishers who had the greatest impact were highly mobile, fighting in open order and relying on individual initiative, often taking to the woods or to rough terrain to snipe at the enemy and harass their formations. They were also used in defence, to protect their own side's close-order formations against attack, with the result that 'a bickering fight against opposing skirmishers was the most characteristic of all their activities' (Muir, 1998, pp. 52–3).

As a general Napoleon had many estimable qualities. He had an unrivalled ability to read a battle and to second-guess the enemy's movements, the patience to prepare carefully before each engagement, and an enviable capacity for winning the trust of his troops and making them feel that he shared both their ambitions and their sufferings. In part this reflects his genius for publicity and propaganda, using everything from honours and promotions to art and newspapers to grab the public imagination, and to seize maximum advantage even from campaigns which ended in failure, like Egypt. But there was much more to it than that. He was notable for incisive decision-taking in the heat of battle, and – in an age when communications were still flawed – he often guessed and gambled. He overwhelmingly favoured the offensive, attacking the enemy with the aim of destroying his troops and of imposing battle as the culmination of manoeuvres. Napoleon did not think defensively; as his great adversary, Wellington, expressed it, 'it was always their object to fight a great battle', while his own was generally to avoid one (Gates, 1997, p. 4). At his best – and especially in the campaigns of 1805 and 1806 – he used speed and surprise to great advantage, and in successive engagements he brilliantly outmanoeuvred his opponents, sweeping the armies of continental Europe before him. But with the passage of time his touch seemed to desert him. He could be rash and headstrong, and his tendency to gamble, to seek out engagement at almost any cost, could result in expensive mistakes. Indeed, Owen Connelly has gone so far as to suggest that he often 'blundered' to victory, beginning almost every battle with a strategic error before charging at the enemy in the hope of winning by sheer force of numbers (Connelly, 1987, pp. 1–2). That is clearly an overstatement, but his later campaigns in

Russia and the Peninsula do demonstrate his fallibility, while a number of the marshals on whom he increasingly came to depend in the field were given to poor planning and catastrophic errors of judgement.

Whatever his qualities as a general and a leader of men, Napoleon cannot be seen as a great military innovator, and nor – though his campaigns continued to be studied admiringly by future generations of officer cadets at Saint-Cyr – did he make any significant contribution to the science of war. In warfare, he declared, there were some principles to be followed, but they were few in number. He recognized the need to keep his army united, to identify the weak spot in the enemy's formation, and to hold back enough seasoned troops for a final decisive assault on the enemy (Serman and Bertaud, 1998, p. 166). More generally, he continued to use and adapt the tactics of the later eighteenth century, in particular the rapid encirclement of the enemy from the wings, which he used to such good effect against the Austrians and Prussians. These were tactics which Napoleon had studied at artillery school at Auxonne in the 1780s, where his teachers laid great store by the writings of the great eighteenth-century French tacticians like Guibert and du Teil, which emphasized the need for speed on the battlefield and the use of massed artillery at critical points in battles (Wilson-Smith, 2002, p. 11). Bonaparte learned these lessons well and would not forget them, studying them on the eve of critical battles and adapting them to the requirements of the larger mass armies he had at his command. As an artillery officer he understood better than most the value of powerful guns in support of the infantry, and he went on to strengthen the role of the artillery within his armies, laying new emphasis on firepower, increasing the number of artillery regiments, both foot and horse, and replacing many of the smaller guns with six- and twelve-pounders (Rothenberg, 1978, p. 143). But in this he was adapting the received wisdom of the day rather than thinking up wholly new approaches to tactical deployment. Significantly, for instance, he continued to deploy his artillery in support of the infantry, who remained the main fighting force within the armies.

The military science of the revolutionary years, like so much revolutionary thinking, had its roots in the ideas and inventions of the Enlightenment. Throughout the eighteenth century there had been a growing awareness of the value of a mathematical and scientific approach to military effectiveness, and experts were increasingly listened to, especially in the wake of crushing military defeats like those at Rossbach in 1757 or Minden in 1759. Armies and navies became increasingly dependent on the design and capacity of their weaponry, from field guns and light artillery pieces to manoeuvrable warships. New technologies played an important role in determining the outcome of war, a fact that may have escaped the attention of some cavalry and infantry officers, but which was critical to the artillery. Artillery officers were increasingly well schooled in mathematics and the physical sciences, to the point where able scholars like Lazare Carnot could combine a career in the artillery with another publishing philosophy and mathematics, while at the Ecole du Génie at Mézières the geometrician Gaspard Monge actively encouraged his young charges to dabble in scientific research and created links with the Academy of Sciences in Paris (Dhombres and Dhombres, 1997, p. 82). When Napoleon arrived to begin his studies at Auxonne, he entered a climate in which the major reformist ideas of the eighteenth century already commanded wide support.

Eighteenth-century strategists, many of them senior or recently-retired generals surveying their own experiences in the field, had written widely on different aspects of military science and the art of war, and by the 1780s theirs were the key texts on which a new generation of military leaders was weaned. Among older writers, Puységur was widely cited, along with the authors whose works were cited in the *Encyclopédie* – such as Turenne and the Marquis de Santa-Cruz – while the *chevalier* Folard argued in his *Traité des colonnes* of 1724 that the Bourbon army was too dependent on firepower, and that to be successful it needed to attack in columns rather than lines and to resort to the use of shock tactics (Bois, 1992, p. 185). Also influential was the Maréchal de Saxe, the victor of Fontenoy, whose greatest work, *Mes Rêveries, ou réflexions sur l'art de la guerre*, was published posthumously in 1757, and who again urged greater use of surprise in the field. The column was more mobile, it brought men rapidly into hand-to-hand conflict, and it facilitated use of the bayonet, in whose potency he profoundly believed. De Saxe roundly criticized the recruitment and discipline of the French armies, which he attacked for sapping morale. It was, he believed, the shortcomings of the *ancien régime* system of recruitment – based on voluntary engagement and periodic *racolage* or impressment, supplemented after 1726 by compulsory militia service – that explained poor levels of motivation among the troops and an intolerably high desertion rate. For it produced an army of unwilling soldiers, and one for which society had little respect. Rather, he suggested, France should oblige every young man, regardless of his station, to serve his prince and his country for a period of five years. He wanted captains made more responsible for the welfare of their men and urged officers to be seen to be fair, a clear criticism of the disciplinary codes in force in the eighteenth century. That, in turn, placed obligations on officers – something that had an unfamiliar ring in a society where 'a young man of good birth sees it as an insult if the court does not entrust a regiment to him by the age of eighteen or twenty' (Saxe, 1757, p. 25).

Even more radical in his attacks on military conventions was Comte Hyppolite de Guibert, whose *Essai général de tactique* of 1772 became one of the reformers' most potent texts. (For the following discussion see also Forrest, 2004.) Guibert pointed out that the wars between nations which were to come would demand very different armies from those of Bourbon France. He criticized the army for being too slow and cumbersome, with its organization in deep columns leaving it vulnerable to enemy attack. To counter this he proposed short attack columns of only three or four men, who would be less exposed to enemy fire and would be able to move quickly from column to line formation (Bertaud, 1997, p. 95). He then reformed army organization by the creation of the division, a standing unit that would remain in place in peacetime, and which grouped together elements of all arms – infantry, artillery and cavalry. His purpose was to increase manoeuvrability on the battlefield, with each division able to act independently and to respond to emergencies and opportunities as they presented themselves. By the end of the *ancien régime* Guibert's advice had been followed on military organization, and the French army had been restructured along divisional lines. But his reformist instincts ranged much more widely, and parts of his work spoke a language that was suggestive of the revolution to come. He dedicated his essay to his country, his *patrie*, 'to the king who is its father, to the ministers who administer it, to all the orders of the state who compose its membership, to all Frenchmen who are its children'. Only when all united and rallied to the nation, he believed, would its power be assured, only when all, 'the master and the subjects, the great and the small, are honoured to call themselves citizens'. For serious military reform demanded changes in the values that guided society: 'Our troops are not constituted militarily. Our values are not military values. That is even more true of our soldiers and officers, who have neither the habit of frugality, nor the patience, nor the physical strength which are the primary constituent qualities of warriors. These qualities are not honoured in our century; rather they are undermined and ridiculed by the dominant spirit of luxury' (Guibert, 1977, pp. 51, 238). To produce effective soldiers Guibert demanded nothing less than a profound change in the cultural values that ran through French society.

The French army of the later eighteenth century had also been provided with improved weaponry, especially in the artillery. Indeed, some of the most significant technological advances of the last years of the *ancien régime* had been in the field of military engineering, with the production of weapons which were more adaptable and simpler to reload, and with a new reliance on the technology of interchangeable parts, something that had become possible as a result of France's as yet incomplete industrial revolution. By 1785 the necessary technology was available, largely through the work of a military gunsmith, Honoré Blanc, who used steel dies to forge pieces of identical dimensions and thus produce a revolutionary new flintlock mechanism. Blanc held out the prospect of cheaper, faster manufacture with less scope for human error. In this he was encouraged by the French artillery service at Vincennes, and especially by Jean-Baptiste Gribeauval, who had been impressed by the Austrian artillery he had seen while serving in the Seven Years War, and was determined to reorganize musket production throughout the kingdom (Alder, 1997, pp. 1–4).

The result was not just standardized weapons, but more accurate ones too, in which the gunners could have confidence. Better casting methods led to lighter and more manoeuvrable cannon, while the use of pre-packaged rounds increased the fire rate. Artillery began to play a much larger role in battle plans, and by the time of the French Revolution France could boast the best artillery in Europe (Black, 1999, p. 195).

All this might seem to constitute a powerful case for a rather conservative view of the Revolutionary and Napoleonic Wars as the last of a line of traditional conflicts between European states. The tactics and weaponry were scarcely revolutionary, having evolved gradually across the eighteenth century in response to military setbacks and to innovation elsewhere, most notably by Frederick the Great. And some of the major changes of the period – in particular the reliance on the bayonet and the almost mythical appeal to *l'arme blanche* – resulted less from tactical astuteness than from a dire shortage of firearms (Lynn, 1984, p. 279). Some have argued that the reasons for going to war were different, that this was, as the revolutionary leaders claimed, a struggle between mutually intolerant ideologies rather than a bid for short-term gain. But even if the French may at times have been carried away by their own rhetoric, there is no reason to think that the other protagonists in the wars – Russia, Prussia, Spain, Austria or Great Britain – chose to resume hostilities for other than the most traditional reasons, because they saw the opportunity to secure a coveted stretch of land or to seize commercial advantage, or because they adjudged the French army to be in a satisfactorily weakened condition, with mutinies in the ranks and as many as a third of the officer class resigning their commissions. In 1791 it seemed a timely moment to launch themselves into what many assumed would be a brief encounter; the Austrians were convinced that France would give up without a fight, while in Prussia Frederick William II's aide-de-camp, Johann Rudolf von Bischoffwerder, urged his fellow officers not to buy too many horses since 'the comedy will not last long' and they would be back home by the autumn. In the circumstances it was an easy mistake to make. What is more surprising is that the war party in France could also have persuaded themselves that victory would come quickly, with the nation in arms invincible and the peoples of Europe rising spontaneously to welcome the French as liberators. Nonsense it may have been, but it proved to be highly persuasive nonsense in the excitable atmosphere of the Assembly (Blanning, 1986, pp. 116, 108–13).

Yet the revolutionaries' faith in the concept of the nation in arms was not misconceived, and Clausewitz was right to believe that in this respect at least the French Revolution had changed the face of warfare for ever. This was a war fought on a scale that was without precedent, both in a theatre of war which extended from Lisbon to Moscow by way of Italy and the Nile, and in the numbers of men it consumed. The French were able to mobilize a much higher proportion of their population than had been possible in previous eras, fielding between two and three million soldiers over the period, and were able to sustain huge losses; nearly 900,000 men died during the Napoleonic campaigns alone. They achieved this by transforming the methods of recruitment on which they and other eighteenth-century states relied. They got rid of the notion of a personal service to the monarch or the local nobleman, and with it, briefly at least, the heavy reliance on foreign mercenaries. After experimenting with a volunteer army, the revolutionaries turned to a series of special levies – the *levée des 300,000* of March 1793 and the much larger *levée en masse* of the following summer – so that by 1794 they had raised an army which, on paper at least, numbered three-quarters of a million men. The *levée en masse* also introduced the notion that the whole of society was geared up for war, whether as combatants or in ancillary roles. 'The young men shall go to battle', read the decree; 'the married men shall forge arms and transport provisions; the women shall make tents and clothes, and shall serve in the hospitals; the children shall turn old linen into lint; the old men shall repair to the public places and preach the unity of the republic and hatred of kings' (Stewart, 1951, pp. 472–4). All could not figure in the front line – the health of the economy and the maintenance of food supplies made it vitally important that the labour force was not denuded of men – but all had a contribution to make to the war effort. And the size of the army recruited in 1793 was such that the men raised by the *levée en masse* continued to provide the bulk of the troops France required until the end of the decade.

From 1799, moreover, with the *Loi Jourdan-Delbrel*, the Directory introduced the first annual conscription, which, after a brief medical examination, placed all those young men aged 20 to 25 who were deemed fit for service in five classes, with the youngest destined to march first. In this way Napoleon's generals could decide each campaign season how many fresh troops they needed. The number actually taken and incorporated into battalions varied hugely from year to year, until, in the dog days of the Russian campaign, he was able in 1812–13 to conscript a million men, though at huge cost to agriculture and the economy. Like the revolutionary generals before him, Napoleon had mass armies at his command, and this both changed the character of the war and gave the French a military advantage which few would have predicted in 1791. It was this *masse*, vitally, which allowed the French to seize the initiative, and which, combined with revolutionary zeal and renewed self-belief, enabled them to recover from early setbacks and turn the war around, inflicting heavy and unexpected defeats on the traditional armies of their opponents in 1792, and exporting the revolution beyond their own frontiers in the years that followed. So it was this *masse* that allowed Napoleon after 1799 to wage wars characterized by high mobility, the deliberate seeking of battle, and frontal and flanking attacks that had relatively little regard for casualties. With the capability always to replace any men he lost, soldiers became more dispensable, and the human costs of war grew massively in consequence. The carefully-nurtured image of a general who cared for the welfare of his troops contrasted grimly with the mortality statistics as line after line of infantry were thrown into battle.

The size of the armies and the ways in which they were recruited brought other changes in their wake. Size affected military tactics, since large and often raw battalions required a different approach, one where enthusiasm and spontaneity played a greater part than precise manoeuvres. It also made it necessary to reorganize the military in such a way that the older, better-trained soldiers could pass on their wisdom to the young volunteers or still younger conscripts, and so that rivalries between different kinds of troops did not undermine harmony in the armies. This led in the revolutionary period to Dubois-Crancé's proposal to get rid of the separate identities of the old line army and the new volunteers, unifying them into a single force – two-thirds volunteers, one-third line – by means of the *amalgame*. But the organizational challenge did not stop there. Huge armies travelling long distances from home had other needs too, of which provisioning, uniforms and boot leather, supply trains, horses and donkeys, military hospitals, field surgeons and efficient postal communications were only a few. These were essential support services which extended far beyond the traditional requirements of the eighteenth-century military, and which stretched the resources of an eighteenth-century state. They also required organization, a staff organization sufficiently sophisticated to direct such large bodies of men. Here the French are widely acknowledged to have led Europe even before the outbreak of the revolution in 1789. From the ideas of Pierre Bourcet at the end of the *ancien régime*, through Carnot's introduction of the *bureau topographique*, to Berthier's reorganization of the army field staff in 1796, French staffing structures were admired for their efficacy. Napoleon built on these reforms, and faced with the challenge of managing and supplying the *Grande Armée* he developed his personal staff, or *maison*, into a staff within a staff. The military department of the *maison* – known as the *cabinet* – was divided into discrete secretarial, topographic and intelligence sections, which allowed the emperor to collect considerable information on the enemy and the lie of the land before he became embroiled in any military engagement. He continued to rely heavily on the skills and experience of Berthier, now his chief of staff, and on thorough reconnaissance, which many see as central to his military success (Rothenberg, 1978, pp. 209–10).

That Napoleon could fill and refill his armies with fresh recruits was not a reflection of the popularity of soldiering, nor did it imply a huge groundswell of support for his policies. Rather it is testimony to his civil administration, to the efficiency of the prefectoral system, and to a decade of local government reform under the revolution which had the effect of extending the outreach of the state. The state was crucial here. Conscripts had to be persuaded to turn up to the *conseil de révision*, just as parents and village mayors had to be dissuaded from sheltering draft-dodgers or from providing food and work for deserters. Conscription might be well on the road to becoming the rite of passage it would be for so much of the nineteenth century, but that did not make it any more popular, especially once army service became divorced from any sense of national or ideological commitment by the individual. It required firm policing, whether by local gendarmes or by serving troops sent to organize sweeps of the countryside where deserters were known to be hiding, and it called for the use of *garnisaires*, soldiers billeted on the families of those missing from their battalions, while deserters risked exemplary punishment. In short, it was solved not by the call of duty but by raw power, the flexing of the muscles of what Howard Brown has called Napoleon's 'security state' (Brown, 1997, pp. 661–95). During the revolution and empire we know that hundreds of thousands of young men sought to escape the service to which they were condemned, and that some regions of the country were notoriously reluctant to provide soldiers. Deserters often lived rough or relied on the charity of friends and neighbours to escape the authorities; others turned to begging and crime, or joined the armed bands that roamed the countryside terrorizing travellers and threatening farms and livestock. Bringing them and their families to book, and ending what the government saw as a 'scourge' threatening public order and state security, was one of the most difficult challenges faced by the authorities, and posed a persistent threat to the authority of the empire (Forrest, 1989, pp. 219–37).

What is perhaps more impressive, however, is the fact that under the revolution and the empire the French obtained the bulk of the soldiers they sought, and that mass armies were indeed formed in the face of such widespread resentment. With the passage of time, just as the army was made more professional, so recruitment became more routine, something that every 20-year-old in France would expect to face. That undoubtedly made military service, and with it the militarization of society, easier to accept. It also democratized the army, making it more representative of society at large, removing the gulf which had separated soldier and civilian during much of the eighteenth century, and which had produced an image of the infantryman throughout the continent as someone to be despised and feared. Soldiers after 1789 enjoyed greater status in the community, and – though discipline necessarily remained severe – there was greater communication between officers and other ranks, a greater bond of unity within the battalions. The officer corps was no longer drawn from a different world from their men, no longer obligatorily of noble stock as they had been in the corporatist society of the *ancien régime*. The new military constitution placed new emphasis on merit;

merit being defined in terms of skills, education, experience and leadership potential. In his report on the proposed decree in September 1790, Alexandre de Lameth argued that for the majority of military men – nobles as well as commoners – the *ancien régime* army had offered little beyond 'a continual burden of oppression, humiliation and ingratitude'. Commoners had been excluded from the officer corps and had been denied deserved promotions, but provincial nobles had also suffered discrimination, remaining in the lower ranks while less deserving men from the court nobility had an exclusive monopoly of the top honours (Blaufarb, 2002, pp. 66–7). The abolition of the corporate legal and social structures of the *ancien régime* was a landmark moment in the growth of meritocracy, and helped to provide France with a modern army in which careers were open to talent.

The revolutionaries' principal contribution to this process of modernization lay less in the apparent politicization of the armies under the Jacobins – a fleeting change which had already begun to evaporate before Robespierre fell – than in the reward of merit. Of course it can be argued that this was forced upon them by the collapse of the line army they had inherited, and by the resignation of one-third of the officers within the first two years, leaving a gaping chasm in the officer ranks and leading to extraordinarily rapid turnover. This placed the government in a serious predicament, especially once war was declared, since it left the army bereft of experienced officers. By the beginning of 1794, for instance, of nearly 500 officers who had served with Rochambeau in America between 1780 and 1783, only 38 (just over 7 per cent) were still in the army (Scott, 1998, p. 182). The government's response was to throw open officer rank to those talented and battle-hardened *sous-officiers* who impressed their superiors and had the trust of their peers; under the new law junior officers were to be elected by those alongside whom they served and whose lives would depend on their decisions. The change worked well, resulting in rapid promotions and producing a generation of young and able officers who, because of their social position, could never have been promoted during the *ancien régime*. Some went on to become Napoleonic marshals, men of modest backgrounds like Augereau or Lannes. And though Napoleon himself showered his generals with honours and titles and shared none of the anti-noble prejudice of the revolutionary years, he remained largely loyal to the principle that in a modern army, just as in a modern state, careers must remain open to talent. He made no attempt to restore the officer class of the *ancien régime*, and he continued to insist on those qualities of competence and professionalism which had characterized the armies he had led as a revolutionary general in Italy (Bertaud, 1986, pp. 91–112; 1972, pp. 513–36). In this respect, too, the revolution and empire can be shown to have made major changes to the eighteenth-century French army and to point forward to the new century and to a more democratic age.

References

Alder, K. 1997. *Engineering the Revolution: Arms and Enlightenment in France, 1763–1815*, Princeton.

Bertaud, J.-P. 1997. 'The Soldier', in *Enlightenment Portraits*, ed. M. Vovelle, Chicago.

—— 1986. 'Napoleon's Officers', *Past and Present*, 112, 91–112.

—— 1979. *La Révolution armée. Les soldats-citoyens et la Révolution Française*, Paris.

—— 1972. 'Le recrutement et l'avancement des officiers de la Révolution', *Annales historiques de la Révolution Française*, 210, 513–36.

Biard, M. 2002. *Missionnaires de la République. Les représentants du peuple en mission, 1793–95*, Paris.

Black, J.M. 1999. *Warfare in the Eighteenth Century*, London.

—— 1994. *European Warfare, 1660–1815*, London.

Blanning, T.C.W. 1986. *The Origins of the French Revolutionary Wars*, London.

Blaufarb, R. 2002. *The French Army, 1750–1820. Careers, Talent, Merit*, Manchester.

Bois, J.-P. 1992. *Maurice de Saxe*, Paris.

Brown, H.G. 1997. 'From Organic Society to Security State: The War on Brigandage in France, 1797–1802', *Journal of Modern History*, 69, 661–95.

Connelly, O. 1987. *Blundering to Glory. Napoleon's Military Campaigns*, Wilmington.

Déprez, E. and others, eds. 1910–67. *Maximilien Robespierre, Oeuvres complètes*, Paris.

Dhombres, J. and Dhombres, N. 1997. *Lazare Carnot*, Paris.

Forrest, A. 2004. 'Enlightenment, Science and Army Reform in Eighteenth Century France', in *Enlightenment and Revolution. Essays in Honour of Norman Hampson*, ed. M. Crook, A. Forrest and W. Doyle, Aldershot.

—— 2002. *Napoleon's Men. The Soldiers of the Revolution and Empire*, London.

—— 1989. *Conscripts and Deserters. The Army and French Society during the Revolution and Empire*, New York.

Gates, D. 1997. *The Napoleonic Wars, 1803–15*, London.

Guibert, J.A.H. de. 1977. *Ecrits militaires, 1772–1790*, Paris.

Lynn, J.A. 1984. *The Bayonets of the Republic: Motivation and Tactics in the Army of Revolutionary France, 1791–1794*, Urbana.

Muir, R. 1998. *Tactics and the Experience of Battle in the Age of Napoleon*, New Haven.

Paret, P. 1992. *Understanding War. Essays on Clausewitz and the History of Military Power*, Princeton.

—— 1985. *Clausewitz and the State. The Man, his Theories and his Times*, Princeton.

Règlement. 1792. *Règlement concernant l'exercice et les manoeuvres de l'infanterie. Du 1er août 1791*, Paris.

Rothenberg, G.E. 1978. *The Art of Warfare in the Age of Napoleon*, Bloomington.

Saxe, Maréchal de. 1757. *Mes Rêveries, ou réflexions sur l'art de la guerre*, Paris.

Scott, S.F. 1998. *From Yorktown to Valmy. The Transformation of the French Army in an Age of Revolution*, Denver.

Serman, W. and Bertaud, J.-P. 1998. *Nouvelle histoire militaire de la France, 1789–1919*, Paris.

Soboul, A. 1959. *Les soldats de l'an II*, Paris.

Stephens, H.M. 1892. *The Principal Speeches of the Statesmen and Orators of the French Revolution*, Oxford.

Stewart, J.H. 1951. *A Documentary Survey of the French Revolution*, New York.

Wilson-Smith, T. 2002. *Napoleon, Man of War, Man of Peace*, London.

12
A Wider Perspective: War outside the West

Jeremy Black

The central conceptual problem with military history is how to acknowledge, appreciate and analyse its diversity. This problem stems from the linked characteristics of the presentation of the subject in western work, with its tendency firstly to focus largely, if not exclusively, on western developments, and secondly to consider those elsewhere in terms of western paradigms and the interaction of non-western powers with the west, these latter two factors being closely intertwined, although, of course, analytically different points (Black, 2000; 2003a). Thus, for example, the focus in discussion of military revolutions is the west, the definitions are western, and in so far as non-western powers feature it is in order to record the success of their western counterparts (Knox and Murray, 2001). There is, indeed, a circular quality in this analysis, which is a serious methodological limitation, and one shared by an empirical failure to even note developments in other cultures.

It might be thought that their discussion in terms of conflict with the west addresses this issue, but that is far from the case. Here there is a linked empirical and methodological problem, in that there is a tendency to treat what is frequently marginal as if it were central. Thus, for both China and Persia, conflict with western powers in the period covered by this book was episodic and relatively minor. This was not the case for the Ottoman Turks, but with them it is necessary to recognize the secondary nature of conflict with Christendom (as opposed to with other Islamic powers) in the sixteenth century, the first four decades of the seventeenth, and for the 1720s, early 1730s and 1740s, the last a period that tends to be neglected in Ottoman military history (but see Olson, 1975).

To turn to another example, Geoff Mortimer's excellent synopsis for this book included the following reasoned response to the sort of views I have just outlined:

> The counter-argument, while acknowledging the regional importance of all these theatres of war, is that they are of relatively little global significance

in an era increasingly dominated by western military technology and the export of western power with it around the world. It was, after all, the Europeans who established colonies and seized territories in the Americas and Asia rather than vice versa. This also contrasts significantly with an earlier period in which Arab armies conquered and colonized Spain and the Balkans, western crusades signally failed to achieve their objective, and eastern Europe trembled before the Mongol incursions of Genghis Khan and his successors.

This analysis invites several comments. First, it assumes that non-western powers should have behaved like their (or rather some of their) western counterparts. For example China and Japan, both of which, alongside Korea, displayed considerable short-range naval capability during the Korean War of the 1590s (Turnbull, 2002), did not seek to match western colonialization, but, rather than treating that as evidence of failure, it is necessary to consider the goals of these and other non-western states. This illuminates the contrast between the trans-oceanic colonization and power projection of the Atlantic European powers, and the far more land-based character of non-European powers and their eastern European counterparts, even though some of the former, such as China, Japan and the Ottoman empire, had lengthy coastlines (but see Hess, 1970, and Brummett, 1994). Neither China nor Japan made an impact in the Pacific, either by launching a programme of voyages of exploration or by creating settlement colonies across the ocean or around its rim. This does not, however, indicate a failure of administrative capability. Indeed in the 1750s China achieved a success in the Eurasian heartland that exceeded those accomplished by Russia that century, when it overcame the Dzungars of Xianking, demonstrating an impressive logistical capability that was the product of a sophisticated administrative system (Perdue, 1996).

The absence from the oceans appears a failure in Atlanticist terms, but these are scarcely appropriate as a means of judging societies that did not share these assumptions. Furthermore the extent of European participation in and control over European–Asian trade links has been exaggerated; this is true of maritime trade, but overland links remained important and were dominated by Asians (Chaudhury and Morineau, 1999). Indeed the western merchants struggling to gain entry to oriental markets, or financing their purchases with bullion exports, would have been as surprised as the Dutch expelled from Taiwan in 1661–62 or the Russians driven from the Amur valley in 1685–89 to be told about western dominance.

This perception can be sharpened up by rethinking the world in 1500 and 1800 in terms of equal-population cartograms, which provide demographically weighted maps that are far more useful than the conventional equal-area maps. Furthermore these maps would suggest that western power was less central than the use of equal-area maps would imply. This is an important perspective, because the subliminal quality of cartographic images conveys impressions of importance that help dictate conclusions about success. In many respects these are misleading. Rethinking the world spatially, in terms of equal-population cartograms, very much revises the impression of western success. For example, the conquest of much of Siberia, and, late in the period, of part of Australia, become relatively inconsequential, as indeed does that of eastern North America. Instead the European achievements that repay attention are those toward the close of the period, particularly if the conquests of the Aztec and Inca empires are adjusted to take note of the impact of smallpox and other diseases on their populations (so that their size in terms of equal-area cartograms is reduced). The British conquests in India in the second half of the eighteenth century are crucial in demographic terms. As yet there has been no extensive rethinking of world history in terms of equal-population cartograms, but it is important at all levels. It would also repay attention at the European level, not least because such an approach would ensure that more attention is devoted to Italy than is usually the case in accounts of seventeenth and eighteenth-century European warfare. Furthermore, an emphasis on gaining control of people helps underline the importance of sieges.

Outside Europe, as already indicated, the demographic approach encourages a re-conceptualization of European expansion, but it is also important in relation to conflict between non-western powers. This is true both at the macro and at the micro level. Inevitably, more attention is devoted to China, and indeed conflict within the country is, at this level, more significant than that between many European states. This is especially true of the ultimately unsuccessful Sanfen rebellion of 1673–81. This 'War of the Three Feudatories' was begun by powerful generals who were provincial governors, especially Wu Sangui, who controlled most of south-western China and who rebelled in 1673, followed, in 1674, by Jingzhong Jimao and, in 1676, by Zhixin Kexi. These feudatories overran most of south China, but were driven back to the south-west by 1677 thanks to the use of Green Standard troops – loyal Chinese forces. Earlier, Manchu units had failed to defeat the rebels, and this failure, together with the success of the Green Standard forces, helped in the consolidation of Chinese administrative techniques, personnel and priorities. Wu died in 1678, but the rebellion did not end until 1681. It had come close to overthrowing the Manchu, but Wu and his allies were unable to translate their success in south China into the conquest of the north. In terms of the number of combatants and the scale of area covered, this war was more important than the contemporaneous Dutch War. The rebellion was particularly serious because it arose from within the structure of the Chinese state as altered by Manchu conquest. Wu was a key Ming general who had joined the Manchu in 1644, and he played a major role in the Manchu conquest of southern China in the 1640s and 1650s, being rewarded with considerable power and autonomy (Kessler, 1976). In contrast, eighteenth-century risings in China, although still large-scale and important, especially the White Lotus rebellion of 1796–1805 in Shaanxi, and the Miao revolt in Hunan and Guizhou in 1795–1805, were not from within the political structure.

Alongside space, it is important to add the variable of time. It is all too easy to assume an early modern situation described and analysed in terms of the use of gunpowder weaponry and naval force projection. This runs such episodes as the conquests of the Aztecs and the Incas in the early sixteenth century together with battles such as Plassey (1757), in order to produce a single situation that can be analysed in one fashion, an approach that encourages an emphasis on technology. This is misleading. Firstly it underrates the chronological as well as the geographical distinctiveness of episodes of western success, and therefore the need to consider them separately. Such a disaggregation reduces the temptation to run together the largely patchy empirical evidence that tactical changes, in the shape of the invention of the volley and the redeployment of firepower, made much difference in practice to the outcome of battles.

Secondly it fails to judge chronological developments alongside those in the non-west, and to understand their mutual dynamism. Thus the globalization of which western power projection was an important aspect involved a strong degree of mutual dependence. If it was westerners, and especially in the eighteenth century the British, who organized the new systems, they could not do so in a unilateral fashion. Instead, mutual dependence and power projection were in a dynamic tension, frequently shifting in balance. Rivalry between the western powers was important in this, not least in affecting the options for syncretic relationships. Rivalry with the Bourbons in the eighteenth century, and even more with revolutionary and Napoleonic France, led to an emphasis in Britain on power projection, which helped reshape the terms of mutual dependence with non-European countries (Ingram, 1981; Mackesy, 1984, esp. pp. 144–7; Förster, 1992). However the nature and chronology of this reshaping varied greatly, as the contrasts between British relations with China and India, and later China and Japan, indicated. In the nineteenth century, rivalry with Russia helped drive forward a similar process (Yapp, 1980).

Having made these theoretical points, it is time to turn to war outside the west in order to ask what were the master elements in the narrative. Here again there is the issue of significance, in particular the question of whether lasting impact is the key topic to pursue, and if so how to define 'lasting' and 'impact'. For example, the fate of Safavid Persia, overthrown by the Afghan Ghazais in 1722, offered a dramatic episode, but its wider significance is unclear. The fate of Safavid Persia was important in the Persian Gulf, as well as to Oman, Afghanistan, northern India, central Asia, the Caucasus, and to the

Ottoman empire, all of which experienced the campaigning of Nadir Shah of Persia in the 1730s and 1740s (Lockhart, 1935–37). Nevertheless it is difficult to see this as playing a formative role in the nineteenth or twentieth-century world, not least because neither the Afghan control, which lasted until defeated in 1729, nor the empire of Nadir Shah, proved lasting; indeed the latter was very much an expression of individual military drive. More generally, the states of the region between the Ottoman empire and Hindustan were unable to coalesce lastingly to provide a strength sufficient to thwart the growing interest and power there of Britain and Russia in the nineteenth century.

Such a *longue durée* approach might appear to render redundant much of the history of the non-west, but it is also necessary to consider its application to the more conventional cast of military history. If the Persia of Nadir Shah, the campaigns of which have received insufficient attention, is to be dismissed, possibly alongside Alaung-hpaya of Burma in the 1750s and Tashin of Siam in the 1770s, both of whom had major successes, then it can be asked why Napoleon is worthy of consideration, as his empire rapidly ended in failure and certainly did not set the geopolitical parameters for the western world. Again, if the context is institutional continuity, not individual genius, then it is worth asking why modern German military history deserves attention, as the General Staff presided over the disasters of two world wars, disasters that culminated in the unconditional surrender of Germany, the dissolution of the German military, including the General Staff, and the partition and occupation of Germany.

These issues invite debate, and they certainly underline the questionable character of any Eurocentric emphasis for land warfare. The situation is different on the water, at least for deep-draught naval capability, although there is also need for study of this question, more particularly for shallow-water capability. The suggestion above of a cartographic re-conceptualization can also be extended to the watery sphere, with a need to place the emphasis on rivers, lakes, deltas, estuaries, lagoons and inshore waters, alongside the oceans that dominate western attention and analysis. Thus, for the seventeenth century, it is important to consider not only the revival in the Ottoman fleet, which covered the massive invasion of Crete in 1645, and the Chinese fleets that helped drive the Dutch from the Pescadores Islands in 1604 and 1624 and from Taiwan in 1661–62, but also the formidable navy with well-gunned warships that the Omani Arabs created after they captured the Portuguese base of Muscat in 1650 (Murphey, 1993, pp. 198–200; Setton, 1991; Blussé, 1973; Boxer, 1926–27; Bathurst, 1972, pp. 99–103). In terms of amphibious operations, the most impressive in the seventeenth century were by non-Europeans: the Ottomans against Crete; Coxinga, the Ming loyalist, against Taiwan, followed, in 1683, by the conquest of Taiwan by the Chinese under Admiral Shi Lang; and, albeit against weaker opposition, by the Omanis against Mombasa (Boxer and Azvedo, 1960, pp. 59–73, 81–3).

In South Asian waters, Mataram, Aceh, Mughal and Magh fleets all played a local role, although Sultan Iskander Muda of Aceh was defeated when he attacked Malacca, then Portuguese-controlled, in 1629. Large squadrons of Mughal riverboats carrying cannon played a major role in defeating the fleet of Arakan in 1666. In the eighteenth century substantial navies were deployed by only a handful of non-European powers, principally the Ottoman empire, the Barbary states of north Africa, the Omani Arabs, and the Maratha Angria family on the Konkon coast of India. The ships of these powers had a greater range than war canoes and approximated more closely to European warships, but they lacked the destructive power of the latter; the Barbary, Omani and Angria ships were commerce raiders with the emphasis on speed and manoeuvrability, whereas the heavier, slower ships of the line of European navies were designed for battle and stressed battering power. When, in 1735, the Pasha of Ottoman-ruled Basra defeated a Persian naval attempt to seize the port, he did so by commandeering British ships.

In some parts of the world, canoes were important. These boats were shallow in draught and therefore enjoyed an inshore range denied to European warships. Their crews usually fought with missile weapons, increasingly muskets, and some canoes also carried cannon (Wright, 1976; Sandin, 1967). Areas where canoes were particularly important included, firstly, inland waterway systems, especially in Amazonia, the eastern half of North America as well as its Pacific coastal region, and the valleys of the Brahmaputra and Irrawaddy, secondly, coastal systems, particularly the lagoons of west Africa, and thirdly, island systems, such as the Hawaiian archipelago (Tregaskis, 1973). By the end of the eighteenth century, the fleets of outrigger canoes of the Betsimisaraka and Sakalava of Madagascar raided as far as the mainland of northern Mozambique. As yet these and other forces are not only largely unstudied but also scarcely mentioned in general accounts of naval power and warfare. Thus a definition of capability is asserted rather than discussed, a common problem in military history.

To turn to another approach to significance, geopolitical links were created and contested throughout the period. Alongside those that commonly dominate attention, it is necessary to focus on the creation of two relationships that were to help define the succeeding centuries, and were thus an important part of the legacy of the period. The conquest of Egypt by the Ottomans in 1517 is generally treated with far less prominence than the achievements of Cortes against the Aztecs, but the battle of Raydaniyya on 23 January, with the victory achieved in less than twenty minutes, helped define the western Islamic world; it was the Omdurman of its age, and yet much more significant. From Egypt the Ottomans rapidly extended their power along the coast of north Africa, down the Red Sea, and into the Arabian peninsula, underlining their prestige by gaining the guardianship of the Holy Places (Hess, 1973).

This linking of the Turkic and Arabic worlds helped to give the Ottomans the resources, energy and confidence to press the Safavids hard to the east and to drive forward against Christendom to the west, and it created a geopolitical system that in large part lasted until World War I, a reminder of the late onset of 'modernity' if seen in terms of western control. Egypt itself was not to be wrested from the Ottomans until the nineteenth century, and then initially by Mehmet Ali, the Viceroy, and only in 1882 by Britain. The earlier European impact – Napoleon's conquest in 1798 and the British counter-invasion in 1801 – was short-lived, and a British invasion in 1807 was unsuccessful.

The second relationship of lasting importance was the overcoming of the steppe challenge by the Chinese in the 1750s, an achievement that helped to define the modern world. The challenge of nomadic power was finally overcome when the Chinese crushed the Dzhungars, and China gained strategic depth (Barfield, 1989).

Mention of the Ottomans and the Chinese underlines another important aspect of the achievement of major non-western powers and suggests another way in which they can be judged: the range of physical and military environments in which they had to operate. Thus the Ottomans fought not only the Safavids and the Mamluks, but also the Europeans on land in Europe, north Africa and Abyssinia (where the Portuguese helped the Abyssinians), and at sea in the Mediterranean, Red Sea, Persian Gulf and Indian Ocean, as well as fighting a series of less powerful polities ranging from Bedouin Arabs to opponents in the Caucasus.

The roots of this success in multiple capability can be compared and contrasted with those of European Atlanticist powers. Like that of the latter, Ottoman capability drew on a military system that required a considerable measure of organization, especially in logistics (Finkel, 1988). However the Ottoman military was arguably more effective (here a comparative methodology is required) in combining the strengths of different systems: organizational/ bureaucratic and fiscal strengths, alongside tribal forces, including allies and tributaries, especially the Crimean Tatars. The diversity of the Ottoman military structure was an inherent source of strength, one linked to the breadth and depth of its recruitment system.

Similarly in China, once conquered by the Manchu in the mid-seventeenth century, the combination of effective forces and successful logistical and organizational systems made the army particularly efficacious and able to operate in a range of environments. The banner system enabled Mongols, Chinese and Manchu to work together as part of a single military machine. Organization meant not only military structures, but also the ability to evolve and maintain a military organization which was adapted to the realities of the political situation, not least in its capacity to cope with the multiple crises that war brought. In short, the powers best able to wage war were those which got close to a synthesis of military organization and political/administrative capacity, although that was far from being a fixed relationship, not least because political parameters varied depending on the goals of the war in question. The eighteenth-century British navy and the early eighteenth-century French army were good examples of well-adapted military organizations, as, more generally, was the military of the period, whereas the situation had been less happy across much of Europe during the period 1560–1660 (Parrott, 2001; Black, 2003b). Military organization should be understood not as necessarily superior in any objective way, but rather as adaptation to the particular political and social realities of the state. This is a point that reminds us of the need to study specific detail, and which thus challenges simplistic attempts by political scientists to offer a typology of states based on the relationship between war and political developments.

The European powers were to deliver something similar to the Manchu banner system outside Europe, as a result of hiring, co-opting or allying with local forces ranging from the sepoys in India to Native American tribes. However the emphasis, as also seen with the use of the sepoys, was on standardized operating procedure focused on infantry volleys. This relative uniformity has customarily been seen as an aspect of western superiority, but this needs reconsideration. It is by no means clear that this uniformity provided an adequate adaptability which permitted an effective response to different environments, and indeed this lack of adaptability can be linked to failure. Geoffrey Parker has recently claimed that 'time and again, infantry volley fire enabled western troops to defeat far larger numbers of non-western adversaries'. Indeed he cites Wellington as his evidence for this providing the basis of British strength in Asia (Parker, 2003, pp. 13–14). Yet alongside success came failure, for example the British defeats at the hands of the Marathas at Wadgaon in 1779 and by Mysore at Perumbakam in 1780. Furthermore, successful campaigning required an ability to combine British firepower with the logistical capability provided by Indian entrepreneurs, while Indian cavalry could also be important, as the British conflicts with Mysore in the 1790s indicated. The tipping point toward European success in India came then and in the following decade. Until the 1790s British success, although important, especially in Bengal, was far from a flowing tide, and there had been significant setbacks. Indeed it was unclear how far Britain would dominate post-Mughal India, as the East India Company was only one among a number of powers.

With the benefit of hindsight, it is possible to explain British success in terms of a number of factors that suggest an inevitable course. These include the fact that (with the exception of brief periods of French challenge after 1761) Britain was the sole power in India with a naval capability, transoceanic range, and maritime commercial resources. Indeed it was not until early 1942, when a Japanese fleet briefly entered the Indian Ocean, that this situation was to be seriously challenged. In the early modern period, there was no equivalent non-western power, certainly not China or Japan. The closest was Oman, but the attacks mounted on Portuguese India in the late seventeenth century – Bombay was attacked in 1661–62 and Bassein in 1674, while Diu was sacked in 1668 and 1676 – were not sustained, and the Omanis concentrated instead on the East African coast, where they sacked Mombasa in 1661 and captured it from Portugal in 1698. Naval capability and commercial interests played a role in another characteristic of British power in India, namely its wide-ranging nature. With their three Presidencies based at Bombay, Calcutta and Madras, the British were present on both the Arabian Sea and the Bay of Bengal coasts, and had a range denied such Mughal-successor powers as the Gurkhas, the Nizams of Hyderabad and Haidar Ali of Mysore.

In terms of battle, it has also been argued that the British mastery of firepower tactics, and their emphasis on infantry and artillery, were crucial. The western impact in India was seen in the spread of flintlock rifles, bayonets, prepared cartridges and cast-iron cannon, and it was in the late eighteenth century that the advantage swung in India from cavalry to infantry armed with firearms, while artillery also became more effective. Superior firearms – flintlocks mounting bayonets – and effective tactics were important in this shift.

The trend thus seems clear, and indeed the eagerness with which several Indian rulers sought to adopt European weaponry has attracted attention. That in turn creates another way to approach their failure, namely that they saw that they had to innovate, but failed to do so successfully. Indeed westernization appears to have had detrimental military and political consequences. Warren Hastings was content for Indian states to try to emulate European infantry formations because he was confident that they would never succeed, and that it would take resources away from their cavalry and slow them up in the field. As Maratha armies became more professional, so the strategy based on living off the land became less feasible. Furthermore the new infantry and artillery formations proved expensive, leading to developments in revenue administration, banking and credit that created serious political problems.

The situation appears clear, but there is a danger that the analysis conforms to the standard approach to military history, with its misleading tendency to attribute to winners all the strengths of superior political and military systems and greater resources, together with all the skills of vision, strategic know-how, preparation and back-up, whereas losers tend to lose because they lose. There is a need, particularly but not only at the operational level, for continued reference to chance, and for the frequent use of terms such as 'perhaps' and 'maybe', and also for a measure of scepticism about the attribution of inevitability to long-term military history. This is especially important for India in this period because it saw the most significant conflict between Europeans and non-Europeans.

At the same time there is a danger in reading from the particular to the general, and it is unclear how far the results seen in India were of wider applicability. As yet there has been no serious study of conflict between western and non-western powers across the world in the 1790s to 1810s. Such a study could focus on western successes, such as the American victories at Fallen Timbers (1795) and against the Creeks in 1813–14, Napoleon's victories in Egypt and Palestine, or Russian success against the Ottomans in 1806–12, but it is also worth noting failures, such as the British in Egypt in 1807. Indeed, outside (lightly-populated) North America, it was only in India that major territorial gains involving large numbers of people took place. The Russians gained Bessarabia from the Ottomans at the Treaty of Bucharest in 1812, but this was marginal to Ottoman power, although it did take the Russians closer to the Balkans.

In India, the British won a number of important battles, but these did not conform to the image of western warfare in terms of defensive firepower bringing down attacking numbers, as had been the position at Plassey. Instead, as at Fallen Timbers and at Horseshoe Bend (1814), and also with the standard Russian campaigning mode against the Ottomans, the emphasis was on the operational offensive and the tactical attack, while the use of bayonet charges was important as well as firepower. It is difficult to produce a comparative weighting of the two, both because of a lack of information (and research) and also due to the very confused nature of some battles, especially Arthur Wellesley's victory over the Marathas at Assaye in 1803. The attack was important there, as it also was in Wellesley's victory at Argaon (Argaum) in 1803, Lake's victory over the Marathas at Farruckhabad in 1804, and Malcolm's victory over the Marathas at Mahidpur in 1817. British tactics, based on firing once or twice and then charging, had had an impact in India from mid-century. On the battlefield, speedy attack helped to compensate for numerical inferiority, while at the operational level it was only through the use of the strategic offensive that the British could hope to counter the Maratha cavalry (Weller, 1972, pp. 275–6). Attack, in the shape of storming, was also important in the capture of fortified positions, such as the Mysore capital Seringapatam in 1799, the Maratha fortresses of Alegarh and Gawilgarh in 1803, and, in the East Indies, the sultan of Yogyakarta's *kraton* (royal residence) in 1812.

This might simply suggest that western military superiority has to be considered in a wider fashion, to encompass offensive as well as defensive conflict, but this approach is complicated firstly by the quality of the Maratha cannon (and the skilful and brave nature of its use) and secondly by the non-military weaknesses of the Marathas, which compromised their effectiveness (Cooper and Wagle, 1995). Weakened by serious divisions, the Marathas suffered from an inadequate command structure and from a lack of money that hit discipline and control, just as divisions among their opponents had helped in the conquest of Bengal (Gordon, 1994; Cooper, 1989, pp. 36–8, 1992; Khanna, 1990; Bennell, 1997).

The latter point directs attention to the wide range of factors at issue. The British may well, as has been argued, have benefited from the degree to which they were less willing than earlier conquerors to absorb Indian political and military values (Bayly, 1993; Alavi, 1995, p. 4). Their administrative goals and methods certainly seem to have been different (Sen, 1998), and it has been argued that in the cases of Mysore, the Marathas and the Sikhs there was an 'inherent weakness ... that seriously impeded their efforts at adopting the western military system ... for all of these powers were essentially feudal in origin and had very little time to make the transition to a stable monarchy with a centralized bureaucracy'; conversely the British were able 'to adapt and innovate on the basis of a vastly superior organizational and governmental infrastructure' (Barua, 1994, p. 616).

However it is important to be wary of judgements that assume a ready superiority in western governmental systems, a point that emerges in comparative discussion of Europe and China (Bin Wong, 1997; Pomeranz, 1999). Indeed the East India Company was nearly bankrupted by the campaigns of 1803–04, so that it recalled Richard Wellesley, the Governor-General, and sought peace with the Marathas. In the absence of a systematic comparative study of Britain and the other Indian powers, and indeed of Britain's Indian wars in the period, it is rash to make statements about military or governmental effectiveness or superiority. The results were notable but the causes are less clear.

For all major powers, success owed much to sensible tasking, the ability to adapt in response to challenges, logistical capability and skill in managing combined-arms operations. Europeans faced major disadvantages in meeting these requirements when operating outside their homelands, although these could be lessened by winning local support, as, very importantly, with Cortes in Mexico and, over a longer time-span, the British in India. For example, in 1774 the British destroyed the Rohilla state in cooperation with Awadh. To this example can be added the role of winning local support in the successes of the Mughals in India, the Manchu in China, and a host of other non-westerners, providing a reminder that there was no clear analytical division. Indeed, the willingness to win acquiescence in conquest, or at least cooperation with the creation of a new hegemony, was crucial to success, both western and non-western.

This approach is far removed from the usual stress on weaponry, but, aside from the problem that that approach mistakenly equates war with fighting, the focus on weaponry provides only limited guidance to military, and even battlefield, capability. More generally, it underrates the continued importance of cavalry, and, in particular, first of horse-archers and then of cavalrymen with firearms (Gommans, 1995a, pp. 271–3, 1995b; Bryant, 1996, p. 32). Infantry gunpowder weaponry only brought so much change because, rather than a transformation of tactics or operational assumptions, there was often an attempt to use new weapons to give added power to existing practices, which was in part a response to social norms. Across the world, the notion of effectiveness was framed and applied in terms of dominant cultural and social patterns. The analysis latent in most military history, which assumes some mechanistic search for efficiency and a maximization of force driven by a form of Social Darwinism, does violence to the complex process by which interests in new methods interacted with powerful elements of continuity; it also overlooks the manner in which efficiency was culturally constructed, and the lack of clarity as to what defined effectiveness in force structure, operational method or tactics. All of these are topics that require research.

The emptiness of the technologically-driven account is shown by the most important conquest of the seventeenth century, that of Ming China by the Manchu. Nothing in the western world compared to its scale or drama, and there is something strange about the standard account of military history, with its heavy emphasis on the Thirty Years War and its near total avoidance of the contemporaneous conquest of China. The point can be repeated for the subsequent centuries, with the conquest of the Dzhungars, the Taipeng rising and the Chinese Civil War. The Manchu triumph was a victory for cavalry over the then military system of China, with its emphasis on positional warfare, and was also a victory in which political factors, in the shape of a lack of Chinese unity, were important (Wakeman, 1985). Barton Hackler has referred to 'the common view of a straight-line historical development from the Greeks to us', and such a linear concept of military history might see this as another triumph for barbarians, and thus as an anachronistic development that did not deserve subsequent scholarly attention (Hackler, 2003). However this is a mistaken approach, flawed by its assumption of a unitary model and a pattern of linear development. There is also an implicit racial stereotyping at work, which indeed bedevils much of military history and contributes to the Eurocentricity that is a serious problem.

Thus the history of this period invites an explicit engagement with methodological issues, and one that puts aside western paradigms. Alongside the spreading role of firearms in, for example, eighteenth-century Madagascar, it is necessary to note campaigns and battles where firearms were far from decisive. Thus, at Amed Ber in 1787, an Ethiopian army equipped with cannon and thousands of muskets was defeated by the cavalry of the Yejju.

By then, however, the world was changing. The Chinese victory over the Dzunghars and the Russian conquest of the Crimea in 1783 showed that this was not simply a matter of the rise of the Atlantic powers. Instead it is necessary to address cross-cultural comparisons and contrasts, while, at the same time, moving away from the mistake of assuming that the period can be read as a whole, and indeed that knowledge of what was to come helps to establish relative capability, which can then be used to explain success. Even more is this the case if war is understood as an attempt to enforce will, with battle treated as an important aspect of it (generally at least) but as in no way coterminous with conflict.

The last invites attention to the capacity of different systems for engendering and sustaining syncreticism. This is not that far removed from European military history; alongside the victories of Louis XIV it is necessary to consider the way in which conquered provinces, such as Artois and Franche-Comté, were assimilated, and the same is true for Peter the Great with Estonia and Livonia. This helps to make military history an aspect of total history, and other branches of history an aspect of military studies, which is indeed the correct conclusion.

References

Alavi, S. 1995. *The Sepoys and the Company. Tradition and Transition in Northern India, 1770–1830*, Delhi.

Barfield, T.J. 1989. *The Perilous Frontier: Nomadic Empires and China, 221 BC to AD 1757*, Oxford.

Barua, P. 1994. 'Military Developments in India, 1750–1850', *Journal of Military History*, 58, 599–616.

Bathurst, R.D. 1972. 'Maritime Trade and Imamate Government: Two Principal Themes in the History of Oman to 1728', in *The Arabian Peninsula. Society and Politics*, ed. D. Hopwood, London, 89–106.

Bayly, C.A. 1993. 'The British Military–Fiscal State and Indigenous Resistance. India 1750–1820', in *An Imperial State at War. Britain from 1689 to 1815*, ed. L. Stone, London, 324–49.

Bennell, A.S. 1997. *The Making of Arthur Wellesley*, Himayatnagar.

Bin Wong, R. 1997. *China Transformed: Historical Change and the Limits of European Experience*, Ithaca.

Black, J.M. 2003a. *War. An Illustrated World History*, Stroud.

—— 2003b. *Kings, Nobles and Commoners. States and Societies in Early Modern Europe. A Revisionist History*, London.

—— 2000. *War. Past, Present and Future*, Stroud.

Blussé, L. 1973. 'The Dutch Occupation of the Pescadores (1622–1624)', *Transactions of the International Conference of Orientalists in Japan*, 18, 28–43.

Boxer, C.R. 1926–27. 'The Siege of Fort Zeelandia and the Capture of Formosa from the Dutch, 1661–62', *Transactions and Proceedings of the Japan Society of London*, 24, 16–47.

Boxer, C.R. and Azvedo, C. de. 1960. *Fort Jesus and the Portuguese in Mombasa, 1593–1729*, London.

Brummett, P. 1994. *Ottoman Seapower and Levantine Diplomacy in the Age of Discovery*, Albany.

Bryant, G.J. 1996. 'The Military Imperative in Early British Expansion in India, 1750–1785', *Indo-British Review*, 21, 18–35.

Chaudhury, S. and Morineau, M. eds. 1999. *Merchants, Companies and Trade: Europe and Asia in the Early Modern Era*, Cambridge.

Cooper, R.G.S. and Wagle, N.K. 1995. 'Maratha Artillery: From Dalhoi to Assaye', *Journal of the Ordnance Society*, 7, 58–78.

Cooper, R.G.S. 1992. 'Cross-Cultural Conflict Analysis: The "Reality" of British Victory in the Second Anglo-Maratha War, 1803–1805', doctoral thesis, University of Cambridge.

—— 1989. 'Wellington and the Marathas in 1803', *International History Review*, 11, 31–8.

Finkel, C. 1988. *The Administration of Warfare: Ottoman Campaigns in Hungary, 1593–1606*, Vienna.

Förster, S. 1992. *Die mächtigen Diener der East India Company. Ursachen und Hintergründe der britischen Expansionspolitik in Südasien, 1793–1819*, Stuttgart.

Gommans, J. 1995a. 'Indian Warfare and Afghan Innovation during the Eighteenth Century', *Studies in History*, 11, 261–80.

—— 1995b. *The Rise of the Indo-Afghan Empire*, c. *1710–1780*, Leiden.

Gordon, S. 1994. *Marathas, Marauders and State Formation in Eighteenth-Century India*, Delhi.

Hackler, B.C. 2003. *World Military History Bibliography. Pre-Modern and Non-Western Military Institutions and Warfare*, Leiden.

Hess, A.C. 1973. 'The Ottoman Conquest of Egypt and the Beginning of the Sixteenth-Century World War', *International Journal of Middle East Studies*, 4, 55–76.

—— 1970. 'The Evolution of the Ottoman Seaborne Empire in the Age of the Oceanic Discoveries, 1453–1525', *American Historical Review*, 75, 1892–1919.

Ingram, E. 1981. *Commitment to Empire: Prophecies of the Great Game in Asia, 1797–1800*, Oxford.

Kessler, L.D. 1976. *K'ang-hsi and the Consolidation of Ch'ing Rule, 1661–1684*, Chicago.

Khanna, D.D. ed. 1990. *The Second Maratha Campaign, 1804–1805: Diary of James Young, Officer Bengal Horse Artillery*, New Delhi.

Knox, M. and Murray, W. eds. 2001. *The Dynamics of Military Revolution, 1300–2050*, Cambridge.

Lockhart, L. 1935–37. 'Nadir Shah's Campaigns in Oman, 1734–1744', *Bulletin of the School of Oriental and African Studies*, 8, 157–73.

Mackesy, P. 1984. *War Without Victory. The Downfall of Pitt, 1799–1802*, Oxford.

Murphey, R. 1993. 'The Ottoman Resurgence in the Seventeenth-Century Mediterranean: The Gamble and its Results', *Mediterranean Historical Review*, 8, 186–200.

Olson, R.W. 1975. *The Siege of Mosul and Ottoman-Persian Relations, 1718–1743. A Study of Rebellion in the Capital and War in the Provinces of the Ottoman Empire*, Bloomington.

Parker, G. 2003. 'Random Thoughts of a Hedgehog', *Historically Speaking: The Newsletter of the Historical Society*, 4, 13–14.

Parrott, D. 2001. *Richelieu's Army. War, Government and Society in France, 1624–1642*, Cambridge.

Perdue, P.C. 1996. 'Military Mobilization in Seventeenth and Eighteenth-Century China, Russia, and Mongolia', *Modern Asian Studies*, 30, 757–93.

Pomeranz, K. 1999. *The Great Divergence: China, Europe and the Making of the Modern World Economy*, Berkeley.

Sandin, B. 1967. *The Sea Dayaks of Borneo: Before White Rajah Rule*, London.

Sen, S. 1998. *Empire of Free Trade. The East India Company and the Making of the Colonial Marketplace*, Philadelphia.

Setton, K.M. 1991. *Venice, Austria and the Turks in the Seventeenth Century*, Philadelphia.

Tregaskis, R. 1973. *The Warrior King: Hawaii's Kamehameha the Great*, New York.

Turnbull, S.R. 2002. *Samurai Invasion. Japan's Korean War, 1592–98*, London.

Wakeman, F. 1985. *The Great Enterprise. The Manchu Reconstruction of Imperial Order in Seventeenth-Century China*, Berkeley.

Weller, J. 1972. *Wellington in India*, London.

Wright, L.R. 1976. 'Piracy in the South-East Asian Archipelago', *Journal of Oriental Studies*, 14, 23–33.

Yapp, M.E. 1980. *Strategies of British India: Britain, Iran and Afghanistan, 1798–1850*, Oxford.

Index